*Parables
of Sun Light*

Parables
of Sun Light

OBSERVATIONS ON PSYCHOLOGY, THE ARTS, AND THE REST

RUDOLF ARNHEIM

UNIVERSITY OF CALIFORNIA PRESS
Berkeley   Los Angeles   London

Cover painting: Paul Klee, *Departing Steamer* (1927).
Reproduced by the kind permission of Billy Wilder.

University of California Press
Berkeley and Los Angeles, California
University of California Press, Ltd.
London, England
© 1989 by
The Regents of the University of California

Library of Congress Cataloging-in-Publication Data
Arnheim, Rudolf.
  Parables of sun light.

    1. Art—Psychology.   2. Aesthetics.   I. Title.
  II. Title: Parables of sunlight.
  N71.A677   1989   701'.1'5   88-27898
  ISBN 0-520-06516-0 (alk. paper)
  ISBN 0-520-06536-0 (pbk.)

Printed in the United States of America
1 2 3 4 5 6 7 8 9

PREFACE

Not quite arbitrarily, this selection from my notebooks begins with the year 1959. A Fulbright year spent in Japan opened to me a world of new images, which awoke an equally new world of thoughts. This indeed is the formula for what is included in this volume: I have avoided mere images, I have avoided mere thoughts; but whenever an episode I observed or a striking sentence I read yielded a flash of insight I had not had before, I wrote it down and preserved it. These jottings are not a diary. They do not present me as a subject but as a mere supplier of symptomatic experiences—experiences that are meant to stand as self-sufficient miniatures, bits of theory kept alive by the senses through which they were transmitted.

Indirectly, therefore, all these *images raisonnées* reflect their settings—my travels to Asia and Europe, our American cities, the lakeshore of our summer months—and also the voices of my wife, my friends and colleagues and students, the strangers, and the ever-present cat, all of them transformed into echoes. It is also in the nature of such a blend of life and thought that professional disciplines are not kept neatly to themselves nor is their number limited. Psychology and the arts are the first to attract my attention, but there is no way of excluding philosophy, religion, or the natural sciences. This medley of topics can be handled only because a collection of notes licenses some recklessness one could not afford in systematic prose. The hit-and-run technique of gathering lets items pass unchecked and uncensored that otherwise may have ended up on the cutting-room floor. In no way do I suggest, however, that I am presenting lightweight material. To my mind, many of the items offer challenges calling for deeper probing. Many ideas first jotted down in my notebooks were later used in one of my books and therefore do not appear here; and, conversely, the principles dominating my books are reflected in the episodes recorded in the present collection.

Also, I was not willing to leave my writing in the shape in which, *au courant de la plume,* it had flown from the pen the day I first put it on paper. I owe my readers as clear and concise a formulation of each piece as possible. Everything has been severely selected, trimmed, and rewritten. Each thought is entered at the date on which it occurred to me, but much of the wording is new.

Having been happily pushed around in the world during a long life, I have always talked and listened and learned in a plurality of languages. In a documentation as personal as this one, this polyphony inevitably shows up. Hence the frequent foreign quotations, which I am leaving in the original languages because so much of what matters is in the quality of the speech. Even so, for readers wanting to check on the factual content of these quotations, I have added translations, mostly my own, which appear at the foot of the page.

Had some of these writings not been published before, I am not sure the impulse to keep them up would have stayed alive through the years. I am most grateful therefore to the editors of *Salmagundi,* my good friends Robert and Peggy Boyers, for having published occasional installments therein ever since 1972.

I also want to express my thanks to my editor, Ernest Callenbach, who once again has helped me with his sympathy and critical wisdom. He has been, for many years, my indispensable middleman to the readers and, beyond the call of duty, my patron, audience, and friend. Once again also I am much indebted to Mary Caraway, who clarified and fine-tuned my sentences with devotion and understanding.

The book's title, *Parables of Sun Light,* is taken from Dylan Thomas's "Poem in October," where he talks of the revival of

a child's
Forgotten mornings when he walked with his mother
Through the parables
Of sun light
And the legends of the green chapels
And the twice told fields of infancy

If there is something the many thoughts collected in this volume have in common, it is that I owe them to the senses, and most of all to vision, the child of sun light.

✿ 1959

Since the Soviet rocket circled the moon and returned to the Earth a few days ago, my perception of our celestial satellite is beginning to change. No longer do I see it in a class with the lamp on the ceiling, with places at a distance where I will never go. Now the moon looks like a landmark on the horizon, distant but reachable. A path leads through space to the outer world.

Different ways of viewing hewn stones. "And if thou wilt make me an altar of stone, thou shalt not build it of hewn stone: for if thou lift up thy tool upon it, thou hast polluted it" (Exod. 20:25). The stone's geometry can be seen as its nature: it is regular, crystalline, rational. Or, its straightness may denounce the violence of human interference, incompatible with the sacrosanct.

Niels Bohr, speaking about complementarity, is concerned with "two statements that are both true although they contradict each other." Whether this can happen in physics, I do not know; but it cannot happen elsewhere. "Intuition" and "intellect" may be complementary in the sense in which two angles can add up to 180°; but they

1

are not complementary in Bohr's sense, because they do not contradict each other. One can reach the midpoint of a mountain slope by descending from the top or by climbing up from the bottom; but there is no contradiction. Only statements can contradict each other; facts cannot.

On board ship, the rhythmical rocking is perceived as the progress of time. When the boat finally stops, it is as though time is stopping. Later, on land, time seems to stand still until the sense of voyage has been forgotten.

When we visited the Imperial Palace in Tokyo, the guide said, "This gate used to be three hundred years old!" Wood architecture can decay fast and is replaced when needed. The reconstruction of old buildings, so disappointing in the West, is successfully practiced in the East. Taste, style, and the method and criteria of workmanship have changed so little over the centuries that an old building can be remade authentically. Identity is preserved not by the matter of the wood but by shape, once invented and then reembodied from time to time.

Struggling with his *l*s and *r*s, the young Japanese insurance agent filled out our application form, describing our house as "wooden dwelling covered with mortal."

The stage of the Kabuki-za Theater in Tokyo occupies the long side of the house. Long and low, it can display crowd action without crowding. Figures can be distanced from each other by generous intervals without losing contact. Even when only one or two actors perform, they do not seem lost, because all distances are in accord with the dimensions of the stage. I saw a prince in a long conversation with the ghost of his dead retainer throughout which the two actors were separated by a distance of about one-third of the stage. They seemed close enough, and the total expanse looked appropriate, even though the prince was supposed to be held prisoner in a temple.

Sometimes a ceremonious scene fills the entire breadth of the stage, but the stage can also be divided into more than one setting. An interior and an outside garden may be shown in juxtaposition so that the garden is not merely a background espied through a window or door but serves to counterpoint the scene as the coordinated partner of the interior.

18 October

Pasternak's novel would be a better book without Dr. Zhivago himself, who is not really made to exist. In a work of art, a figure comes to acquire presence by the function it fulfills. There would be no chess game if the knight were not defined by his moves, the bishop by his. Dr. Zhivago is given no such function. His withholding himself has no effect upon the total setting. In fact, that setting itself is no more than a patchwork of scenes— magnificent scenes sometimes, because Pasternak is a gifted miniaturist. But a collection of scenes is no novel.

The principal failure of the book, however, is the absence of history. Never does his story resound with that most momentous happening of our times. It is as though an American during our Revolution would complain, "All this dreadful shooting, and the brutality, and the waste of perfectly good tea!" The doctor does not measure up to the immensity of the event of which he is condemned to be a part. Not surprisingly, the book finds much success with the kind of liberal who wants freedom but does not quite know what for.

A chess game at the stage of one of its moves illustrates the contention of the psychologist Kurt Lewin that no forces can be active in a given situation other than those contained in it then and there. Knowledge of what happened before can be illuminating but is not indispensable. The past need not act upon the present.

26 October

The impersonation of women by Kabuki actors looks shocking at first. An elderly, paunchy gentleman plays the part of the maiden. The squeaky voice he affects does not sound feminine but like a takeoff. Soon, however, one realizes that these first impressions are misinterpretations, derived from our expectation of an "illusion" style of staging. For us, a young woman on the stage must appear to *be* a young woman. The Kabuki theater, however, is highly stylized throughout. The male actor does not intend to produce the illusion of a particular woman; rather he represents femininity. Art is creation, not illusion. Baiko, the famous impersonator of women, may be an elderly man, but Matisse and Maillol, creators of lovely female figures, were no more girlish than he. The impersonations of the *onna-gata* are no more unnatural than the tiny mouths of the courtesans in Utamaro's prints.

Taking your hot bath in a wooden box, you feel at home with the touch of the wood, which is a product of nature like your own skin. The unnaturally hard smoothness of our tubs!

A modern school of flower arrangement (*ikebana*) goes far beyond the traditional style by abandoning organic materials and working in metal, glass, and stone. An exhibition of the Sogetsu school of *ikebana* gave me much to think about. Many of the works were simply what we would call abstract sculpture, made with welding equipment and using various objets trouvés. But by being exhibited in the company of traditional flower arrangements, these new works revealed an unsuspected ancestry.

In the West, abstract art developed from the gradual rarefaction of subject matter. In the East, it derives from three practices of abstract shape: flower arrangement, calligraphy, and the color schemes and textures of ceramic glazes. In consequence, Japanese abstract artists seem to be more at home with the modern media than are their Western colleagues. And the little old ladies in kimono, the devotees of *ikebana,* did not stop their attention when the exhibition presented them with inorganic displays.

A display of Japanese erotic art, ranging from a powerful twelfth-century scroll (painted, I believe, by the master of the rabbit and frog scroll of the Kozanji Temple in Kyoto) to Utamaro and Hiroshige and their modern imitators. Seeing the detailed representations of the human genitals, I realized how decisively the visual image of any object is shaped for us by the form it acquires through pictorial tradition. The penis was perhaps the only object in the world of which I had not seen such detailed artistic depiction. Suddenly it emerged from a twilight of vagueness and assumed a precise visually defined character and expression, half tree trunk, half serpent—sharpened, translated, interpreted.

Because of this transfiguration of the subject matter into artistic form, I felt no trace of smuttiness in these pictures. The ancient scroll, in particular, conveyed a frantic struggle for satisfaction with almost desperate ferocity. The huge genitals portrayed the disproportion of a mind overwhelmed by sex. Proudly equipped with their gigantic members, these men looked absurdly overburdened. And as the tricky males and females grappled with each other, they offered the tragicomic spectacle of Homo sapiens unwisely enslaved by a ridiculous-looking activity.

On an advertising pillar in Fukuoka at night, outlined by neon lights, the large star pattern of a snowflake rotated slowly. What an opportunity for abstract sculpture! I remember Henry Moore telling me that safety regulations prohibited him from mounting his sculptures atop the London Time-Life Building on vertical axles, which would have made them mobile.

20 November

We say "He kissed her hand," whereas "he kissed her" means that he kissed her mouth. The person is in the face. But, when "he touches her," he may be doing so anywhere on her body. In touching, body meets body. A kiss aims at the core.

In the ideograph for rain (Figure 1) the sky dominates as a detached line, separate from the field on which the drops fall. Children make the same separation when they paint the sky as a blue strip separated from the ground by empty space.

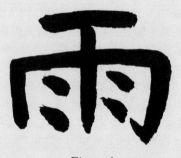

Figure 1

22 November

To be pushed and crushed by the hundreds and thousands of persons milling through the National Museum to see the Shosoin Treasures from Nara was a disheveling but heartening experience. The remarkable interest of the common man in these fine works of ancient handicraft!

However, can a single, small object in a mass culture still serve the function of art? Try to get a glimpse of an inlaid box or precious manuscript over several rows of heads while you are shoved past the showcase! Formerly, few persons saw such objects or knew of them. By now, as the privilege is extended to all, nobody can see them. I thought of this also in the Uffizi and the Louvre. The Mona Lisa, although in full sight, is no longer visible, precisely because she can be seen by everyone.

25 November

In Yasujiro Ozu's film *Ukigusa* [*Floating Grass*] the theme of restless wandering is represented at a very slow pace, like a heavily grinding wheel loaded with weights. The effect is obtained by carefully composed pictures, static and definitive in aspect. Each speaking actor is so compellingly framed by the walls, lanterns, and flowers of the background that he cannot move and often does not move. Much dialogue is presented in straight frontal shots, the two or three partners appearing singly and successively at the same place and in the same position. Instead of locomotion there is replacement. Picture postcard shots of the harbor and its white lighthouse open the film, and similar empty settings are insisted upon throughout. The immobility of the "floating" world, which causes the tragedy of the story, is conveyed by the restraint of external action.

31 November

On the square-shaped No stage the persons not involved in the action—that is, the musicians and singers—are lined up along the sides. Actors also sit frontally or on the side when they are waiting or otherwise quiet. Action, however, is almost always conducted diagonally: then the actors face the corners of the stage, and the spa-

7

tial axes of the dialogue are at an angle with the basic
framework of the square stage. Obliquity expresses
action.

2 December

Chinese and Japanese poetry must be seen to be understood. A word like the Chinese *chu,* meaning "a feeling of
harmony and friendship," is nothing more than an identifying sound chip, but it is written as a combination of
two signs, one standing for person, the other for center
or middle. The visual image of the ideograph renders the
life-giving service of etymology.

A powerful admonition to us teachers appears in a foot-
note to an article on the Chinese philosophy of education.
In its original, mysterious English: "In a fable about the
musical-instrument maker Ta-Sheng, a chapter of the
Chuang Tzu, one cannot make a good instrument, one
can only discover it. After having been discovered, it is
then manufactured, thus the operation is from Nature to
Nature, that is, the Nature which is hidden in the prototype. It may be said that this story expresses also the idea
of Chinese education."

14 December

Gestalt psychologists might refer to the solfeggio way of
naming musical sounds, which asserts that the absolute
pitch level of a tune does not matter. Do-re-mi means
conceiving of musical structure purely in terms of relation.

19 December

To express a climax of emotion, the Kabuki actor crosses
his eyes and thereby shortens the distance between the
pupils. For the viewer this contraction heightens visual

tension, a device related perhaps to the facial expression of the fierce temple guardians in sculpture, whose eye axes converge strongly, concentrating the glance intensely upon a nearby target. In the actor on the stage the convergence of the eyes seems to exclude any focusing upon the outer world and to withdraw attention to the inward experience of passion and thought. Compare this with the Buddha figures, whose eye axes run parallel, bent on the infinite.

In the Kabuki theater, the stage surrounds the audience; in the No theater, the audience surrounds the stage. In Kabuki, the encirclement overwhelms the audience, which sits as though on an island, attacked by the surf of the action. In the No, the audience is gathered around the play as though around a lovely exhibit, to be explored actively.

The visible accesses leading to the stage—the *hashi-gakari* of the No and the *hana michi* of the Kabuki—provide the stage action with arrival and exit, crescendo and decrescendo. They also add time to the play in space.

Two examples of how intimately life and writing are connected in Japan: (1) During a recent devastating typhoon, hundreds of people, among them fifty children, were stranded on a mountain in Nara prefecture. The helicopter flying over Yoshino Mountain noticed the children standing in lines forming the ideograph for "Help!" (2) The *ronin,* or masterless samurai, who took their famous revenge early in the seventeenth century, were forty-seven in number. But since forty-seven is also the number of the syllables in the syllabary, the *ronin* in the Kabuki performance of *Chushingura* carried small wooden tablets, each showing one of the katakana characters. Is this identity of number coincidental? In fact, the full name of the play is *Kanadehon Chushingura.*

9

🌿 1960

Mary noticed that the Japanese dogs have Oriental faces; so do, she says, Eskimo dogs. Is this the result of selective breeding? Julian Huxley, in *New Bottles for New Wine,* has a photo of the Heike crab, which developed a distinct samurai face on its shell because the specimens showing the face were consistently thrown back into the water by superstitious fishermen. Thus, by selection, the face was bred in. Did something similar happen to dogs among Mongols? Or is the Oriental dog face more nearly the original one, and it is we who bred a Western look into our dogs?

17 January

Concerning the psychology of memory. When Mary opened a can in our Tokyo kitchen the other day, she felt, with the strength of a hallucination, that our cat Charcoal was rubbing her leg. She was about to bend down to him when she remembered with a start that he was no longer with us. The Japanese can opener was of an old-fashioned type, the same she used to have at home until about the time Charcoal died, a year ago; shortly afterward she started using a more modern tool, screwed to the wall. She used to open very few cans except those of cat food, so neither for the cans nor the opener was there much competitive association. The mental slate was clean for the association to establish itself between can opener and cat. Add to this that Mary used to open cans of cat food not only at home but anywhere on our travels and at our summer places: no particular locality was tied to the operation, and thus the Tokyo kitchen did not interfere with the cat scene. When the links of an association are free of other ties, the mechanism seems to work best.

21 January

At what time in the history of thought and in what sort of culture arises the vision of the other mind enshrined in the fortress of the other body, unreachable and unable to reach? Shakespeare has it, and so does much modern literature. Alienation chills much modern portraiture.

But who saw it first? In the *Kagero Nikki,* written in the tenth century, people speak to each other through poetry sent by messenger. This lets them keep their distance and hide their thoughts without having to lie. A man who, in a poem written in artful calligraphy and attached to a symbolic twig, says that his sleeve is wet with the dew of the night even though in fact he shed no tears and slept well is not lying. The loneliness of the men and women in that Japanese chronicle is supreme. Did they believe that there can be no understanding?

I visited a German musician, now over seventy, who has lived in Japan for nearly thirty years and was the conductor of the Tokyo orchestra but has never tried to learn the language. He says it prevents unnecessary discussion.

Koi means "love," but also "carp." Therefore a carp will serve as a symbol of love. Japanese poetry and customs are full of such puns, in which the word becomes flesh.

The red lobster, a part of the bundle of decorations put on the doors and stores for the New Year, is probably derived from an apotropaic phallic charm, just as the horns and corals in Italy call up the generative power of sex as a defense against the evil eye.

In Plato's time, the Supreme Maker was thought of as a craftsman. Nowadays we describe the work of the craftsman as a kind of divine creation. The theorists seem to shoot either too low or too high.

2 February

A haiku made to test my impression that the first and the third lines should describe a state of being while the second, longer one gives the action:

> Ears and eyes at night
> Patter of wooden sandals
> But I see no street.

6 February

The least touchable object in the world is the eye.

Trying to write Chinese characters, I am hampered by not placing the separate units of a character closely enough together. This same tendency to keep separate objects clearly apart shows in children's drawings and other early art. Children have difficulty in interrelating objects in space, for instance, in putting a human figure close enough to the tree from which he is purportedly picking apples. Since one falls back on earlier formal devices when problems occur at higher levels, I find myself battling with the childlike need for separation when I am struggling with complex shape.

> Kabuki lobby
> The paper flowers in bloom
> Promising magic.

8 February

> Over the wine cups
> Two probingly drinking eyes
> Signaling friendship.

9 February

R. H. Blyth's book on haiku irritates me because he is one of the theorists who pride themselves on believing that poetry can be dealt with only by poetry and who therefore feel guilty about engaging in their undertaking. He keeps stopping short of the analysis he is pledged to offer and instead talks about poetry coyly, like an old maid talking about sex. He does not know that all things in this world, not just poems and paintings, are untouchable. Any sight, any noise, any experience has a virginity of its own. Philosophy and science do not violate it if wise thinkers are at work. Even the artist respects the gulf. The portrait of a flower leaves the flower unharmed. It is the lack of respect for nature that makes people have too much respect for poetry.

The symmetrical Greek cross with its arms of equal length represents the Platonic cosmos—a formidable referent; whereas the Latin cross of the Crucifixion recalls the sacrifice of the Savior but does not truly symbolize it by its shape. Instead I wonder whether the Latin cross with its short horizontal arms and longer spine is not essentially an image of man, a humanistic symbol challenging the cosmological version of the Greeks. There are human figures inscribed in the ground plans of churches based on the Latin cross. Perceptually the Latin cross resembles the human figure strikingly, and of course each crucifix shows the visual coincidence of man and cross. The Latin cross, then, would symbolize the humanization of religion accomplished by Christianity, which made the god a man and man the god.

11 February

The phone receiver
Chattering on the table
Unheard and unhugged.

12 February

On distant islands
Women combed her golden hair
The man hears her tale.

14 February

On the faint picture
Kneeling she plays the flute
Unreachable tune.

19 February

One of the few still-active carvers of Buddha figures says that unlike other art products Buddhist images do not bear the signature of the sculptor, because "the sculptor does not make the images but is caused to make them."

24 February

The Japanese call "grandson quotations" the kind of reference not derived from the original source but from some other author who used it first.

3 March

The ukiyo-e woodcuts are not reversed in the print. They appear as the artist designed them because the engraver pastes the drawing on the woodblock facedown. This requires thinning the paper to make it transparent. They seem willing to take the trouble to avoid the reversal of left and right.

4 March

The irritating notion that the beholder should complete through his imagination what the artist left undone is refuted by the sumi paintings, so fond of incomplete objects. Try to complete the rocks whose base is lost in the mist or to populate the "empty" spaces with more rocks or woods, and you will find that your clumsy moves destroy the delicate balance and thus the meaning.

The traditional Japanese gardens were normally designed in the left-to-right direction. The view begins with a dominant object on the left, for example, with a cascade, and moves, often with the flow of the water, to the right. This is called "strong-hand" composition, as distinguished from the "weak-hand" way of placing the dominant on the right. The "origin" belongs on the left. Similarly, Western painting is composed on a vector from the left to the right.

8 March

Upright rocks often "symbolize" waterfalls. The representation of nature by nature is something to which I believe we have no parallel in the West.

11 March

"The wise find pleasure in water, the virtuous find pleasure in hills" (Confucius, *Analects,* bk. 6, chap. 21).

For a right-handed person the motion of writing from
the left to the right is expansive, i.e., the arm moves away
from the body; but the left arm's motion to the right is
constrictive. Centrifugal motion makes for a feeling of
freedom. Is one of the reasons for left-handedness that
the person finds constriction congenial—the closing up of
the shell?

20 March

Very Japanese, the gracefully hesitant attitude of thinking
depicted by the wooden Miroku-Bosatsu in the Koryuji
Temple. He does not quite rest his chin on his hand as
does our own robust *Thinker,* nor can he quite do without the protective support of that delicately petaled hand.
Rather different is the expression of the similar bronze
figure, unkindly hidden behind curtains, at Horyuji. His
head is held upright, and he is less absorbed in his thinking. He is an enthroned monarch, attired with graceful
thought as though it were nothing but one of his attributes. No particular occupation holds him. His face has
the archaic beauty of the best Greek bronzes.

1 April

What formal devices convey an ending or closure? When
Shakespeare marks the ending of a speech by rhyming
the last two lines he does more than just introduce a signal of change. He stops the waves of rhythmic alternation
by repetition. Constriction is another way of indicating
the end. The façade columns of Greek temples as well as
those of some Japanese temples, such as the Toshodaiji
near Nara, have intercolumnar spaces diminishing from

the center toward both sides. The decreasing intervals produce a gradual compression directed toward a final zero interval—which, however, is not reached. The endlessness of equal intervals, the deadly metronome beat, is avoided.

Experimenting with a sound hammer, Professor Sagara found that when a series of regular beats is presented, subjects hear them grouped by uneven numbers, such as five and seven in twelve beats. Did the Japanese preference for odd numbers influence this result? The experiment should be repeated with American subjects.

To indicate that the ancient Japanese read pictures, as we do, from the left to the right, I draw attention to one of the paintings in the Tamamushi-no-zushi Shrine at Horyuji. The small panel combines three phases of a story. At the top left, Sakyamuni takes off his clothes on a sort of jumping platform; further to the right and halfway down, he dives into the tiger's den; and in the lower right-hand corner he is being eaten by the tigress and her hungry cubs, for whose survival he sacrifices his life.

27 April

After watching Jean-Louis Barrault play the intrigant in Marivaux's *Fausses Confessions,* it occurred to me that the servant, this favorite character of comedy, is an embodiment of fate. He manipulates the powdered aristocrats (who populate the plot) by stirring up their passions, although his social inferiority makes him as invisible as the black-clad and hooded puppeteers on the Japanese *bunraku* stage. By the time of the French Revolution, the servant figure becomes Beaumarchais's Figaro, an image of the underdog as the rising social force; and Strindberg's valet Jean in *Miss Julie* still embodies the threat of proletarian vitality. Even so, by acquiring the flesh and blood of social status, the earlier function of the figure has been diminished.

3 May

Modeling in clay suggests limbs, noses, breasts, and eyeballs to be added to the trunk of the figure. Carving discloses the same shapes negatively by freeing them from the matter around them. The spatial relief of the best sculpture combines both conceptions.

26 May

At the time of the *Genji Monogatari,* illness, whether physical or mental, was still considered the action of hostile powers. Princess Aoi, who is possessed by her rival, Lady Rokuji, dies suddenly without any physical cause. The characters of the story waste away like wilting flowers. There is no diagnosis or physiology, and the chant of the priests is the chief medicine.

6 June

One of the pioneers of the Japanese kindergarten movement began as a devout priest who spied for his government on the Christians in Yokohama and Nagasaki. While keeping contact with the foreigners, he became interested in their activities and ended up a convinced follower of Fröbel. When he died, after having been the director of the Ochanomizu kindergarten in Tokyo for thirty years, his disciples erected on his grave a stone monument consisting of the basic shapes of Fröbel's play blocks, the cube, the cylinder, the sphere, and the cone— a Cubist sculpture in the 1890s, anticipating Brancusi.

9 June

The boss on the forehead of the Buddha Amida statues seems to be meant as light-giver and light-receiver at the same time. It is a third eye, the spiritual eye, but also a beacon emitting light. There is no contradiction in this double function. According to early theories (of Plato and others), vision is an encounter between the gentle fire pouring forth through the pupil of the eye and the counterfire emanating from the object to be perceived. To the spontaneous mind, seeing is an emission of energy.

As long as in flower arrangement the plants are used the way they grow naturally, care is taken to keep the center of the visual weight at the bottom of the composition, near the vase. The pattern thins out radially upward and sideward. But recently, when the style of *ikebana* moved away from nature, the weight tended to become more evenly distributed all over the composition, just as we observe it in modern painting and sculpture.

12 June

They, too, have "droodles." A Japanese friend showed me this one, meaning "earthworm crawling over a razor blade" (Figure 2).

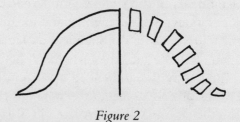

Figure 2

20 June

When I was surprised to find iris included among the medical herbs in a garden in Sapporo, I was told that Japanese girls like to put iris in their bathwater because the plant is believed to enlarge the breasts. Some also use the long leaves to measure the results of the practice.

When a boy, usually at about twelve years of age, enters the progressive high school of Jiyu-gakuen, he is asked to spend much of his first month on carpentering the desk and chair he will be using during the years of his stay at the school. Thereby his place in the new setting becomes something he created himself and has his affection. He also comes to feel that he is embarking on a long, solidly supported journey toward scholarship.

23 June

Books were objects of worship, endowed with magic powers, and even one generation ago some fathers taught their sons to raise a book respectfully to their foreheads before opening it. The mere possession of books was considered precious and beneficial, and a library was essentially a storehouse of sacred powers. After the Second World War, when the new era began, it took a law to change this traditional notion to Western style "library service."

9 August

When I was a young boy, I was tortured many nights by a frightening image from a trashy crime story called *The Student of Oxford,* which I had read in German. In the story a mad professor, disturbed by any loud student who threw his boots against the walls, would sneak after him and kill him. Often I had to call my mother in the middle of the night to have her relieve me of the evil spell. Why just this story among the many horror stories I must have read at that age? I grew up to be a professor whom nobody could induce to commit murder—except, perhaps, a noisy neighbor.

Sometimes we change the nature of an object simply by putting it in a different category. Japanese bathing seems repulsive to many a Westerner because we think of a bathtub as a large washbasin. Who would want to use the wash water after another person? The Japanese, however, think of their *ofuro* tub as a small swimming pool, which commonly serves more than one person; and they feel as disgusted by our method of bathing in our own soapy waste water as we would if somebody scrubbed himself in a swimming pool.

19 August

While at work on an essay about landscape design, I took a walk to clarify a problem in my mind. Marching through the suburban streets, I was so absorbed in my thoughts that I was all but blind to the gardens and tree-lined streets that illustrated precisely the problem I was wrestling with.

In Rousseau's *Nouvelle Héloïse* the narrator, after learning about the care Julie takes not to disturb the birds in their natural setting, comments caustically, "So afraid were you to make the birds your slaves that you have become theirs!" Whereupon Julie, with the shiny cleverness of an eighteenth-century heroine, retorts, "Spoken like a tyrant, who thinks he cannot enjoy his freedom unless he interferes with that of others." What an answer to the notion, Freudian and otherwise, that one is frustrated unless there is no constraint!

22 August

Now and then the thinking of the child surfaces in the adult. I wanted to move the bathroom scales to another place in the house. But I thought that I would not be strong enough to lift them because "they weigh up to two hundred pounds."

29 August

I must record the date at which I first observed this symptom of our rapid degeneration. Every Wednesday

night some young doctors would meet to play good
chamber music, Bartók, Beethoven, Haydn, in the home
of a friend of the arts. An audience of about twenty persons—students and older women, some American, some
European—gathered regularly. I was invited to attend.
When the music began, nearly half of the listeners, who
were seated around the musicians, got up, selected a
book or magazine from the shelves, and sat down again
to read, quietly and politely, through the entire performance. The sight was that of a well-behaved clientele in
the waiting room of a dentist. Thus, music has departed
from us. It can no longer be listened to; it only fills the
room with agreeable sound. "Music as wallpaper," as a
friend of mine calls it.

28 September

In the posture of meditation the hands of the Buddha are
locked together in a state of inactivity; but the arms, con-
joined by the hands, present a closed loop of circulation,
through which mental energy, issuing from the head,
seems to course incessantly. A similar version of secluded
internal life is found in Modigliani's portrait figures,
whose eyes are often without pupils. The eyes of the
Buddha also do not focus on any external target.

How can we tell whether the picture of a person represents a general type or the portrait of an individual? The
ten disciples of Buddha look like faithful portraits of ten
particular gentlemen but probably represent ten types of
behavior. Generally, when a type is intended, it is more
likely to determine the total expression. A Venus is all
Venus, but the Mona Lisa cannot be said to be all smile.

The gestalt tendency toward simplest structure makes us
hear a musical interval such as C–E as based on the tonic
C even though it could just as well be the fourth and
sixth of G major or the minor third and fifth of A minor.

These other percepts, however, would involve reference to an outer base and thereby introduce a tension that the law of simplicity makes us avoid.

Science means to explain, not just to "predict and control." The latter attitude is a product of American pragmatism. It constricts the aspirations of human curiosity by suggesting that once you can predict, you no longer need to explain.

7 October

After a demonstration the great Kabuki actor Baiko gave at our college, he told us in discussion that their acting style looks unrealistic only to the uninitiated. He showed us that although he will use his fan instead of a cup to take a sip of sake, he will strain his neck and lips to keep the imaginary liquid from dripping.

23 October

There are no exceptions to the laws of nature. If the law prescribes the shape of Figure 3a and we encounter instead Figure 3b, then either the law is invalid or the apparent exception is actually of the shape 3c—meaning that additional factors modify the law-abiding shape of the specimen. The law, being an abstraction, is rarely realized in its purity.

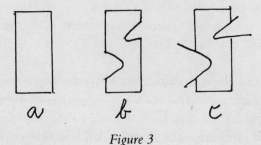

Figure 3

The Temple of Sanju-sangendo in Kyoto contains 1,001 statues of the Kannon because, I was told, the number 1,000 signifies infinity. Since infinity, however, is a concept, it is bounded by a finiteness of its own, which is overcome by the added 1. Now the figure is truly infinite.

13 November

Some people suffer from cancer of the intellect. Their reasoning has grown wild, losing its connection with reality and purpose. To put it another way: their thinking and talking is like a motor running out of gear because it has become uncoupled from the car it is meant to drive.

14 November

The heliotropism of sunflowers should make psychologists see what Wolfgang Köhler meant when he refused to let behavior be parceled out between inherited and acquired components. No inherited mechanism, transmitted by the genes, makes the flower turn to the sun, nor has anybody taught it to do so. Rather, an inherent tendency toward a balanced distribution of energy moves the flower's head into the one position that guarantees the symmetry of solar justice to all its parts.

21 November.

Pondering over a proper translation of Basho's lines

> Iwa ni shimi iru
> Semi no koe

I realized that in the phrase "The voice of the cicada penetrates the rock" the transitivity of the verb holds two quite different meanings. Penetration describes either the cicada's intention or an invasion happening to the rock.

25

This ambiguity must be inherent in all such verbs and must be overcome by the writer when the difference matters.

26 November

When an ignorant translator rendered Freud's term *Aktualneurosen* as "actual neuroses," he deceived readers into believing that Freud was referring to real, bona fide neuroses, to be distinguished from merely apparent ones, such as conversions, which were to be thought of as illusions or fakes. The very opposite is true. Freud meant by *Aktualneurosen* those neuroses caused by purely physical disturbances, such as sexual dysfunction. *Aktual,* not a happy term even in German, is used by Freud to indicate "physical" rather than "psychological"; by contrast, the conversions are the *real* neuroses, whose symptoms derive directly from psychological causes.

18 December

In his chapel at MIT, Eero Saarinen defeats the necessary unity of inside and outside by covering its cylindrical shape on the inside with a wavy screen, folded like a piece of corrugated cardboard. If one accepts this wavy enclosure as the inner wall, there is no way of perceiving outside and inside as aspects of the same building. Unity could be preserved only if the internal wall were taken to be an insubstantial lining, but doing so would contradict the substance of the stone and negate its function as an enclosure.

28 December

In the sciences there is no such thing as the profession of the critic. Nobody is admitted as a judge of the work of others unless he himself does acceptable work, which, in turn, is criticized by his fellow scientists. Hence criticism

among scientists is more competent, somewhat more
responsible, and taken more seriously by the criticized.
Consider here that the criticism of artists by artists has
special values but also peculiar weaknesses. In the arts the
truths are many.

❧ 1961

22 January

Our times will be judged by future historians, if there are to be any, as the last gasps of a dying civilization. They will recognize the achievements of our scientists and a few of our artists as the admirable products of an aged spirit. My own work, analytical and critical, is the kind for which late minds are well suited.

8 February

A striking example of perceptual restructuring can be derived from Sakurabayashi's experiments on the effects of long inspection (Figure 4). By removing two sections of the circle, one changes the character and relations of all the remaining parts. The "butterfly" has a new symmetry axis. Two of the radii cease to be contour lines and become antennae. The center is no longer in the middle. Etc.

Gestalt theory gets itself into trouble when it demands that the scientific description of a gestalt cannot be adequate unless it is a gestalt itself. This criterion is impossible to meet: the human mind creates gestalten in per-

29

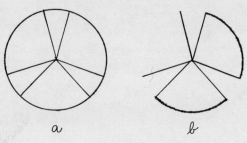

a *b*

Figure 4

ceptual experience but not in reasoning, which always takes the form of a conceptual network. Reasoning can do no better than connect isolated items. The neurophysiologists will have an easier time accounting for these networks than for the field processes needed to supply an adequate counterpart of perception.

12 February

My dentist tells me that sometimes when he runs into another person while trying to get through a door, he finds himself saying "Open, please!" instead of "Excuse me!" Does this simply mean that because both situations present obstacles to be overcome, he equates them and replaces the reaction to the more frequently occurring one for the less frequent one? Or are our perceptual experiences geared to their essentials rather than to their individuality, so that when these are as similar as door and mouth we tend to react similarly?

The approach of behaviorist psychology points conspicuously to a particular philosophical and social ideology. It starts its inquiry with the other person, observed externally, rather than with the self, experienced internally. It values physical action more than thought. To account for such bias, one must look beyond the arguments of science.

30

13 February

Hierarchical composition in painting wanes with the advent of democratic middle-class society. Coordination as a principle of social relation is foreshadowed by Flemish artists like Brueghel; and in the age of the French and American revolutions Hogarth fills the picture frame evenly with struggling creatures.

19 February

Mere balance is not enough to meet the demands of pictorial composition. Plenty of paintings are held together by nothing better than the equipoise of their weights.

28 February

The Freudian mechanism of projection matches its mechanical model too closely to do justice to the subtleties of the mind. A mental burden cannot be borne as simply as Atlas shoulders the terrestrial globe. Some rationale must be found to make the unloading possible. Often there is a reinterpretation: It is not I who hates me, it is they who do! Or the person relieves the internal pressure by generalizing his own deficiency: Not only am I myself dangerous, everything in this world is! This leads to the paranoiac view of the world as a bundle of threats.

21 March

A former student of the great German historian Friedrich Meinecke told me of the old gentleman's first visit to America. "This is quite an event!" he said. "It is the first time in my life that I have been abroad." The student seemed to remember that Meinecke had been in Italy and reminded him of it. "Oh Italy—that's not abroad! That is a part of the Roman Empire."

Five-year-old Carolyn believes that as she is growing up, her mother will correspondingly get younger, so that in due course their roles will be reversed. She transforms the one-way street of time into a symmetrical two-way arrangement, and she is not slow to warn her mother of the eventual consequences.

23 March

There is something distinctly Platonic about Jung's archetypes. The primordial matrices lie beyond the formation of the individual's thoughts. And just as in the Platonic world there cannot be more kinds of things than there are immutable ideas, so are the conceptions of the Jungian mind restricted to their underlying molds.

24 March

I remember that the scroll on the wall of my hotel room in Nago on Okinawa bore the inscription "White Smoke, Black Smoke," a calligraphic reminder of the title of a novel that deals with a mother too poor to see her daughter off to the port of Naha. To console them both, she set fire to a heap of pine needles so that the daughter would see the white smoke when her boat passed her little hometown of Nago. In turn, the mother saw the black smoke of the boat. Thus the story is brought down beautifully to the simplified visual image of two clouds of rising smoke, embodying the upward motion of vows and wishes, the unison of mother and daughter across the distance, the contrast of the blackness of sorrowful departure and the whiteness of a mother's comforting devotion.

25 March

Amateur performances achieve a curiously surrealist effect by the unintentional discrepancy between what the

players are and do and what they are supposed to represent. As they look and behave differently from what their
parts would require, as they tumble from one character
or attitude into another and react inappropriately, they
render their presentation mysterious like a weird dream
and thereby produce an aesthetic delicacy for connois-
seurs. They create an uncanniness similar to that discovered by the Surrealist painters in cheap nineteenth-
century wood engravings and exploited in their collages.

I noticed recently the first definite intimation of aging
when I found that the paper of some of my books, old
manuscripts, notes, and letters is beginning to crumble.
Whatever symptoms I had observed about my mind and
body could always be explained as a mere fluctuation, a
change of character or capacity rather than a diminution
of strength. But the agony of the paper, which retains so
much of what I was and am, this indeed is the irrefutable
and irreversible announcement of senescence.

12 April

The solution of a problem is often hampered when one
focuses too narrowly on the trouble spot. The exclusion
of one's own self, in particular, tends to block insight.
One tries to manipulate the situation, to change the other
people involved in it, but one's self remains outside, untouchable and untouched.

24 April

From the very first day, the young cat mother is familiar
with her kittens. They must be totally unexpected, totally without precedent in her experience, yet she holds
and licks them as though they were a part of her own
body. We have read about the wisdom of instinct; but
to see it in action!

13 May

I had learned that in music before 1800, a trill starts on the upper note, not on the lower one as in the more modern practice. Only recently I discovered that I was cheating by playing the first note of the old trill as a kind of upbeat or appoggiatura, thereby leaving the base of the trill on the lower note. And only then did I understand how much of a Baroque device is the old trill: it creates tension by withholding the next step of the tune through a syncopation.

15 May

As the only son and the oldest child of a family in which I experienced little hostility, I have lived my life as a friend among friends. The few persons who have ever harmed me were alien exceptions. And the basic assumption of gestalt theory—that every dynamic whole tends toward an optimal structure—has supported my belief that every human mind struggles toward the good.

17 May

I should have suspected that weaning is hard not only on the child but also on the mother. Michiko sits on a chair peering at her four kittens in the basket. She mews desperately. She no longer feels like being with her children but is miserable without them.

6 August

Letter writing flourished before the days of the railroad because persons who wrote to each other tended to live closer together and meet from time to time. What one can say to strangers, or to those who have become strangers by distance, is better printed than postmarked, because it concerns everybody. The letters exchanged between Goethe and Schiller or Flaubert and his mistress drew much of their life from being bridges between interrupted conversations. Today the airplane has brought us closer together again; but the telephone replaces writing, and chatter replaces speech.

7 August

As I was writing the last sentences of a new book, a large gray heron strutted along the water's edge with the dignity of a No actor. I finished my paragraph and rushed down to the beach, but the bird with the spindly legs and the curved neck had vanished like a ghost, promising longevity to my work.

10 August

In reporting on what I see, I behave like the artist, who offers his observations without consulting others. The presumptuous trust in one's own eyes and brain is a risk worth taking in the sciences as well as in the arts.

11 August

Animals that survive by escaping danger have their eyes on the sides of their heads, whereas those who live by attack have frontal eyes. This suggests that man, with his frontal eyes, is a creature of initiative rather than response—initiative being the human version of attack.

15 August

Did Goethe know that *Et in Arcadia Ego* refers to the presence of death when he made that maxim the epigraph of his *Italian Journey*? In a letter of 29 May 1817 to his friend Zelter he explains that he used it because Italy is so humdrum a country that he preferred to have nothing to do with it unless he could find his own reflection there, as

35

though in a rejuvenating mirror. This would seem to call for the reading "I, too, am in Arcady," rather than "I am even in Arcady."

20 August

When an American stalks out of the water to go back to his towel on the beach, he says, "I am going in," whereas a German would say, "I am going out." The one thinks of the beach, the other of the water. Many of the cultural contradictions by which relativists make a living are no more profound than this one.

Kay told about a boy who was accustomed to seeing his father off at the airport. When he himself got on a plane for his first flight, he asked after a while, "Daddy, when are we going to get smaller?"

3 September

I understand that the Alaska Eskimo, who never developed a written language, have now taken to sending each other tape-recorded messages. They thereby skip a phase of culture that, though dominant worldwide for some five thousand years, may be about to end. Before much longer, transmitted talk may well replace written and printed language even among ourselves.

4 September

What is the message of vertical harmony, developed in Western music after the Middle Ages and apparently absent from all other musical systems? It is not merely a matter of "enrichment" through the addition of another dimension. In monodic music the sound-object preserves its identity unaltered as it climbs and descends along the skyline of the tune. In harmonic music the sound-object undergoes modification within itself while it moves through time. It manifests discord, concord, tension, relaxation. Harmonic music portrays the agent as changing during the action which it performs and by which it is molded. Identity loses the simple trait of invariance. Being becomes process modified by happening and action. An age of innocence is over.

At the international congress of art historians a young scholar spoke about the heroic portrait in the fifteenth century. He showed that the lion, the prototype for such portraits, appears in two temperaments, namely, as the ferocious hero and as the clement hero. This reminded me of a similar ambiguity in the bull of Picasso's *Guernica:* he is the sturdy savior and at the same time the ferocious beast.

19 September

Things placed next to one another without insulation will influence one another. This happens not only in highly organized wholes but also in a chaos of accidentally assembled pieces. Be careful, therefore, when you use mutual influence as the criterion of wholeness.

30 September

In a recent paper on the *homo pictor,* Hans Jonas asserted that image making is the distinguishing trait of man. This works well for representational art. But which traits of nonfigurative art would persuade us that it was done by a human being? If we entered a cave on an unknown planet—to adopt Jonas's thought experiment—and found an abstract painting on a rock, formal harmony and order alone would not prove that the work had been done by a human being, since these qualities are not entirely absent from the handiwork of animals. Good abstractions, however, do possess significant form, even though they do not depict the things populating the earth. If they seem to display this sophisticated quality, they might give the nature of their author away.

29 October

Plato says in the *Theaetetus* (181C–182) that there are two kinds of movement, the change of place and the change within the object itself. What I said earlier about music can be formulated to mean that music without harmony conveys movement only of the first kind, whereas harmonic music presents locomotion and internal change as interdependent aspects of a more complex process. In the history of narrative and dramatic literature also, there comes a time when the interplay of invariant characters is replaced by the mutual influence of character and action. Compare Boccaccio with Shakespeare.

4 November

Self by boundary must be distinguished from Self by focus. It takes an infant a while to straighten out the different territorial claims of what is part of himself and what belongs to somebody or something outside. The Self as the focal center is established earlier: it is the place where feelings are located and from which wishes and acts issue. In human cognition everywhere, distinction by focus precedes distinction by boundary and remains the more important. Quibbles about what belongs where and to whom should be left to pedants whenever feasible.

12 November

Crookedness, weakness, depravity must be represented in the arts as deviations from a norm implicit in the work itself. In visual images also, obliqueness can be perceived only in relation to the framework of vertical and horizontal. When deformations of the mind or the body are presented without such reference, they change into monsters, curious, repellent, and essentially uninteresting.

At one of the annual conventions of the American Society for Aesthetics much confusion arose when the Society for Anesthetics met at the same time in the same hotel.

23 November

Some years ago the president of the Japanese Association of Mystery Writers assumed the name Edogawa Rampo. The two words have pleasant linguistic connotations, meaning something like "Old Tokyo River rambling." Actually, however, they are a phonetic adaptation of the name Edgar Allan Poe. The Japanese, like many old civilizations, are fond of punning. The aged mind plays with shapes, remote from the significations of the practical world.

Jefferson's Rotunda, built for the University of Virginia, was gutted in 1895, and its interior was entirely disfigured during the restoration. Intended by Jefferson to be a library, it now stands empty. One day a sight-seeing lady asked the old janitor what the building was used for, and he is said to have answered, "Why, lady, we use it for a rotunda!" The story would make a good introduction for a book on the purposes of art.

24 November

Sometimes an element of an artistic conception becomes a complete work in its own right. Picasso singled out the head of the wounded horse in *Guernica* and turned it into a separate painting. Michelangelo's *Moses* survives the aborted project of the tomb for Pope Julius II, of which it was to be one of the corner figures, and Rodin's *Thinker* was made for *The Gate of Hell*. In literature we have the

39

brief item about a mother killing her son unknowingly, read, if I remember correctly, from a piece of newspaper by the prisoner in Camus's *L'Etranger*. This theme was extended into Camus's play *Le Malentendu*. Dissertation topic for a gestalt psychologist: What happens when a part becomes a whole?

26 November

One-sided learning is not necessarily corrected even by a situation that calls patently for the opposite behavior. Ordinarily, cats learn more easily to open a door by pushing than by pulling. Michiko, however, received her instruction from a kitchen door that opened toward the inside. Now, no longer a kitten, she copes with any door she finds ajar by means of her pulling technique, which accomplishes nothing when the door needs to be pushed but pinching her paw. Her eight-month-old son, born in another house, pushes and pulls without trouble, depending on which way the door opens.

Pornographic pictures have always had a difficult time showing what is intimately hidden in the embrace of two bodies. Unless they rely on transparency, as did Leonardo in his anatomical drawings of sexual intercourse and as is still customary in the folk art on washroom walls, it takes desperate acrobatics to disclose the concealed kernel of the sexual union. Paradoxically, the artist must pull apart what he wants to show together.

22 December

Once people realize that the gods have no needs and that therefore there is nothing one can give them, the faithful can hope to influence the gods only by depriving themselves of something. Offering turns into sacrifice.

✿ 1962

1 January

Is it not curious that the same exclusive reliance on what
the senses tell us made an empiricist like Berkeley deny
the existence of matter in favor of existence in the mind,
whereas it led our modern behaviorists to abandon everything mental in favor of the purely physical?

13 January

The automobile and the telephone are defeated as instruments of individualism by being applied to the needs of a
mass society. The automobile fulfills man's desire to
move over the surface of the earth all by himself; but by
becoming accessible to everybody, automobiles have paralyzed our streets. Individualism is possible only in
plenty of empty space. Similarly, telephones block their
own paths of individual communication when everybody
is talking: the phone is too often "busy." Private enterprise cannot but strangle itself.

10 March

If Edward Sapir is correct in saying that "the lowliest
South African Bushman speaks in the form of a rich sym-

bolic system that is in essence perfectly comparable to the speech of the cultivated Frenchman," is there likely to be such a thing as primitive art—i.e., simple images conceived by complex minds—unless such images are kept simple on purpose, as our own posters and icons are at times?

6 June

The term *still life* ought to be reserved for arrangements of things not held together by a natural context. Chardin organizes his kitchenware for the purposes of his painting, whereas the Roman mosaics showing the leftovers of a meal strewn on the floor are not really still lifes. The still life is somewhere in between ornament and genre painting. It is a modern principle because it eschews realistic justification. Cézanne's or Matisse's nudes populating landscapes come close to still life arrangements of vegetation and human bodies. Those scenes are no more likely to occur anywhere outside art than Chardin's displays on the kitchen table. And in a sense, all nonrepresentational compositions also are still lifes.

8 June

What better demonstration of the figure/ground effect in perception than the shape of the human eye itself! As long as the pupil is seen as a dark disk in front of the colored iris, it is indeed looking at its target. But when at closer inspection and aided by our knowledge of anatomy we see the pupil as "ground," as a dark hole in the iris, the eye becomes frighteningly empty. It no longer sees; it looks blind, at best receptive. Remember also the kind of eye that shows no ground, such as those of some birds and animals—black buttons that do not "look" because they do not indicate an outward direction. Only the head as a whole, pointed, cocked, or turned, displays focused attention.

Perhaps what is disturbing about the color purple is not
the combination of blue and red but the equal presence
of two colors. Is not a similar disturbance created by an
orange in which red and yellow are equally strong or
even by a green in which the blue balances the yellow?
Perhaps the mind needs dominance to avoid ambiguity.

18 June

Adam's fall is made possible by the rebellion of Lucifer. It
takes a lack of perfection in the very governance, a crack
in the workmanship of the Creation, to make such mis-
behavior of the creature possible. Adam's sin is but a reflection of the tragic conflict within the nature of nature.

19 June

Certain poor translators tend to omit those small but
vitally telling words by which one expresses the logical
links between statements, the *but* and *although* and *nevertheless*. This happens because they tackle the text sentence
by sentence and do not bother to trace the sequence of
the argument. Hence the reader is faced with a succession
of periods that can be understood one by one but do not
hang together.

22 June

To any space-oriented person, it is one of the mysteries
of time that a change occurring in one short moment may
cast its consequences upon the entire duration. Take an
object out of a room, or change a spot in a painting, and
the effect is reversible and mainly local. But a second of
inattention in the mind of a person crossing a street, and
his life will be wiped out forever.

I am still of the opinion that movies, like children, should
be seen, not heard.

23 June

Vygotsky says in *Thought and Language* that the Russians have two words for the moon, one deriving from the Latin word for "caprice, inconstancy, fancy" and referring to the changing phases, the other meaning "measurer."

When Albert Michotte reported his observation that it is impossible to convey the perceptual experience of "being attracted by" through the behavior of abstract shapes, he does not seem to have remembered a grand example confirming his observation. Our experience of "falling" does not involve any sense of being attracted by gravity: falling is the passive letting go of something not held in place, not the effect of being pulled. Attractive power does not reveal itself to the senses. But how about magnets? There indeed knowledge seems to overrule perception.

24 June

Some notes left from Japan:

• On a poster I deciphered a long word written in hiragana: *Motabotaresu*. I finally figured out the meaning with the help of the picture above the text. It was "Motor boat race."

• "Last night all *denki* sayonara!" said the hotel maid in her fragmentary English. She was telling me that the electricity had been off everywhere.

• *Boy-san* [Mr. Boy] is the proper way to address a sleeping-car porter. A remnant of British colonialism embellished by Eastern politeness.

28 June

Traditionally, the color black is defined either as the opposite pole to white or as the absence of whiteness.

Something similar is true for the theology of evil. "Evil," says Augustine, "is the privation of good."

2 July

My experience with wood carving makes me suspect that, at least in the work of an amateur, the stages of formal development repeat themselves to some extent in the genesis of each work. Not that a mature artist will start each time at the very bottom of the ladder of complexity. Yet I find in my own case that I keep producing flat, shieldlike faces, simple outlines, undifferentiated rims of eyes and mouths, and right-angular corners before I proceed to modify these simple shapes into subtler ones.

4 July

So much does reading depend on the recognition of familiar shapes that when I look at unknown characters— Chinese ideographs, Greek letters, phonetic signs—I am not only unable to read them, which is natural enough, but I cannot even decipher them visually. I am left admiring the keen eyesight of those who can cope with the small print.

6 July

Perhaps the kinship of skin and leather has escaped me until now because in German they are named with different words. The Italians, for instance, can use *pelle* for both. And is the inverted gender of the words for sun and moon the reason why *il sole* (and *le soleil*) is a radiant hero whereas *die Sonne* dispenses motherly warmth?

31 July

I find that I do not give nature credit for geraniums and hydrangeas. They have so much geometry that I treat them as products of man and therefore as easy to make and of dubious taste. They do not count as a part of the garden.

11 August

In the smoldering remains of the house, they had made neat piles of still usable boards, bricks, metal pipes, all charred. It looked like the result of a piece of second-rate research.

12 September

The uncorruptible integrity of the work of art. Picasso talks smilingly about the tragedy of a painter who likes blonde women but finds that his pictures call for figures with dark hair. Friedrich Engels, in a letter (of April 1888) to the writer Margaret Harkness, speaks with admiration about Balzac, who found himself compelled to describe the necessary and deserved downfall of the noblemen even though it was they who had his sympathy. And a Catholic student of mine invented and danced a ferocious inquisitor, which forced her to recognize a crisis of her religious conviction she had tolerated half-consciously but not dared to tackle.

25 September

It is comforting for teachers and writers to know that there are persons who profit greatly from misunderstanding what others say to them. By taking something they hear to mean something that fits their own thinking in some fashion, they find themselves enriched, confirmed, contradicted, or merely stimulated and thus draw genuine enlightenment from a communication that was never sent out.

1 October

Few drivers will run through a red light, but almost
everyone will exceed the legal speed limit sometimes.
The reason for the difference would seem to be that red
and green differ in principle, whereas permissible speed
and prohibited speed are distinguished only by degree.
Unfortunately, many wicked things are only quantita-
tively different from the commendable ones—if one goes
a little farther one has gone too far. If this were not so,
living sensibly would be much easier.

8 October

The smoke detection system in the new public library
where Mary works turned out to be so sensitive at first
that twice when the staff lit cigarettes in the offices, the
county's entire fire department was mobilized. Some
sense organs created artificially by man respond more re-
liably to a dangerous nuisance than do the senses people
are born with.

What statisticians call a *normal distribution* is the universality of a trait modified by the dispersion that the imperfec-
tion of nature imposes upon the underlying lawfulness.
This dispersion around a mean is like the stray hits
around the bull's-eye. Why is such a distribution called
normal? Certainly not because it is the usual one. Normal
distributions are fairly rare. They occur where a natural
trait is relatively unmodified by other factors, inborn or
environmental. It is the trait that is the norm, pure and
undisturbed.

30 December

Artistic truth? I just read a whole book of examples of
kitsch in German literature. Their main characteristic was

that they are untrue. Graham Greene once wrote that it is the duty of the novelist to tell the truth: "By truth I mean accuracy—it is largely a matter of style. It is my duty to society not to write 'I stood above a bottomless gulf' or 'Going downstairs, I got into a taxi,' because these statements are untrue. My characters must not go white in the face or tremble like leaves, not because these phrases are clichés but because they are untrue." Let me talk irresponsibly for a moment. Rilke, a great poet, was also one of the most talented liars in modern literature. He wrote, for example: "und, umrauscht von seidenen Rotunden gingen ihm die vielen Engel nach." This means, roughly: "and surrounded by the rustle of silken rotundas, the many angels followed him." This is untrue, not because it is metaphoric but because it is cheap cosmetics. Certain passional upsurges in Tchaikovsky or Rachmaninoff are untrue, not because "the composer did not feel them"— which we have no way of knowing—but because they do not follow from their antecedents. Rossetti's anemic maidens are not true nor are the plumbing contraptions Fernand Léger presents as human figures. Marilyn Monroe in her own restricted way was true, but Marlene Dietrich hardly ever was. As the Italians say, "Si vede subito che non è vero niente!"*

* "One can tell right away that it is not true at all!"

9 January

The principal reason the phallus has not been represented in Western art is that in our tradition it cannot mean anything but naked sex. Also, however, it is almost impossible in realistic art to integrate with the human figure a small, independent item. The effect is as ridiculous as that of a statue smoking a cigar. The dancing satyrs on Greek vases or their imitations in certain drawings by Picasso deliberately suggest the comic, grotesque, or absurd; and the ludicrous effect of Jacob Epstein's phallic alabaster Adam unintentionally confirms my observation. The problem becomes manageable in stylized art such as African sculpture, where the size of such an organ can be increased to match that of a leg or forearm. It also profits from a stylistic base of right-angularity, which permits noses, breasts, or phalluses to stick out at the visually simplest angle.

To be getting old: gradually the lava has shaped the cone of the mountain, but the cone has also cooled and hardened. The hope is that there is a core of fire left, and now and then at least the top still sputters with some flames and brimstones. Otherwise the only reminder is the modest crown of smoke.

20 April

In his watercolors Cézanne treats the paper surface not as empty space but, on the contrary, as the intact world, still undivided and integral. He must have felt that tampering with the integrity of the world calls for extreme caution. To create objects, he often limits himself to making trenches between them. He leaves the centers of things untouched so that the uniformity of their whiteness safe-guards the unity of the whole. When he wants to use the local colors, which distinguish objects from one another, he leaves them to the last—the opposite of what a naive painter would do.

21 April

A compositional detail of Leonardo's *Virgin and Child with Saint Anne* may be said to support Freud's interpretation of the painting. Has it been observed that the determined left arm of the grandmother breaks, at a harsh right angle, the connection between the face of the mother and that of the child, cutting the line of their glance as though the woman in the background were indeed a rival inter-fering with the tie between mother and child? This motif hardly makes sense religiously, but it supports Freud's suggestion of the double mother. The remote real mother stands in the way of the stepmother's concern with her husband's child.

8 June

When we moved from the house to the apartment, the cat Kuro was badly disturbed. At the house we had kept him from the few carpeted rooms so that he would not scratch. Now suddenly the forbidden floor cover was everywhere. Temptation was universal, and so was the threat of punishment. Like a hermit haunted by a thousand women, chased by his superego, Kuro watched us in panic from a corner, dashed madly through the entire place when we approached, tried a frantic scratch here and there as though driven to sin rather than willingly committing it, and was off again immediately in flight from retribution.

A person may be willing to sacrifice some superiority he possesses as the price for being accepted. One of my students, working at a home for the blind, observed that inmates with partial sight would try to hide their ability and insist that they were getting around "by intuition." They were afraid that unless considered totally blind they would not "belong."

21 June

In his novel *La Modification* Michel Butor transposes all outer existence to the plane of the mind, thereby going beyond Proust, since Proust retains a physical base that defines the remembrances as mental and subjective, different from what *is*. Butor does not undo the dimension of time, but chronological sequence is surely overruled. The sequence of the narrative flashes back and forth, directed entirely by connections dictated by the sovereign mind. The mind draws on the reservoirs of past, present, and future with complete freedom from the path of history. The three realms of time, while differing from one another with regard to nearness or distance, confinement or openness, finality or opportunity, are no longer temporal in the true sense, since they do not follow one another.

22 June

In Neoplatonism the metaphors of art become flesh. The relation between the signifier and the signified is no longer purely mental; it becomes an existential connection built into the hierarchy of all being. The lower echelons of material things serve as images of the highest by embodying them. The dependents are also the proclaimers and explainers. Art does not dwell in the world as a stranger; the lone reflector among the reflected, it is now creature and image at the same time.

I am told of a child who insisted that seven times zero does not make zero but seven zeros. Although the word *zero* signifies nothingness, it is yet a thing in itself. To keep the thingness of words out of the world of material things is not an easy task for young minds.

23 June

Michel Butor reverses not only the direction of time; he also upsets movement in space. As the protagonist of *La Modification* travels from Paris to Rome, he recalls the opposite trip, from Rome to Paris, and he thinks of Paris as an alternate point of arrival. The recalled return trips counterbalance the trip in which he is engaged at present; but rather than simply neutralize its dynamics, they immerse the reader in a crisscross of opposites, a confused, undirected agitation, somewhat like the churning textures of Jackson Pollock. The goals themselves are also subjected to "modification." Rome and the traveler's mistress in Rome were the promise of freedom and rejuvenation; but as his obligation toward his wife grows, he finds that Rome becomes another center of constraint and defeat— in fact, the primary one—from which he now escapes with a sense of relief back to the slavery of his marriage in Paris. Thus the antagonistic geographic directions exchange their meanings: traveling to Rome becomes like traveling to Paris and vice versa, so that the confusion of the geographic directions is increased by an exchange of the relations between the actions and their meanings.

30 June

It had seemed to me that speech, to be poetic, would have to refer to the sensuous base of words. But what about concepts that no longer connote such life-giving relation to the world of the senses? Or might they still? To pick an example at random, consider John Donne's line "To night put on perfection, and a woman's name." What makes the abstract terms poetic? The meaning of "perfection" carries with it the sensory qualities of completeness and fullness, and "name" also has a tangible sense of finality. Even abstractions, to be understandable, have to be concrete and, hence, can be poetic.

5 July

After observing Butor's interference with the chronological sequence in his narrative, I was interested to find his remark in an article on Proust that the famous view of the three clock towers of Martinville, freed from their actual locations by changing perspective grouping and therefore "détachés de leurs servitudes quotidiennes, comme s'ils étaient devenus oiseaux,"* could be interpreted as a prefiguration of that female trinity Gilberte, Albertine, and the Duchesse de Guermantes. A liberation from time, says Butor, seems foreshadowed by their liberation from spatial location. And in fact, space is free from the sequential constraints that enslave appearance in time. In the dimension of time, one must swim against the stream with a troutlike effort to gain some of that freedom even in the imagination; in actual living it is entirely excluded. This is why some modern artists assault the dimension of time while indulging in the freedom of space. All that needs to be overcome in space is the continuity: we can decide to skip from place to place, as is

* "detached from their daily chores as though they had become birds."

done in the movies, or to fuse the noncontiguous, as is done in Cubist painting.

25 July

Seldom more than once every summer there appears between the dunes in the depression of the road that leads from our cottage to the beach—the heron! Elevated beyond the daily events by his rarity, he stands isolated between the symmetrical dunes against the empty foil of the water, framed and set off as though sheerly for the purpose of indicating his special significance. The hieroglyphic simplicity of his profile makes him an embodiment of his own image. He seems to be the portent of something weighty to come, a sign or message remote from the daily traffic.

2 August

The Taoists teach us that giving oneself up to a superior movement is not the same as being swung around as indifferent dead weight. It is the swing of the dancer's compliance with the music. I came across this sentence in Goethe's *Wilhelm Meisters Wanderjahre:* "Are you permitted to even think of yourself in the midst of this eternally living order as long as there does not arise in you, too, a magnificent motion rotating about a pure center?" We are told that man's ultimate role is to comply.

Getting older, one comes to suffer not only from forgetting but also from what looks like the opposite of losing contact with the memory traces, namely, from being flooded by an onrush of nonpertinent associations. This can interfere with concentration. The causerie is an old man's format of exposition. It is possible that this lack of intellectual stringency is nothing more interesting than a physiological loosening of the mental sphincters, resulting in an overall permeability. But it is also possible that both the loss of memory and the excess of it derive from the same cause, namely an increasing detachment from what matters in the outer world.

5 August

Five-year-old Jimmy said, "God is rich. Some men die with their wallets in their pockets, and God takes them."

Hegel's belief that art can embody the spirit only when it represents the human figure is based on the prejudice that the essence of a thing is tied to the thing's image—a prejudice of representational art. Instead, what endows an object with a humanlike spirit is the complexity of form and response analogous to that of our mind. A single nerve cell with the intelligent thicket of its dendrites or the network of a tree's roots may be more congenial to the nature of a mature human being than are certain effigies of man or woman that because of their simplicity remain below the highest human level although they may be beautiful and very valuable to us.

In his discussion of early architecture, Hegel speaks of mazes, "paths, between walls, mysteriously intertwined, entangled not for the silly task of finding the exit, but rather for meaningful circumambulation among symbolic enigmas." If you compare this seignorial contempt for the pragmatic with the dogged efforts of the hundreds of American psychologists who limited their quest for wisdom to watching an animal go after its food and drink in a maze, you see a difference between two cultures.

7 August

Mary suspects that the use of discarded junk in modern art is related to the Puritan reluctance to waste things. Why throw away a perfectly good egg carton?

Günter Grass's young Oskar in *The Tin Drum* agrees with Hegel that the nature of a tower implies no necessary limitation of its height. When Oskar reaches the top of the tower, he would like to continue climbing, "but the staircase had given up prematurely. He understood the nonsense and powerlessness of tower building."

Oskar also confirms Hume's skepticism about causality when he believes that the soprano in the Wagner opera is screaming with pain in protest against being hit by the spotlight. The interpretation fits all the facts of the moment perfectly.

For the benefit of the Freudians one ought to collect instances where sex is not the final target of the symbol but is itself used as a symbol for an ulterior meaning. Hegel quotes from Herodotus to the effect that Sesostris used to erect a phallic column in every country he had conquered. If the people had put up little resistance, he also had a vagina engraved on the monument.

The post-and-lintel construction in architecture is in no way a visible representation of the physical statics controlling the relation between support and load. Apart from its practical convenience for the builder, it is rather like a child's simplified drawing of a tree or human figure. In nature, where physical forces determine the shape of the objects they bring about, complex curvatures reflect the actual configurations of these forces. Pier Luigi Nervi refers to flower cups, leaves, eggs, shells, etc., and explains that only our modern building materials make it possible to apply these functional shapes to architecture. This is what led him to create his beautiful vaults and columns, which "feel" like nature because they stylize the configurations of natural forces.

8 August

When the Apollo of the Belvedere moves his head freely, he expresses, according to Schopenhauer, the independence of the human intellect. One could extend this observation to hand gestures, which somewhere along the historical development of Greek sculpture begin to display their independence from the wrist. As a loosening of the relation between part and whole, such formal emancipation could be read as a symptom of growing individualism.

⌊One cannot simply recommend the full development of all human potentialities as the desirable conduct of life. The various sources of possible experience get in one another's way when they are simply enumerated. The comedian W. C. Fields, when told by his doctor that he would lose his eyesight if he did not stop drinking, is said to have replied, "The stuff I drink is far superior to the things I get to see!" Consider the instances in which a deficiency—blindness, deafness, celibacy—enhanced a person's experience. What is needed is a hierarchy of values reflecting the complex interaction of a person's needs. ⌋

9 August

In an experiment on the sorting of color chips, a student of mine found that kindergarten children grouped a pale blue under blue but not a pink under red. There was some indication that this happened because the English language has a word for pale red but not for pale blue. In daily life, children who did not know the word *pink* seemed to call pink things red. There may be a similar inconsistency in other languages. German has *rosa* but *hellblau*. Does this mean that perceptually pink is less directly related to red than light blue is to blue? If so, why? If not, what makes for the peculiar linguistic practice?

When a tall building fails to offer man-size detail, our estimating glance cannot develop the structure from its elements to its height. Instead we reduce the actual expanse to a size more in keeping with human measurements, that is, we see large as small. So-called monumental architecture tends to defeat its ambition when it assumes that the omission of the small produces the large.

15 August

One reason I have always refused to learn to drive a car is that, to an unusual extent, I perceive my environment as pure shape or color. My eyes get caught by some peculiar-looking thing—an inversion of an object or a combination of shapes that do not belong together—and I savor it without any urge to know what I see, what it is a part of, and what is going on around it. This behavior of mine is, of course, the opposite of using vision for information and protective orientation. It may be thought of by some as "aesthetic perception," although in fact it is by no means typical of artists, who, on the contrary, tend to be observant and readily capable of identifying the things they see.

Only on rare occasions can one observe what happens when an art object appears not as a man-made image but as a part of life itself. The other day in Washington we were having lunch in a large hotel dining room when suddenly a fashion model started to move among the tables. Before I realized what she was, I noticed the peculiar perfection of the woman and the heightening and overevidence of her appearance, obtained by heavy makeup and a domineering and stylized hairdo. She also displayed an unusual concentration on holding herself together and walking at a straight and even pace. In the crowded dining room she was completely detached, like a painting on the wall of a museum on Sundays. The effect was that of an apparition, a sleepwalker. Even after I recognized her for what she was, the spell of unreality remained. She was intensely superreal, more strongly present than anybody else and at the same time an immaterial image.

2 September

The mind's action can be reduced to the concepts of driving and steering, that is, to motivational and cognitive processes. The term *steering* well describes the purposive character of all cognition, which guides the organism as a whole. Emotion—that is, the level of tension or excitement—is not a constitutive element of mental action but merely a property of a configuration of forces. When a rope is pulled in two opposite directions, is the tension of the rope a constituent of the happening, just like the two vectors, or is it merely a consequence of the antagonism? Stress measures the strength of the pull but does not add an actor to the play of forces.

4 September

The Massacre of the Innocents is often represented with Herod in attendance and watching the scene from his throne. In this way a merely causal connection is made visible through the simultaneous presentation of the commander and the execution of his command.

It would be amusing to extend Hogarth's notion of fitness to nonrealistic art. I seem to observe that even in the world of Cubist boats and buildings, one can distinguish between those that are fit to function and those that are not. Feininger's boats sail properly and his crooked buildings stand up, given the crooked laws of statics that govern his world. In the work of Picasso the same is true for his disfigured horses; and among his nudes I believe one can distinguish between those that hang together organically and breathe and move, wildly unrealistic though they may be, and some others that look like monstrous miscarriages of nature.

Architecture not only exhibits expression but also imposes expression. The low entrance door to the Japanese teahouse forces the visitor to humble himself as he enters.

7 September

What psychological and perhaps physiological factors make a person speak habitually at a certain speed—a speed that varies characteristically from person to person, just as everybody seems to have his own finger-tapping speed? At an international congress we were asked to slow down our delivery. This hampered me severely. I was not making my points with my usual spontaneity.

11 September

I confess that sometimes I profit more from statements I consider untrue than from truths that strike me as shallow. Thus Freud's imagination and intellectual discipline keep stimulating my thoughts even though I believe practically nothing of what he says. Such propositions are like Swiftian fantasies that enlighten us about the existing world by means of worlds that are pure invention.

18 September

If the lids of the human eyes opened downward instead of upward, the downcast eyes of modesty and bashfulness would be upcast eyes. Perhaps the direction of the lid closure is not related to gravity at all, but it does go nicely with the rest of bodily behavior, which expresses withholding and yielding by downward motion.

21 September

The useful objects we manufacture are supposed to be standardized. Unfortunately, they have as much capricious individuality as humans. In every hotel room the shower has its individual personality. You have to find out by explicit experience how it works, when it works, what relation there is between hot and cold and at what times, and also how the contraption responds to stimula-

tion, that is, to the handling of its faucets—whether they
have to be handled roughly or gently, etc. By the time
your mind has become shrewd enough to handle such
objects, you are ready to cope with humans.

29 September

Nature is made up of orderly islands not always designed
for getting along with one another. There is a beautiful
order to the pollen sent out by plants and their recipients.
Beautiful also the sensitive service of the human nose,
which lets the person distinguish between good and evil.
But when the pollen meet the nose, the cosmos breaks
down. And all of us, plants, animals, and humans, labor
forever like *bricoleurs* to patch up the seams.

12 October

The mind is a very incomplete recorder of all that is
going on in the organism. Much of what we see or learn
drops from awareness, to be retrieved from the storehouse of the nervous system only when it is needed. The
psychoanalysts rarely had the courage to admit that the
place where memory hoards its acquisitions can only be
the brain, not the mind. And in the psychology of perception we are reluctant to realize that our laws only describe what we see and hear—we will not obtain explanations until we dig down to the processes of physiology.

17 October

I wonder what Josef Albers meant when, in his book on
the interaction of color, he wrote this absurd sentence:
"Color is almost never seen as it really is—as it physically
is." Did he, of all people, not realize that there is no objective perceptual equivalent to the wavelength of light
energy? The "reality" of a color is certainly never seen,
since it is never free of the modifications of context. How

its reality can be described nevertheless—since things that do not exist cannot influence one another—is the great epistemological problem of gestalt theory still to be tackled.

2 November

When in the first act of Verdi's *Don Carlo* the king and the queen enter the church to pray at the altar where they notice the prince, they seem to be apparitions despite their substantial presence. This happens because they are not singing. Something similar happens to silent characters in stage plays. So dominant is the principal medium of song or speech that whoever does not partake in it becomes unreal.

28 November

When I walked through the park one hour after President Kennedy was shot, the trees and buildings began to look as though they knew it. They responded by an oppressive silence. I was perceiving their usual quietness as the absence of the commotion called for by the world-shaking event.

The strongest impression, as in the past at similar occasions, was the improbability of the event, the mind's resistance to something so thoroughly unanticipated. The awareness of what had happened tried to assert itself by momentary stabs but was rejected like an intruder. The world did not admit the hole torn into it. But, retroactively, the figure of the president became that of a man who would die early. The shadow of his fate was suddenly visible on our image of his cheerful face.

2 December

When a great emergency occurs at the head of the nation, there is a spontaneous impulse to short-circuit the intricate connection between the citizen and his government. I heard that, at the news of the president's death, students in some colleges took their cars and drove to Washington, D.C., having no particular purpose in mind but simply feeling they had to be there. This immediacy of contact was experienced by the millions of people, young and old, who sat in front of that instrument of social short circuit, the television set.

23 December

What Max Wertheimer has shown in his gestalt interpretation of the *modus barbara* in logic can be applied to other forms of the syllogism as well. A student of mine complained about being unable to work with her English teacher: "I resist agreeing with her on anything because that would make me feel that I am a dreadful old spinster like her." The syllogism "If A contains P and B also contains P, then A equals B" is logically incorrect because identity cannot be established by just one common property. But, says the gestalt psychologist, when a single trait is experienced, rightly or wrongly, as pervading the entire whole, then partaking in that trait indeed means absorbing the whole.

$$\mathcal{Y} \quad 1964$$

3 January

At the hospital they have a shorthand language of euphe-
misms. Having an operation is referred to as "going up,"
regardless of whether the operating room is on a higher
or a lower floor. "What are you going up for?" is asked
when they want to know what kind of an operation you
are scheduled to have. The meeting with the surgeon
thereby acquires an awesome overtone of ascension. By
avoiding mention of the unspeakable, they also give it a
tinge of religious majesty, revealing the association of
medicine with meeting one's judge and maker.

4 January

Thrown upon the snow
With shivering silver threads
The old Christmas tree.

14 January

After my nose operation Dr. C. said, "What a pleasure
now to reach all the way straight through your nose!"
The suspicion came to me that doctors have a simplified

65

model image of what the architecture of the body ought
to be and that they use surgery to straighten out crooked
passages, to improve symmetry, and to make shapes
more perfectly accessible. A sinister aesthetic conspiracy
hidden from our anesthetized eyes.

25 January

Tobacco has been recognized as damaging to health, and
a warning against smoking will be issued by the government. Soon it may be discovered that driving automobiles also endangers the lives of too large a percentage of
the population, and here again an official warning may be
in order. This is all to the good as long as they do not
find that life in general is too dangerous to be permitted
to exist.

6 April

I had come to feel, unwisely, that the material weight of
books burdens the spirit with a humiliating ballast. For
me to learn about another person's thoughts, why do two
pounds of paper have to be produced, wrapped, and de-
livered? How much more congenial are the electronic
flashes carrying thoughts from one mind to the next! But
as I watched what the new technology is doing to the
care of formulation, the survival of statements, the respect for established wisdom and precedent, I found myself looking back nostalgically at the leather tomes
chained to the lecterns of the Laurentiana, and I returned
gratefully to the medieval equipment of paper and pen on
the solid desk in my study.

12 April

The poet gave a reading. The glance of her dark eyes was
precise, and so was her black hair, simply sculptured in
the manner of an ancient Egyptian woman. Otherwise,

however, her appearance had a remarkable indistinctness. The contour of her face was not quite traceable, the mouth was not clearly defined, and the body in the envelope of a simply hanging dress seemed to sway in somewhat independent segments. This elusiveness, far from being unattractive, gave the impression of an apparition one could not hope to take hold of, flexible enough to respond to many different aspects of the world but ready to assume a defined shape in full response to any stirring from within. This was confirmed when she began to speak. She looked completely collected and present. She did not seem to be reading, yet she held her eyes steadily on the paper, as though in firm obedience to a persistent command conveyed to her by her poems. In response she generated the words inside, giving birth to them almost one by one. Soon also her body fitted itself to a kind of bell-rope swing, and she became the inspired "medium" of what she had written.

25 April

A very similar floodlight device may have very disparate effects: it spiritualizes a Rembrandt painting but highlights the sensuality of a Caravaggio. It is not simply the difference of the subject matter that, in the one, draws us to the transcendental source of the illumination and, in the other, caresses the flesh of the young bodies like a lover. There is also a difference in the texture of the receptive surface: the lacquer smoothness of the skin in the Caravaggio, as opposed to the breaking of the light as it is partially absorbed and consumed like a nourishment by Rembrandt's earthbound bodies.

26 April

Does van Gogh build his color composition on a yellow-violet axis with the yellow standing for the central generating force, the light, the sun, the flowers, and the wheat and with the complementary violet standing for the counterforce, the recipient, the antagonist, the victim?

20 May

Children seem to rely spontaneously on the isomorphic similarity of shape in objects and words. A colleague of mine tells me that his young son, playing around with his pajamas and pulling the legs inside out, showed them to his father exclaiming, "Look, Dad, japamas!"

12 June

I have never memorized the names of the four suits of playing cards for any length of time, although I do retain their images as four distinct and identifiable visual concepts. It is otherwise with birds. I may know a species quite well visually, but I feel uncomfortably incomplete unless I can connect its appearance and song with its name. The difference makes sense: I take no interest in card games and therefore have no need to talk about them. Birds, however, are a staple of our conversation.

One of our students, although gifted as a dancer, had never been truly successful because inhibition braked her movements. Liberation came with a choreography for which she used a wooden frame, which served to enclose the human figure but also stood for a mirror when two dancers faced each other. It also functioned as a door and swung around past a standing figure. Finally the frame became a toy tumbling and being tumbled about, catching and releasing a victim much as a lasso does. I have rarely seen a more successful exploration and overcoming of constraint.

7 July

What is the historical difference between, say, tuberculosis and Hitler? Both killed millions of people, but the illness remained historically neutral—except when it killed great artists in their youth or became a symbol of social alienation in *The Magic Mountain*. The Black Death and the earthquake of Lisbon each shook the Western worldview for centuries. So will Hitler have done, not simply by his deeds as such but by their meaning as an attack on the foundation of the human mind.

9 July

It is not good enough for the functionalist to point out that the flicker's body is most appropriately designed for his woodpecking business. If we are discussing architectural design, we also want to know why the flicker has black speckles on his chest and why he wears a red cap and yellow tail feathers. Here the analogy with nature lets us down. It was the aesthetic problem, after all, for which a theoretical solution was needed and which the functionalists undertook to supply. We did not need them to tell us that a building should be practical.

16 July

One can have shapes without color but not colors without shape. Van Gogh's detailed descriptions of the color schemes that he gives in his letters are remarkably useless unless one sees at least a sketch of the picture to which he's referring. One needs to know how much space is given to each color, and which colors border upon each other. What are the shapes of the color patches and where within the frame are they located? One also needs to know what subjects the colors depict. All this makes it extremely difficult to go beyond the most elementary relations when one talks in the abstract about color composition. No comparable problem exists for shapes. There are art historians who prefer black-and-white slides for their lectures not just because most color slides are such monstrous liars but because what the professor wants to show comes across more clearly without the colors. The practice may be deplorable, but the shapes are willing to cooperate.

No longer any need for Latin? But how can you ignore it if it survives in the very language you are using? What becomes of your English if in *reveal* you no longer sense the *velum?*

A painter doing a still life for a group of amateurs to show them the technique of oil painting applied a light horizontal layer of green to indicate the ground cover. A young boy observing this asked, "Isn't grass painted up and down?" It reminds one of how much sophistication it took to make the brushstroke independent of the object. Surfaces, of course, have always been daubed. But when it comes to shaping an object—when was this freedom acquired in the history of painting?

18 July

You are not necessarily a double-tongued hypocrite if you speak positively to a man about his work but call it inferior when speaking to others. Talking to the man himself, you discuss his work within the range of what he intends to do and can do; by general standards, you may have to judge it differently. One gets different sights by viewing a scene from the ground floor and from the top floor, but those two sights do not contradict each other.

20 July

In the world of our bodies there is no getting away from the horizon. When we rise, the horizon rises with us, and it descends with automatic obedience as we descend. A painted horizon frees us from our earthbound condition.

Should the critic "grade on the curve," as they do in the public schools? In practice, this despicable procedure is almost unavoidable, since much of the artistic work offered to the public day by day is bound to be inferior. One cannot growl in the low register all the time and thereby defeat the very raison d'être of one's own occupation. Because of this necessity, bad fare is called palatable in every edition of the paper.

25 July

When van Gogh attempted to symbolize the four seasons by pairs of opposite colors—for example, by making green and red stand for spring or black and white for winter—did he equate the color circle with the design of nature, the way the Pythagoreans saw the numbers of the *tetractys* as underlying the universe?

5 August

After injuring my chest in a minor accident, I was observed walking around with one of my shoulders pulled up. I was unaware of doing this, but I did notice a stiffening of my neck and muscular pain caused by my distorted posture. When I tried to correct my bearing, my subjective sensation was not that of straightening out what was crooked but, on the contrary, of pulling out of symmetry what I had come to accept as the balanced position. What better illustration of mental maladjustment, which compensates for a psychic trauma and is therefore experienced as the maintenance of normal balance. As a distortion, however, it causes symptoms of pain, for which the sufferer can find no explanation in his mental state. (Notice that it takes no "repression" to bring about this unawareness!) Relief can come ultimately only from correcting the imbalance.

At the age of twenty-five Jean-Jacques Rousseau confesses to being constantly obsessed by the fear of death. This compares with what a person nowadays may begin to feel at seventy. But the difference goes further. We know with some precision how threatening a given physical condition will be, whereas in the eighteenth century people were afflicted by symptoms of whose causes they and their doctors had only the vaguest notions (for instance, "un polype au coeur"). Beset, often for years, by ills for which no cure was known, the average person had to live with the daily threat of the final blow. No wonder Jean-Jacques wrote: "Nous sommes si peu faits pour être heureux ici-bas, qu'il faut nécessairement que l'âme ou le corps souffre quand ils ne souffrent pas tous les deux, et que le bon état de l'un fait presque toujours tort à l'autre" (*Confessions*, bk. 6).*

The steady stare of the jealous man in Edvard Munch's lithograph was on my mind as I was reading Robbe-Grillet's novel on the same subject. But whereas Munch at least leaves the view of his martyr unobstructed, the pun in Robbe-Grillet's title *La Jalousie* reveals that the true torture of the haunted man comes from the lack of full evidence, the scene visible only through the slats of the venetian blinds.

24 September

It has taken all these many years to make me realize that the phenomena of perceptual grouping must be described as dynamic relations. "Proximity" is not just a matter of connection or separation by distance. This is most evident in the arts. In Rogier van der Weyden's *Saint Luke*

---

* "So little are we made for happiness down here on earth that by necessity either the soul or the body is in pain when they are not both suffering, and that when the one is in good shape, this almost always does harm to the other."

Portraying the Madonna the spatial gap that keeps the Virgin remote from the saint is effectively counterpoised by the tightly joined couple of sightseers on the distant bridge. Expression comes about as visual tension, which pulls one of the pairs apart while compressing the other.

30 September

I have argued that in Picasso's *Guernica* the bull represents the surviving spirit of Spain because without this affirmation the message of the painting would be purely negative and therefore unsuitable for its purpose. As a great precedent one could refer to typical representations of the Deposition of Christ, where again a scene of pure destruction and death needs to be counteracted by indications of Christ's immortality and the stability of the faith. See the upright figures of bystanders, the introduction of verticals, the uprising trees.

7 November

A child drew a cemetery with a balloon rising from each gravestone. The balloons, she said, are the stomachs of the dead. "When someone dies, their stomach flies to heaven." Asked who had told her so, she referred to the maid, who reported she had told the child that the soul rises to heaven when one dies. And where is the soul? "Here, where the stomach is," the maid had responded. I am reminded of what Flaubert says of the "coeur simple," his maid, Félicité: "Pour de pareilles âmes le surnaturel est tout simple."*

12 November

One does not grow or age gradually. Rather, one stays in an age-group for some time and then shifts to the next,

* "For souls like this one, the supernatural is quite simple."

often quite suddenly. As the aging man says in Nathalie Sarraute's *Portrait d'un inconnu:* "On change de catégorie, hein?"*

Experiences involve the fusion and separation that in the infusoria is called conjugation. Temporarily at one with somebody or something outside of yourself, you leave a bit of your own and receive new matter in return. You may worry about the intensity of the momentary spending and the disturbance of being invaded. Yet your ability to give and to take is beyond expectation, and you emerge from the encounter rearranged and biologically refreshed.

The dissolution of the solid block of material, which came as such an innovation in the sculpture of recent years, was anticipated by the architects of the nineteenth century. The steel skeletons of the Crystal Palace or the Eiffel Tower transform the solid volume of the traditional building into webs of girders in open space—very much like what happens in the constructions of our sculptural welders.

Scenes from Eskimo life were shown to children with the intention of having them think and ask questions about the practices used by the primitive nomads. Why do they eat pieces of ice; why do they build weirs for fishing; why do they hold their bow drills in their mouths, etc.? It occurred to me that an unspoiled and unprepared child, before getting involved with such technical questions, would be caught by the larger problems of why some human beings behave and look so strangely, why they are so animallike, wearing furs, holding things with their teeth,

* "You switch to another category, don't you?"

tearing raw meat and eating it without knives and forks
in the open land among rocks. It seemed to me that good
thinking involves matters of priority that ought to be re-
spected. Not to wonder about the awesome differences
within our species and to busy oneself instead with technical detail indicates intellectual poverty, which should
not be encouraged. Blinders need to be handled with
care.

19 November

It makes little difference to a boat whether it is loaded
with stones, books, or persons. They are all heavy
things, differing from one another in secondary ways. To
the rest of us, this is a case of grouping different things
by a common property. In the logic of boat language one
word, like *cargo,* would suffice for stones, books, and
people.

2 December

From the beginning of Western thought there has been a
distinctly different evaluation of seeing and hearing in
their relation to knowledge. Sight conveyed external appearance, and special efforts had to be made to defend it
against the accusation that it misleads us. The Pythagoreans associated sound with mathematics. Sound pene-
trated the deceptive world of the phenomena—mostly a
visual world—and disclosed the essence of things. It
grasped directly the permanent truth. Sight was imagery;
sound was imageless music. Any distinction of the two
senses in our culture starts from this lead.

6 December

Size difference serves visual expression only when it is
perceived dynamically. It is not enough for the pharaoh

to be tall and his courtiers and underlings to be small. Such a translation of a social difference into a visual one will serve only the intellect. Unless we are made to see the ruler as a rising power and his underlings as pressed into inferiority, art will not speak.

14 December

Would there be any truth in saying that psychology was created by the Sophists to sow distrust between man and his world?

22 December

On the relativity of distance: if in an all-but-empty restaurant somebody takes the table next to mine, he has come very close indeed—so close that a special reason must justify his choice. If the room is filled, the distance between two neighboring tables separates us sufficiently.

1965

1 January

Late in the evening, half asleep, I was reading in "La crosse en l'air," a poem by Jacques Prévert, a reference to Pope Pius's father (culminating in the magnificent line: "La pipe au papa du Pape Pie pue")* when I found myself suddenly puzzled by the thought of how it was possible for a pope to have a father since popes are not supposed to have sons. It was as though at a primitive level of thought a genus had genetic connotations: popes must be born of popes, as horses are born of horses. Pertinent here perhaps the Aristotelian notion of the genus breeding the particulars.

Snow crowns all loftiness with white. It is a kind of substantial illumination. But what it contributes to the clarification of shape by distinguishing between above and below, it undoes by adding volume to volume. There is no continuity between the darkness of the tree branches and the whiteness of the snow covering them. Therefore, even when the snow has hit the trees from one side only,

* "The pipe of the dad of Pope Pius smells."

I do not notice the illusory illumination effect obtained with paint on the stage.

18 January

When in Venice, looking out from a second-floor window on the island of San Giorgio, I was astonished to realize that the Giudecca was only a stone's throw away. In the kind of visual schema one forms of geographic maps according to the gestalt laws, I had neatly detached the island not only from the Riva degli Schiavoni but equally from the body of streets bordering on the canals. Therefore, to fit an easy comprehension, I had reordered the actual situation, which has the island untidily close to the land.

In a photograph a parakeet embryo struck me as looking four-legged. A moment's reflection told me that the forelegs must be the rudiments of the wings and that the wings of birds must be their forelegs. This revelation, coming embarrassingly late in my life, gave me the opportunity to watch the ensuing restructuring of my view of birds. Suddenly birds looked like upright fourleggers walking on their hind legs. Their wings came to resemble the gesticulation and coping of our arms, and our arms in turn appeared as potential wings. I sat down and made a whole sheet of drawings of phantastic creatures, upright birds and winged humans.

23 January

A philosopher pointed out to me that when one listens to a cry of pain, "the person is heard in the cry." In our discussion I referred to the wailing of a dog run over by a car and the screeching of a car mistreated by a teenager. The car is somewhat humanized by seeming able to scream in pain, and the howl of the dog would indeed sound different if it were taken to come from a person.

A human cry is heard as the utterance of someone normally constrained by convention, which makes the outburst more appalling than that of a dog. Also, since we are endowed with language, the sudden replacement of speech with the primitive outcry of suffering announces the ultimate catastrophe, the loss of being human.

24 January

We are willing to sacrifice much comfort to symmetry, especially as long as we are not thinking. I kept my paper-cutting machine standing in the center of a small table, leaving not much of a margin on the sides. As a result, the cutoff part of a sheet of paper would drop to the floor. For how many years have I patiently collected those cuttings from the floor, until it occurred to me to place the contraption off center and thereby obtain the table space needed to keep the cuttings from dropping!

In the system of graphological analysis developed by Ludwig Klages the crucial criterion of a handwriting's *form level,* that is, the degree of its excellence, is determined intuitively by a synoptic evaluation of the overall structure, its richness, its rhythm, substance, intelligence. The score of the form level determines for every single trait whether it is to be considered as positive or negative, for example, whether control stands for rigidity or for discipline. I would emend this system by suggesting that the form level is not an isolated style quality but the result of a desirable structure organizing the relations between the traits. Every trait becomes negative when it is one-sided. In a fine person, the handwriting indicates a well-developed sense of freedom combined with the necessary control, or a strong concern for oneself combined with an equally strong concern for others, etc. It is this harmonious balance of active traits that creates the good form level of the whole. Could this approach be helpful for an analysis of style in the arts?

22 February

Jacques Yves Cousteau's new film on underwater research gave me a strong sense of well-being, which I attribute mainly to two of its qualities. A sense of freedom emanated from the unrestrained movement in all three dimensions of space. For the swimming creatures, both human and nonhuman, no difference seemed to be left between moving upward or downward. No laborious effort was needed for climbing, and descent was no downfall. Gravity seemed to be eliminated. Then also, for an hour and a half I saw no hasty movement. Everything was gliding smoothly and slowly, except for an occasional quick jolt gesture of attack or escape. This may feel intolerable to some people; it seemed paradise to me.

24 February

A relapse of the bad allergic face rash that spoiled my Italian trip last August. Again the experience of moving around behind the crust of an alien face. To look in the mirror and see somebody swollen, turgid, shapeless, out of character with my own mind. Also a sample of how people respond to a person with an unattractive face. I talked about all this to one of my students. She said she knew the experience. "But I could feel the pulls and squeezes that distorted my real face, and that helped me to preserve the connection between what I was and what I saw."

2 March

A single, small symptom may suffice to specify the difference between two worlds. When the dinner guests entered the home of our friends, the musicians, they were shocked to see two large cats lounging on the dining table. Said the guests, "But, you know, one can *train* cats not to sit on the table!" Whereupon the host replied, "In this house the cats are trained to sit on the table." The guests came from a world of distinctions—distinctions between man and animal, tabletop and floor, eating place and resting place—and were unprepared to face another world, one of careless and relaxed cohabitation.

3 March

I have always gone by the belief that if you try to make sure not to step on anybody's toes, you will have no space left to walk. I have written on philosophy, ignoring the debates that barricade every concept; I have behaved in an Asian country as I saw fit, without heeding the admonition to watch out for taboos; and I have walked through the cobwebs of intrigue and partisanship in academic settings with the half-conscious ignorance of a sleepwalker, intent and able to cling to my own business.

20 March

Some art theorists cannot let go of the axiom of realism. Someone has discovered the Soviet hammer and sickle in the nipples of the running woman's breasts in Picasso's *Guernica*. If an artist's shapes deviate from those of nature, it is taken for granted that they must resemble some other sample of reality. Natural they must be, to keep the albatross in the company of the pedestrians.

21 March

I get irritated by the parochial fuss made by some poets about the poet, the poem, and the nature of poetry in the very poems they are writing. They are exploiting the coincidence by which poetry is written in a medium that can also be used for talking, among other things, about poetry itself. Painters may sound off just as much about their trade, but at least they cannot do it in their pictures.

81

31 March

A young art historian tells me that his German-born professor improved on the sonority of spoken English by the usual confusion of *v* and *w*. When, in his lectures, he extolled the large architectural "woids," the vaults of the Basilica di Massenzio or the Hagia Sophia seemed to truly reverberate. How narrow-mouthed is the correct *v* in comparison!

15 April

One could teach a monkey to paint a red patch every time he is shown a red object, but that would not have taught him the semantics of likeness. The animal would establish a mental association between two kinds of things, and their similarity would facilitate the learning. But to make one object represent another is a different matter—that is where apes and men part company.

16 April

The traditional Japanese stage dancer stresses the diagonal in the direction of his glance and the position of his body. Although tied spatially to the framework of the stage, his mind runs unhampered into a distance where no target stops him. In Japanese painting, also, the architectural shapes move obliquely from infinity to infinity.

28 April

I have played the violin for half a century, but it only just occurred to me that the hand that makes the music is not the left but the right. My attention has always been on the fingers that capture the pitches prescribed by the music, while the right hand merely supplied the necessary sound by "working the bellows." Being absorbed by the difficult task of finding the right spot on the string per-

haps ten times a second kept me from realizing that it is
the right hand that controls the speed, the rhythm, the
dynamic pressures, and all the subtle accents of break and
slur. Perhaps for this reason also the instrument is held
under the left side of the chin so that the more capable of
the two hands remains free to conduct the music.

22 May

Radio astronomers believe they have recorded the faint
stir of the explosion that created the universe. The past
becomes present because it is so far away. We are presented with the past as its messengers keep arriving. If
what we call our history had not been in such a hurry to
disperse its light, we might see Socrates and Napoleon
come and go in due time.

7 July

When Picasso uses a wicker basket to make the rib cage
of a goat, both the goat and the basket abandon their natural character to meet at the metaphoric level where objects deposit their abstract expression. Recently I saw in
the work of a young Greek artist an old shirt and a child's
underpants pasted on a canvas and treated in such a way
as to lose their material distinction and become a music
of moving folds like those of the garments of the marble
Nike tying her sandal. Without this transformation, objets trouvés fail as pathetically as do their forerunners, the
mechanically faithful copies of nature.

26 July

The double function of the eye—emitting power and receiving information—manifests itself in the arts only at
an advanced level. The early icons stare but hardly see.
A nineteenth-century portrait looks at the viewer with
interested curiosity. Rembrandt's figures spell the fascina-

tion of their presence by their way of taking part in the sorrows we share.

When the gopher digs a hole, he engages in a constructive activity, although undermining our cottage is destructive. When our cat catches the gopher, he acts destructively, although feeding himself and protecting the foundation of our house are constructive. Does all this argue for relativism? To judge by the respective opinions of the gopher, the cat, and the homeowner, no values could be more absolute.

20 August

Dante, in canto 7 of the *Purgatorio* (lines 73–81), nicely describes the difference between the colors of a thousand flowers composing a painting and their thousand odors producing an *incognito indistinto,* that is, a mixture of unidentifiable elements. That is why one cannot paint pictures with fragrances.

14 September

In his early years a person is predictable, and in maturity he becomes predictable again. In between, he wrestles with the errantry of growth. Is the task of life that of acquiring what one had originally received as a gift?

26 November

Karl Duncker has told us that to solve a problem, one must establish the "functional value" of the sought-for solution. Before doing this, it seems to me, one has to reduce the problem itself to its functional character. Depending on whether one thinks "the neighbors are too noisy" or "the walls are too thin," one will look for different solutions.

20 December

If natural science has made man smaller by placing him
on an inconspicuous speck of matter, it has also made
him larger by discovering a new universe within him.
Leonardo da Vinci, whose anatomical drawings trace the
miraculous intricacies of man's internal organization, also
illustrated the Vitruvian man, the Neoplatonic reflection
of the macrocosm.

21 December

No religion ought to claim possession of any factual
knowledge of its own. When a culture is in good working order, religion arises from what is considered true by
everybody; but when knowledge advances while religion
stagnates, a split develops between what science knows
and what religion avows. Belief in God is not a religious
prerogative but a hypothesis left from early science.

25 December

A young German painter told me that his Berlin apartment opens to an inner court whose triangular shape is
formed by the backs of three apartment houses. The
court is divided up among the buildings by fences in such
a way that each has its triangular slice. Therefore, the
organ-grinder entering each section of the yard from the
appropriate entrance goes through his program for each
building, and although pennies are dropped only by the
inhabitants for whom he is playing, everybody hears him
three times. The community of sound is overridden by
the separateness of spaces and vice versa.

Faithful believers put God in a realm beyond the mental.
Even George Berkeley, although he denied the existence
of a physical world, had to become a dualist to avoid call-

ing God a product of the human mind. Berkeley made God dwell in God's own consciousness. C. G. Jung plays tricks in the twilight: talking to psychologists, he describes God as one of the archetypes that shape the human mind, which makes Him a mental figment; but for the benefit of the faithful he describes the archetypes also as autonomous forces, which lifts God, being one of them, somehow beyond the mind to a realm of respectable transcendence.

🌿 1966

1 January

There are reciprocal metaphors, where the two items reflect each other symmetrically, neither of them referring
solely to the actual "reality" that is being metaphorized.
When T. S. Eliot identifies the dove of peace with a dive-
bomber, neither the Bible nor the battle prevails. When
Henry Moore creates women that are mountains, his
sculpture does not show a mountainlike woman as does
Baudelaire's *La Géante*. Rather, by raising his image to
the level of the common denominator, Moore synthesizes
the feminine in the monumental with the monumental
in the feminine. What results is a rarified abstraction that
could qualify as a religious vision.

2 January

The notion that the soul is separable from the body
comes about because we do not usually know what is
going on in the brain. In daily experience the mind labors
and travels, leaps and connects, while the body may be all
but motionless, like a container harboring a lively, fluttering thing.

8 January

When I showed my students the recent reconstruction of the Laocoon statue, one of them remarked that the bending of the arms as now established has a bearing on the famous problem of the priest's half-open mouth. The father and the son's right arms, no longer freely stretched as they were in the faulty addition of the sixteenth century, express by their angled elbows a control similar to the one that keeps the mouth from screaming.

10 January

If Ernest Fenollosa is correct in asserting that "in Chinese the proposition is frankly a verb" (*by* = "to cause"; *to* = "to fall forward"; *in* = "to remain; to dwell"), we should no longer be misled by our own languages to believe, as Freud still did in his discussion of dream symbols, that relational concepts cannot be expressed by images. Fenollosa makes his point also for conjunctions. Thus, if instead of saying, "She cleans the house because we are having guests," we say, "Her housecleaning serves to honor the guests," our speech is freed of its dry fillers; it dissolves entirely in the living medium of perceivable action.

17 January

Nothing, I said to myself while I was falling asleep, will have suggested the art of writing to ancient man so compellingly as the sight of the crescent moon, for nothing in nature resembles a written letter as closely as the elegant white sickle on an undisturbed ground.

3 February

The film version of Laurence Olivier's *Othello* showed the actors so closely that I could analyze the facial gesture by

which Frank Finlay as Iago expressed villainy. He kept
his mouth half open—not with the lower lip dropping
loosely (as one would do to express a lack of intellectual
discipline) but by retracting his lip tensely as though to
withhold progress of action. There was alertness, lying in
wait, holding back, which together with the vigilance of
the glance conveyed scheming and dishonesty. Compare
for contrast the open receptivity of the lips practiced as a
sexual lure by young actresses and models.

22 February

The closed and concentric stage of the Greek theater ex-
cludes time from the play. Oedipus's punishment does
not follow his crime; it is implied from the beginning of
the presentation. The frame of our modern stage offers
instead a momentary unveiling of a story emerging from
behind the scene and exiting into an invisible future on
the other side. It therefore suits plays stressing the course
of time. On our peephole stage, the mop-up of the characters at the end of a tragedy—which is a device of ancient drama—has the almost ludicrous quality of a total
liquidation, leaving the future as empty as an express
train at the end of its run. Instead, when the curtain falls,
the play should be felt to continue.

12 April

I was surprised to notice that Jerome, in the Vulgate,
translates the petition for our daily bread in Matt. 6:11
as "Panem nostrum supersubstantialem da nobis hodie."
The Greek original, it seems, has an adjective that can refer to what is beyond the substance but can also simply
mean "what is needed." Even though in antiquity the demand for bread must have been intended literally, Jerome
prefers a wording that transforms it into a eucharistic figure of speech.

89

Light in my window
As I look up from the street
"I must be at home!"

16 May

Turner had to search nature for subjects resembling the
swirls of color congenial to his temperament. He found
them in storms, waves, clouds, flames, smoke, and in the
camouflaging hazes. He could also justify them as mere
sketches, preparations for fully executed works. This
need for realistic justification in his paintings explains the
inconsistency of style that makes him combine a whirl-
pool of waves and storm with meticulous detail in the
shore scene. Although art should have objected, nature
offered them both.

12 August

Ernest Jones says of the verse from the *Aeneid* used by
Freud as a motto for his *Interpretation of Dreams* that it is
"an obvious reference to the fate of the repressed." This
it certainly is: "Flectere si nequeo superos, Acheronta
movebo."* But because the quotation appears on the title
page of Freud's first major work, it would seem to refer
to the author's enterprise at least as much as it does to his
subject matter. Not admitted to the honors of the daylight world, Freud becomes the ruler of the underworld,
powerful enough to move the Acheron. The pursuit of
psychoanalysis presents itself as an act of escape and com-
pensation—the psychoanalyst himself becomes a prime
example of the basic psychoanalytic mechanism.

28 August

Indoors, man towers over most of the objects around
him, indicating that he is the master. Outdoors, he is at

* "If I cannot move the earthlings, I shall stir up the Acheron."

the bottom of the world, overtopped by trees and mountains and also by his own buildings and vehicles, which
are permitted and intended to lord it over him.

Our black cat lay on the window sill, against the black
night outside. When his eyes were open, his body was
visible, dimly outlined; but as soon as he closed them, the
whole cat vanished, leaving only the unbroken darkness
of the window.

We look up to the mountain with humility; but since we
can usually see its top, its greatness is encompassed by
our visual field, which is our empire. Not so in the can-
yons of our city streets, where we are surrounded by
buildings we cannot fully survey. They pass into endlessness beyond the reach of our comprehension. So do the
other dimensions of city life, its numbers, its complexity,
its disorder.

29 August

In a village such as that of Verga's *I Malavoglia* every citizen is thoroughly aware of the existence, both private and
civic, of everybody else. Every person is visible in the total spectrum of his experiences and actions—a wholly
known human being. In a town, a person will approxi-
mate such completeness only within his own narrow
circle. That circle, however, is surrounded and served by
a set of bit players, mailcarriers, plumbers, waiters, who
exist only as their function and by their function.

1 September

After Rembrandt's death
The Parthenon exploded
Is there sense in time?

13 September

With good reasons the heralds of obsolescence praise the
paper handkerchief. But will it do what the embroidered
linen or silk handkerchief did as an implement of human
relations? Could *Othello* be played over a piece of Klee-
nex? This is not a matter of the sturdiness of the material.
The fragile paper fan of vanishing Japan crushes with its
symbolic weight all the metal blades of its modern electric successor.

17 September

Irma Bartenieff's Effort Shape method teaches the dance
students in the Laban manner not to aim for a particular
shape of movement but for the movement impulse. This
makes good sense, because it develops expression from
dynamic action. Instead of performing curves and lines
with her limbs, the dancer makes her body move freely
through space or push space out of her way, plow
through it, press against it, etc. My guess is that the
dancer understands such meaningful action as coming
down ultimately to the antagonistic innervations of flexor
and tensor.

19 September

According to a misconception still prevailing among psychologists, gestalt theory teaches that cognitive insight
comes about suddenly rather than taking time as opponents assert it does; this, although Wolfgang Köhler already rejected the notion that problem solving must be
expected to occur in a flash. In the areas of shape perception or the visual constancies, authors such as D. O.
Hebb have insisted, supposedly as a refutation of gestalt
psychology, that these mental capacities take time to acquire. Actually there is probably nothing in the mind that
comes full-blown, and why should anything be expected

to? What matters is whether the process through which
the capacity develops is one of learning to survey the
structure of a situation, fitting parts into wholes, subdi-
viding wholes, etc.—as gestalt psychologists would expect—or whether it is one of searching memory for precedent, collecting instances, or resorting to some
extraneous rationale.

22 September

In a dream, I am finding my way to the registration desk
of a hotel and am told, "Fill out this card, and also write
your name on this photograph!" The photo is a large
landscape, and I have much trouble writing on it because
the trees are in my way. My letters are getting larger and
scrawlier as I try to adapt them to the shapes of the trees.
Finally I say, "You'd better take this away from me!" In
my waking hours, I have been engaged lately in writing
a chapter on shape perception, in which I have been attempting to explain that perceiving shapes means fitting
them to the unruly stimulus material; the dream expresses my doubt as to whether I (my signature) can
maintain myself in the struggle with this difficult job.

2 October

Suddenly I had to laugh about the human ear—this baroque ornament pasted on the perfectly functional head.

African sculpture is not primarily "early" art, let alone
primitive art. There is nothing primitive about such mastery of shape, such originality of invention, such subtle
control of relations. To be sure, the style is not realistic,
but the particular function of tribal art did not call for
more realistic representation. Also, any firm tradition
tends to freeze shape; and geometric precision conveys
a sense of what is lasting, unalterable, definitively valid.
A circle or a symmetry resists change.

9 October

A new medium may display meaning before any of its applications do. It is easier to sense what kind of medium is needed than to employ it tellingly. This was probably true for the introduction of central perspective in the fifteenth century, merely a new technique for showing depth before it became an enrichment of symbolic expression. It was true for the motion picture, and it may be the case now for the so-called happenings, which mean little or nothing so far but may captivate us as a new idiom of art.

22 October

There is something happily vegetal about Oskar Ko-koschka's paintings. The faces of his portraits have the colors of autumn leaves, and even his cathedrals look as though they were made of greenery. And what other painter in this day and age would still dare to depict a whole city, the whole sweep of a vista. Like the Lord, he stands high up on a hill or tower and surveys the cosmos, as did the German and the Flemish painters of the Renaissance.

> The birds still pecking
> Before my mother's window
> But seeds have run out.

Some works of art are meant to look as though they were made by nobody. Others insist on showing that they were shaped by the hand of the artist. Still others, objets trouvés, derive their meaning from having been made elsewhere and for another purpose.

26 October

One of the great beauties of flying is that an airplane's locomotion feels so slow, although as powerful as the ad-

94

vance of a gigantic steamroller. The illusion is bought at the price of a dangerous remoteness from the ground, but the sensation is real nevertheless. This must be the way God moves: smoothly, relentlessly, yet astronomically slowly.

28 October

Perfection is possible only in works of art and in the gods; and even the gods are works of art.

5 December

The rigidity of circular shape becomes evident when a car is driven along a circular curve. The steering wheel can be held steadily in the same position, inducing the same constant deviation from the car's position at every point of the turn.

14 December

Contours do not belong in sculpture, because in sculpture lines are objects. Alexander Calder's wire drawings are a late sophistication, since they enjoin us to accept the physical substance of the contours, which are so much more tangible than pencil lines on paper, and treat them as a purely visual boundary of physically empty space. Calder's humorous paradox: the physically nonexistent outline of a physically real cow is represented by the physically real outline of a physically nonexistent cow.

26 December

The flames of real wax candles on the Christmas tree create silence because they move without making the noise that such commotion would be expected to make. Not so the electric bulbs. They do not move and therefore create no silence. But the snowflakes outside behave like the flickering flames: they fall noiselessly. Et in terra pax.

28 December

When the meaning of a word is not known, its sound and its ingredients of particular connotation may conjure up a distinct referent. *Antimacassar* is to me a mastodontic battlewagon, and the dictionary's assurance that the word designates a delicate backrest cover is not strong enough to dispel the barbarous vision.

29 December

When you talk or listen to someone, you do not really look *at* him so much as you look *into* him through his eyes, with your glance adapted to a distance beyond his face. The two minds are fastened to each other like two peacefully copulating snails. But some painters look *at* the shapes of their model the way a physician examines the skin of a patient—a breach of social etiquette. It means treating a person as an object.

Curious, by the way, that between the sounds I hear as the words leave my mouth and the sounds my interlocutor hears as they arrive at his ears there is a no-man's-land of silence.

🌿 1967

Long ago I observed that tourists use photography to replace response. If a Greek temple seems to call for an articulate reaction, to snap a picture of it means to do
something tangible about the challenge and to take something away with you. With photographic facilities increasing, the practice has spread to museums. If a Rembrandt leaves you thoughtless and speechless, you can
assimilate it mechanically, acquire it symbolically, shoot
it like a duck. Recently, photostatting has created a similar temptation. I come across a provocative page, I make
a photostat of it. By possessing the paper, I fancy that I
possess the author's thought and naturally shall make intelligent use of it later. Another trap of the devil.

4 January

Marshall McLuhan's theories might lead one to conclude
that there would have been no need for gestalt theory before the invention of the phonetic alphabet. The alphabet
is indeed the mind's first attempt to cut living wholes into
elements that do not respect the structure of the whole
and are self-contained, closed units. Eventually this kind
of blindly mechanical decomposition may have led to a

similar procedure in the sciences. The idea is striking, if
one is willing not to consider the many centuries of intellectual history separating the early invention from the late
practice.

13 January

By wrapping an armchair in sheets of plastic, tying it up
with ropes, and displaying it in an art show, one transforms the object into the image of a tortured prisoner.
When the aesthetic attitude is called up, it automatically
turns the practical function of the object into an expressive one: the chair becomes human, the ropes are fetters,
and their crisscross becomes the visual music of violence.
The demonstration is no great creative achievement, but
it is useful and rather upsetting.

Color influences our manner of handling physical objects.
On chilly days I reach for my red corduroy shirt. At the
American Federation of Arts they used to stain their
packing cases in pastel colors, baby blue or pink, to make
sure that the freight handlers would treat them with care.

21 January

Andy Warhol's film *Eat* shows for half an hour a man
slowly chewing and savoring his morsels. For the viewer,
this changes the motion picture from a pastime to a torture. Instead of shortening time, it lengthens it intolerably. Instead of artfully narrating events, it reveals the
business of life as emptiness. What is worse, the man
seems to do his chewing with a deliberate indifference
to the audience, as though he were sitting on a subway
bench, watched by all; and by displaying his sensuous
consummation in close-up, the film makes us feel guilty
of voyeurism. The human face becomes a private part of
the body, and its shameless exposure is practiced with total nonchalance.

10 February

Marshall McLuhan's confession, "I don't pretend to understand [my theories]. After all, my stuff is very difficult," reveals that the author of *Understanding Media* is thinking of himself as a medium. His unchecked dictations are but another instance of the surrender of intellectual and creative initiative in our time. And like his forerunners, from the Delphic Pythia to our spiritualist mediums, he mistakes his own obscurity for the mysterious wisdom of superior powers.

6 March

Art navigates between illustration and decoration. The illustrator conveys subject matter, moods, theses, jokes, or tricks by whatever pictorial means are needed. Ben Shawn, Magritte, Dali, Wyeth are illustrators, because in their pictures the content is not carried by the power of form, which is the case, for example, in Goya. At the other extreme, form without the substance of content makes the decorator. Aubrey Beardsley spikes the pretty harmony of his drawings by depicting the deformities of the human body that derive from indulgence, evil disposition, or decrepitude. He fits these deformities to his calligraphic ornaments and thereby, one might say, redeems them morally: depravity becomes the spice of beauty.

The automobile driver's horn demonstrates the wealth of expression obtainable by pure rhythm. By varying the intensity, speed, dynamics, and number of tones, the driver—without changing the pitch—expresses the routine warning, the sudden emergency, the anger of impatience or protest, the friendly salute, the noisy merrymaking, etc.

Since any union of egg and sperm is a purely accidental encounter of disparate sets of genes, it is a miracle that the offspring contains so many reasonably well-shaped specimens. One would expect something worse than discord in many cases, namely, a lack of any relation, a hodgepodge of traits, the mutual undoing of shapes. To be sure, one does see plenty of nondescript, unreadable human figures, but I suspect that such lack of character is due more often to a mixture of poor stock.

31 March

It takes an older man some patience to watch a whole civilization work through puberty. Perhaps another ten years of pornographic books and movies will be needed before we'll learn to put up with the human body and the business of sex. After that, let us hope that we shall still have enough time left to try to run the world sensibly.

10 April

By now, most people I meet look familiar. There exists only a limited number of human types.

> Like a maiden's hair
> brushed sideways by the wind
> Willows in the spring.

8 May

For the discussion of intimately personal things the relation between parents and children is too distant and too close. Husband and wife, when they are one body and one mind, can share much. So can friends if they do not see too much of each other. But the trust and affection holding a good family together neither permit nor require total disclosure.

11 May

Probably there is no need to "review" the average work of art. It is no more "news" than the average tree or meal or medication. As long as it does its daily duty, it calls for neither praise nor punishment. Nobody is sent to review the local hardware store. I suspect that this is also the case for pictures and sculptures under conditions more normal than ours.

16 May

The cat Kuro:

> Although he left us
> His shadow sits on the chairs
> And he waits at the door in silence.

8 June

By replacing the right angle with the triangle and the cube with the sphere, Buckminster Fuller occupies the landscape with large crystals, which the wind may blow away. Nearby, designed also for the World's Fair in Montreal, Moshe Safdie has built his Habitat apartment buildings. The Mediterranean architect replaces the traditional compactness of the cubic block with an agglomeration of units, which accumulate but do not fuse. As in the clustered cubes of southern hill towns there is anonymity of shape but individuality by position. No two locations look alike. Each apartment shares as little wall space as possible with its neighbor. The Habitat reef seems to have grown from the earth or to have been thrust out of it. Seen as a whole, it looks like a work of nature, romantic and irrational. In its elements it is rational, geometric, man-made.

> Quite early the thrush
> After the silence of night
> Made the longest speech.

9 June

Of the Latin *supercilium* the English language preserves
only the haughty pride, not the eyebrow. Frequently,
words are adopted from another language at a time when
they have developed a metaphoric superstructure. By
adopting the later meaning without the original one, a
language adds through such loans to its own opacity.

30 July

When one listens to people talking in Henry James's *Bos-
tonians,* one is tempted to envy them their supernatural
lucidity of observation and thought. By holding them
against one's own obtuseness, one forgets that they are
not "real" but mere extracts of the author's reasoning of
a lifetime and that their spontaneity is laboriously prepared.

1 August

So many decades ago, a fellow student of mine, a practically minded and efficient young man, permitted his wife
to go on a canoe trip with me but cautioned her to be
careful: "If you fall into the water, he will not save you; at
most, he will write a sad poem about your drowning!"
His knowing smile has haunted me through a lifetime of
contemplation and theory, questioning my smug insistence that the struggles and victories of the mind are the
true action, the true reality.

8 August

Not unwisely, stories that end well have been called com-
edies even though there may be nothing funny about
their plots while they are in progress. When the desperate
struggle of passions that engaged our Aristotelian anguish
and pity is untangled at a happy end, there is comedy in

the realization that a solution obtained at such an effort was available from the beginning. Hindsight makes us smile.

22 September

Having read proof all my life, I spot misprints as soon as I glance at anything printed. The impression I receive is not that of a missing or misplaced or mistaken element in an otherwise correct whole but rather that of a crippled word. The word as a whole looks pathological—twisted or gaunt, or it may carry the wrong expression, looking sharp and edgy rather than nicely graded, or swollen with an excrescence rather than streamlined. The sick look of that whole prompts me to search the word's particular makeup, which lets me pinpoint the erroneous detail.

For David Hume's notebook: One evening a young boy somewhere in the country banged with a stick against a telegraph pole at the very moment when all the lights went out along the Eastern seaboard because of a power failure. He ran home to confess to his mother that he was to blame for the blackout.

27 September

Half-asleep, I wondered about cutting a corner from any polygon and being left with one more corner than the figure had before, provided the cut touches no corners. A magical paradox: by taking away, you get more!

18 October

I am encouraged by what I once read about Charlie Chaplin's way of checking on his work. When a film, or a part of it, was finished in rough shape, he showed it to a random group of people. Instead of asking, "Did you like it?" he wanted to know, "What did you see?" When their account matched his intention, he was satisfied. In my own writing I find still and inevitably that I am not saying what I think I am saying. When Mary reads my manuscript and shows me my shortcomings, I am comforted by the thought that even Chaplin could not be sure that he was saying what he wanted to say. And in pictures at that!

🌿 1968

13 February

For the first time after having been forced to leave my hometown, I returned to Berlin. On the evening of my arrival, while unpacking my suitcase in the hotel room, I heard a metallic noise and found that a rifle bullet had dropped on the floor. I knew that bullet. It had pierced my bedroom window one night during the German revolution of 1918. But how did this token of past violence happen to appear as an uncanny salutation in the hour of my somewhat diffident return? It took me a while to remember that I had last used the suitcase a year and a half earlier, when I was in Germany shortly after the death of my mother. At that time I found the bullet among my mother's souvenirs and took it with me; and I have carried it with me ever since as a charm on my travels.

An elderly lady who teaches French with the spark of the born teacher said, "One must make sure that the student does not misinterpret the discipline demanded by the language as a rigidity of the teacher's character." A language cannot be blamed for mechanical and often arbitrary regulations. Coming from the teacher, they would amount to pedantry, justifying rebellion.

17 February

I asked Kurt Badt, the art historian, what he meant by "intelligent" art. He answered with the following list:

Artistic intelligence: Michelangelo, Poussin, Delacroix.
Lack of it: Memling, Riemenschneider, Ingres, Kandinsky.

29 April

If, as Thomas Szasz insists, mental disturbances were not to be called diseases, the patient himself would be charged with overcoming his trouble. Such responsibility, although derived from a quixotic theory, might be of some help in psychiatric practice.

9 June

Alice Sheldon suggests a life-oriented arithmetic, such as:

One rabbit + one rabbit = 10 rabbits
One cat + one dog = no animals present
One cat + one mouse = one cat

21 June

The Landmarks Preservation Commission of New York City must certify that the Grand Central Station building will not be "unduly changed" by a skyscraper to be placed on top of it. That change will not be physical but perceptual. One can leave the landmark untouched but destroy it nonetheless by what one puts above and around it.

106

5 July

In information theory it makes sense to call the points of a straight line redundant and treat them as duplications or repetitions. Perceptually, however, this will not do. The structure of a line and that of a point have next to nothing in common. Perceptual redundancy would have to tell us what is structurally superfluous and therefore disturbing.

9 July

For philosophers obsessed with language the world is like an arboretum: every tree bears a nameplate, and once one has read the plate, one has seen the tree.

16 August

Kinetic sculpture does not generally display a time arrow as do the works of the temporal arts, which have a beginning and an end. A rotating sculpture or a mobile with any number of degrees of freedom does not show progress but simply explores the relations within an invariant system.

18 August

In the northern wind
Spiders swaying back and forth
Sitting on nothing.

Gestalt theory deals with formal organization, and only to that extent is it concerned with content. It says, Give me a set of forces, and I shall tell you how they will organize! Gestalt theory prefers order to chaos only in the sense that order is the condition for the creation of almost anything, whereas chaos generates nothing as long as it is defined as the absence of all organization. In the psychology of art one should not assert that an organized work

can result from a "gestalt-free" unconscious substratum,
as Anton Ehrenzweig has tried to do. The Book of Genesis suggests that the world emerged from chaos—but was
the brain of the Creator gestalt-free?

29 August

Steve, a retired engineer, repaired with a few quick moves
the screen installed in our fireplace. I asked him whether
he had handled a contraption of this kind before. No, he
had not. In that case, what let him know how the device
was constructed and how it could be made to work? "It
was made by a human being," was his answer.

The ancient notion that to see is not only to receive energy from the objects observed but to send it out as well
derives convincingly from subjective experience. I am
hesitant to watch the lightning during a thunderstorm
because of a slight, irrational fear that I might attract the
murderous bolts by focusing upon them. Also, more
commonly, to look at a person or object insistently is
much like aiming at the target with a gun and, in fact,
like pelting it with a stream of missiles.

"Auf des Menschen Inneres ist so viel verwandt, dass
seine Oberfläche nur sparsamer begabt werden konnte"
(Goethe, *Farbenlehre*).*

10 September

The first yellow leaves
Or a tardy butterfly?
Passing September.

---

* "So much has been spent on the human inside that the outside had
to be endowed more sparingly."

As we walk along the beach, the sandpipers run ahead of us, picking up frantically whatever they can at the water's edge before our approach shoos them farther. Someday a genius will arise among the sandpipers telling them that they need not keep ahead of us but can take off in a loop and return to the beach behind us, where no human wanderer will bother them in their work.

In praise of simplicity: "Lucerna corporis tui est oculus tuus. Si oculus tuus fuerit simplex, totum corpus tuum lucidum erit; si autem nequam fuerit, etiam corpus tuum tenebrosum erit" (Luke 11:34; cf. Matt. 6:22).*

29 September

A person born blind does not live in darkness. Darkness is a visual experience, namely, the absence of light. The blind have no visual experience.

30 September

An endlessly moving crowd ceases to be a progression in time and becomes a stationary flow. There is no beginning or end to the sea gulls flying west when the wind blows on our Michigan beach or to the Radcliffe students moving toward Harvard along our street in Cambridge in a steady stream, as though they were being dispensed by a girl-making machine.

5 October

It looks as though the style of modern representational painting is not always present in the first sketches for a work but comes with the development of the final shape.

---

* "The light of the body is the eye; therefore when thine eye is single [*simplex*], thy whole body also is full of light; but when thine eye is evil, thy body also is full of darkness."

I noticed this, for example, in comparing Picasso's early sketches for *Guernica* with the style of the completed painting and again recently in Feininger's sketches for the *Ruin on the Cliff*. Feininger's early drawings, done on the spot, show a fluent, spontaneous handwriting, not all that different from the sketches of artists in past centuries. Later, the straight edges come in, the cutting up of the sky, the Feininger Cubism. I suspect that these additions of the Feininger trademark will soon look dated, like ornaments overlaying spontaneous notation; whereas the unimpaired strokes of the first drawings, inspired by nothing but the direct impression, are unlikely to lose their freshness.

One can understand, by the way, why Feininger's attention was so lastingly caught by the ruined Gothic church on the cliff near the Baltic Sea. Nature herself had performed that destruction of man-made shape that he was fond of inflicting on intact architecture in his paintings. He saw in the ruin the impact of outer forces on the integrity of perfect shape and the shape's partial resistance to the onslaught.

16 October

In Ingmar Bergman's film *The Hour of the Wolf* a man demonstrates the length of a minute by checking its exact duration on his watch. It seems incredibly long. Artistic performance is so loaded with significance, and one's attention is so geared, correspondingly, to the offerings of every instant, that a minute serves as the container for many events. The loosely stacked, half-shaped experiences of real life consume much more time per unit of gain, and therefore time passes more quickly.

17 October

Symbolism and the facts of life. We watched Chief Justice Earl Warren at the cornerstone ceremony for the new

building of the Trial Lawyers Association. He dabbed bits
of mortar on the stone with various trowels, each of them
to become a souvenir. When the ceremony was over and
the guests and cameramen had left, one of the workmen
wiped the mortar carefully from the stone, after which he
and his fellow workers set it up in earnest.

In German, commas are placed anatomically at the grammatical joints of the sentence, and there is little freedom
as to where and where not to put them. In English, the
grammatical structure articulates itself, and the commas
strengthen the subdivisions here and there at the pleasure
of the writer, much as a woman will comment on her figure by placing accents as she sees fit.

28 October

Architectural space holds people together and keeps them
apart. It strikes a bargain between what it lets us do and
what it makes us do.

1 November

I doubt that if we were born on the small planet of the
Little Prince, where plane surfaces were lacking, non-
Euclidean geometry would be developed first. Euclidean
geometry comes first not because it fits the local geogra-
phy but because it offers the simplest shapes and relations. On the Little Prince's planet, disturbing discrepan-
cies might be noted until someday its Copernicus would
figure out that the surface of the planet was curved and
that this is why the sum of the angles in the triangle came
out too large. Helmholtz agrees. He says in his *Popular
Lectures:* "Therefore it cannot be allowed that the axioms
of our geometry depend on the native form of our per-
ceptive faculty or are in any way connected with it."
Wolfgang Pauli in his book on Kepler says that man has

an instinctive tendency, rooted not merely in external experience, to interpret his sensory perceptions in terms of Euclidean geometry. Morris Kline, however, falls for the flat explanation derived from the flat earth.

9 November

Perhaps *taste,* in the figurative meaning of the term, derives from the sense of the tongue, because taste gives prominence to the subjective qualities of what is agreeable or repulsive. The sense of taste, more than the other senses, is concerned with what suits the person because its stimuli are things actually introduced into our bodies rather than things merely touched externally or apprehended as dwelling somewhere in the neighborhood. The tongue and the nose are the guardians of the gate.

17 November

That laughter last night
Vanished into nothingness
When the car drove off.

The *Odyssey* is the product of a younger mind than are the books of Moses: Homer is more nearly sensory; the Old Testament is more verbal. Quite in general, sensory imagery is the vehicle of the younger mind, language that of the older. No picture of the Sacrifice of Isaac can rival the psychological complexity of the biblical text, let alone the verbal intricacies of, say, Thomas Mann's Joseph stories. There is an innocence about the painter, a shrewdness about the writer.

20 November

If you want to see two cultures, look at what happens when a god cohabits with a mortal. The Virgin bears a son, the Son of God, the Savior of men. The dove of the

Holy Ghost symbolizes rather than performs the impregnation. A golden ray connects the bird with the virgin across a respectful distance. When Zeus mates with Leda, their daughter is a girl who inherits from the gods not wisdom and virtue but disconcerting beauty and, perhaps, a talent for making trouble. Helen of Troy is the Greek counterpart of Christ. The divine swan does not content himself with a symbolic act. Mary comes to "know" God, but Leda receives the seed of a godly animal.

❧ 1969

I compared Pierre-Auguste Renoir's way of shaping
foliage in two of his landscapes. In one of them he used a
color scheme ranging from a green for the lighted sides
of the trees to a dark blue for the shadows. In the other
landscape, he modulated from green to a complementary
dark red. It seemed to me that the volume obtained with
the latter procedure looked complete, fully closed,
whereas the gamut from green to dark blue made for
an incompletely curved shape—as though only the completeness of the color range created a completeness of
volume.

Kevin Lynch mentions in his book on the image of the
city that place names in the old Florence referred originally to *canti,* namely, to landmarks such as loggias or
pharmacies or lights. Only later were the names attached
to the streets. A similar system prevails in Tokyo, where
the local names refer to small blocks of houses; street
names are mostly the product of Western influence. It
would stand to reason that originally streets were not ob-

115

jects but mere connections between objects and that only with increasing density of construction did the road itself become a string of habitations, worthy of a name.

30 January

Da quinci innanzi il mio veder fu maggio
Che'l parlar nostro, ch'a tal vista cede;
E cede la memoria a tanto oltraggio.*

(*Paradiso* 33.55–57)

2 February

Apparently, Italian artists used the term *pensieri* to describe the first sketch that gave the general idea of the work, done, say, by a master to tell his disciple what kind of composition to develop.

4 February

"On doit tendre avec effort à l'infaillibilité sans y prétendre" (Malebranche, as quoted on the title page of Chevreul's *De la loi du contraste simultané*).*

When around 1930 I wrote a book on film, the nature of the new medium made me start the presentation from visual reality and show in what ways the film image deviated from it. Some twenty years later, for my book *Art and Visual Perception,* I started from the elements of the medium, a black dot placed in a square. The former approach was that of traditional art theory; the latter derived from modern art's emphasis on the immediacy of

---

* "From then on, what I saw went beyond what can be mastered by our speech, which gives in to such a sight; and memory gives in to such exorbitance."
* "One must try hard to be infallible but not pretend that one is."

116

formal expression. One could also approach film theory
the modern way, by taking off from a dot moving across
the screen; but it would take some doing to reach, if only
asymptotically, the mechanical recordings of the photographic image. One would be working against the grain
of the medium.

7 February

In the 1890s, when Freud revealed the manifestations of
the unconscious mind, Mélisande lost her wedding ring
on purpose.

18 February

What I learned from writing in German for so many
years was not so much German as writing. I learned to
write, which helped me immensely with my English.

2 March

When Kandinsky had not yet abandoned all references to
physical subject matter, one had to recognize the objects
to see his composition correctly. I noticed that the lack of
visible order is largely remedied as soon as one recognizes
the buildings, the men on horseback, the roads, and the
water. This made me realize that the shape of familiar objects contributes actively to the compositional pattern, for
example, by creating depth where there would be little or
none without the reference, or distinguishing objects
sharply where little distinction is provided by the paint.
This factor is likely to operate importantly in "painterly"
styles such as that of the Impressionists: the artist, intent
on color and light effects, can leave a part of the organization of shape to the images of the objects represented.

 Kandinsky's abstractions come beautifully into their
own once he abandons the references to nature entirely.
How is one to understand, by the way, that so imagina-

tive a painter reduced his form to a sort of White Russian costume jewelry in the 1920s? Was this return to the decorative style of his beginnings his only way of responding to the formalism of the Bauhaus?

The tantalizing threat created by the first prospect of abstract painting is forecast in an episode in chapter 3 of Joseph Conrad's *Secret Agent,* written around 1908, where a retarded boy is drawing "innumerable circles, concentric, eccentric; a corruscating whirl of circles that by their tangled multitude of repeated curves, uniformity of form, and confusing of intersecting lines suggested a rendering of cosmic chaos, the symbolism of a mad art attempting the inconceivable." The first of Robert Delaunay's *Disques* appeared in 1912.

20 March

The Busch-Reisinger Museum owns a *Saint Jerome* by Joest van Cleve. The painting shows the saint with his hand on a skull and next to him a teakettle boiling, with the inscription *Homo Bulla*—man is but a bubble. Symbolically inclined artists will find their pretexts most anywhere.

10 April

Some of the young college revolutionaries of today have been brought up under "progressive education." In kindergarten and at home they were permitted to break things and to hurt other people without punishment or other appropriate reactions. Now, occupying buildings, destroying property, and manhandling officials, they become indignant when they are opposed by force. Revolutionaries have always fought their adversaries, but they have not disputed their enemies' right to defend themselves. Their academic offspring have been misled by being trained to play the game of society with loaded dice.

7 May

In the arts, time and space become carriers of meaning. Time expresses the relation of cause and effect, showing where things come from and what they lead to. Space symbolizes the structural relations within an existing order.

13 May

My new dentist, the most taciturn practitioner I have ever met, is an impressive instance of the conviction that everything worth knowing about the past can be observed in the present. Without asking me a word about previous history or treatment, he looked at my teeth and started working. Perhaps the mouth is a place where nothing knowable is hidden; but when applied to the human mind, the procedure has proved impractical or at least uneconomical.

The virtues of seeing and hearing complement each other. I am facing a group of eight hotel elevators, four on each side. When a car arrives, a colored signal lights up over the door about to open. At the same time a bell rings. The bell alone would not suffice for precise localization. One would know *that* the lift is arriving but not *where*. On the other hand, because the sound comes from all directions at once, the bell alerts me, no matter in what direction I happen to be looking, whereas I could easily have missed the light signal on one of the doors. Sight specifies the spatial direction of origin; hearing overcomes specificity.

Speculate on what would have happened to painting if the human skin were a bright red rather than a pale pink. Up until the days of Gauguin the nude body depended for emphasis heavily on flamboyant garments or curtains, which animated or deadened the timid tint of the skin. When the Fauvists and Expressionists freed painters from being faithful to nature, the human body could appear a fiery color, presenting itself directly rather than indirectly and stressing its importance as a subject by an ostentatious appearance.

15 May

Freud referred privately to his *Beyond the Pleasure Principle* as "das Jenseits," which is the common German word for "the beyond," the afterlife. He consciously designated death as the principal subject of his book.

"Alcmaeon says that men die for this reason that they cannot join the beginning to the end" (Aristotle, *De anima* 916a33).

15 June

If only our symbol mongers would content themselves with the depth of genuine works of art. Instead, they invest some trivial story or minimal object with unfitting significance. There the poor thing stands revealed in its indigence, the symbols hanging around the empty frame, and the interpreter looks like one of those pathetic schizophrenics who predict the end of the world from the number of buttons on somebody's coat.

In the front porch of Freiburg Cathedral the figures symbolizing the liberal arts are placed next to those of the foolish virgins. A sobering thought.

19 July

The awkwardness of discussing sex with people who get too much pleasure from the talking.

120

As we move from our city apartment to our beach cottage, our senses are suddenly awakened and the whole of the mind is called upon to respond. The bird call is an enriching visit, a caller. The stir of the waves or treetops, the gusts of wind entering the open windows and doors testify to the weather, our weather, on which we depend. Suddenly surrounded by a world of almost total relevance, I think back to our city life as one crowded with irrelevancies. The coming and going in the streets, the noises penetrating the walls pass me by because I have nothing to do for them, against them, or about them. The main response they call for is my need to exclude them.

20 July

Compared with the short stories of our day, those of Turgenev look like Delacroix's battle scenes reduced to the size of medallions. There is constant tragedy. In our own stories the horizon of birth and death has been removed to such a distance in time and space that people live in a state of lukewarm immortality, briefly upset now and then by episodes of loss or even terror and ruffled otherwise by the halfhearted oscillations of daily experience.

29 July

A writer needs to practice "which burning," the purging of relative clauses from his sentences.

1 August

I asked someone how an elderly lady of our acquaintance was doing. "She is all right," I was told, "still the same, just more so." How many of us evolve with increasing age into Daumier portraits of ourselves?

9 August

The goldfinches and chipping sparrows fly across the
dunes only in garlands, never in arcades—graphologically
speaking. It might be possible to elucidate the kinetic difference between those two curves in handwriting by
looking at the muscular dynamics of bird flight.

16 August

When information theorists assert that the value of works
of art depends on their novelty, they can refer to nothing
better than popular entertainment, whose blandness
keeps it from outlasting its newness. It is true that as I
listen every day to a particular section of a Vivaldi concerto used as the "theme" for a radio program, I begin to
resent it, but only because it has been degraded to a logo
and finds me unprepared to listen. Great music or poetry,
of course, seizes us more deeply the better we come to
know it, the more it becomes a part of ourselves. Consider also the obsessions of people whistling the same
tune for hours or being kept sleepless by a haunting
theme; or artists held for a lifetime by the same subject,
the reclining figures of Henry Moore, the sleepwatchers
of Picasso.

I do much of my writing the way Theseus killed the
Crommyonian sow. According to Plutarch, he went
out of his way to meet and engage the animal so that he
might not seem to perform all his deeds just because of
outer necessity. Yet he could not resist the other, inner
necessity, his urge to seek her out. We cherish the freedom to do what we need to do.

18 August

When Mary explained to me that the lakes, beaches, and
hills around our summer place were created by the action

of prehistoric glaciers and the moraines left by them, the large scenery suddenly shrank in size and became the accidental detail of some giant shape and event. The particular formation of a lake or ridge left as the imprint of some ancient upheaval became a manifesto of nature's eternal laws. Not unrelatedly, I was struck at the same time by Herodotus's way of presenting historical events: no historian, he is instead a raconteur of official gossip. This coming and going of warriors and ladies is colorful material for art and science but not the work of a man who perceives in the particular episode the nature of human aspiration and passion, the tragedies of greed, the fear of the stranger, the lust for power. How do true historians succeed in teaching us about the nature of man by telling particular stories? How, for that matter, did Homer?

23 August

Sometimes I feel uneasy in the company of engineers, builders, farmers, craftsmen—persons in constant touch with the physical world, persons who observe with precision, remember what they have handled, and react aptly to the demands of their tangible environment. I myself, on the other hand, am one of the indirect people who speculate about things they have not made and perhaps not even seen. This drawback is possibly related to my early background, a father who was a merchant and a mother not skilled in any basic trade.

2 September

For years I have used a wooden mallet for my wood carving, but only the other day it occurred to me that I have been handling it incorrectly. I have held it with a tight wrist, which carried the clout of the blows directly into my arm, hurting the joints of wrist and elbow. This faulty technique also reduced the impact of the mallet on

the wood. Now, by letting my wrist act loosely, I cush-
ion the effect of the blow on my arm and almost double
the strength of the instrument. Here again, as in so many
other physical skills—swimming, dancing, writing,
even in the use of the speech muscles—the secret of successful motion is in muscular relaxation. The novice is
driven to the wrong procedure because he is wary of the
new task, and the tightness of his attitude produces tightness of the limbs. As the task becomes familiar, one can
afford to let much of the energy flow into productive action.

11 September

The English language is fortunate in making a distinction
between *because* and *since,* the one connoting the cause,
the other the reason—a difference Schopenhauer takes
such pains to explain in his book *Der Satz vom zureichen-
den Grunde.*

> In our dark bedroom
> The wind lifting the curtain
> Reveals one bright star.

19 September

Are *animus* and *anemos* related, the breath of life in Genesis ("et inspiravit animam vivam") and the anemonies,
the daughters of the wind?

Strangely enough, the absurd belief that without words
there can be no concepts is held even by older persons,
who must know from their own experience that one constantly loses names without losing the concepts for which
they stand. I can think with great precision of a flowering
plant that grows on trellises and arbors; its blooms are
crescent-shaped, bunched like grapes, smelling sweetly,
and hang from twisted, knobby branches. I have known
its name for many years in German, English, Italian, and

Japanese, but off and on I cannot think of any of them.
Yet, my concept is as precise and complete as it ever is
when I recapture the designating word.

20 November

The meaning of "identity" held by modern Western
adults may differ fundamentally from what is obvious to
others. In an experiment, Jean Piaget presented a cutout
square in different positions and asked, "Is this still the
same square?" He found that children under the age of
seven denied the identity. Now, a child would have to be
a moron not to see that the piece of cardboard remains
the same when it is tilted. He obviously is talking about
something else, namely sameness of appearance. He says
that the square looks different from a diamond, which it
obviously does. And whether or not physical shape is
more important than perceptual shape depends on who
is talking.

14 December

Beauty is correctly described as what gives order, unity,
and harmony to an image, as long as one refrains from
asserting that these qualities are also what beauty expresses. Order can serve to express disorder, unity to express disunity, harmony to express disharmony. If this is
denied, as it was in some classicist tradition, sterility
ensues.

15 December

A revolution-minded art critic wrote: "What is required
is not the affirmative representation of reality but the
shaping of that reality; which means: the transformation
of it." However, the map, the blueprint, the chart were
not invented by the practitioners of contemplation but by
men of action, who could not act unless they saw. The

125

artist creates the image of the world so that we may see, judge, and perhaps change it.

23 December

Something deeply significant of Goethe's personality must be reflected in the persistent incompleteness of the families he describes in his fiction, for example, in *Wilhelm Meisters Wanderjahre*. An uncle living with two nieces, a father traveling with his son. The absence of wives and mothers is particularly conspicuous. Add to this Goethe's insistence on men distancing themselves from their loved ones for their own benefit, and what you see emerging is the picture of a person who required anarchic liberty to build the solemn shapes of his classical designs for living.

🌿 1970

30 January

All around my heart
The coronary fingers
Gripping me too tight.

From my bed window
Cars circulating in veins
My body extended.

From my bed window
Branchings of sycamore trees
Vessels of my blood.

An example of the adaptation effect. The head end of
the hospital bed rises and lowers mechanically. When it is
lowered after having been raised for a while, the normal
position no longer feels horizontal but as though the bed
were tilting downward.

A Catholic laboratory technician looking at a pot of red
cyclamens on the windowsill of my hospital room exclaimed, "They are just like the outpouring of the Holy
Spirit!" Yes indeed, the "cloven tongues like as of fire"
(Acts 2) on the heads of the twelve apostles, roughly the

number of the red, flamelike flowers in my pot. Once
again I was reminded of the indispensable power of collective imagery, the symbols provided by a tradition
shared by all. How almost beyond human power is any
single artist's attempt to create such images all on his
own!

13 February

I have insisted that in a sensible taxonomy one should not
classify by species but by properties. The question should
not be, In which class does this kind of thing belong?
but, What properties is it made of? Librarians face the insoluble task of where to shelve a book, say, by a psychologist analyzing the effects of furniture arrangement on
the behavior of the users. A reasonable catalog would list
it under several components: the psychological, the architectural, the sociological. But only King Solomon could
decide where to shelve that one book itself.

Goethe on architecture: "Mag man doch immer Fehler
begehen, bauen darf man keine" (*Wilhelm Meisters Wanderjahre*).*

26 February

Age is not a causative agent and, in fact, not a property
of any existing entity at all but simply a yardstick for the
length of time a process has been going on. Age is no
more guilty of the predicaments of the late years than
is the clock on the wall.

1 March

To a melancholy mind, things that belong together come
apart. Georg Büchner in his play *Dantons Tod* has his lan-

---

* "Mistakes are permissible, but one must not build any."

guid hero complain about the double-dealings of symmetry. Danton resents the boredom of doing the same things again and again every day: "It is very sad that, in addition, we consist of two halves, which do both the same, so that everything happens twice" (act 2, sc. 1).

6 March

Any notation for the temporal media of art can serve two different purposes. By simply preserving and reconstructing the static elements of a performance, it can indirectly define the actions in time of which the work consists. Musical notation, for example, lists the tones following one another and thereby shows the beginning and end of each up-and-down movement of pitch. Dance notation also, as far as I know, gives the fixed body positions indicating the beginning and end of each movement and thereby implies the motions to be executed. In architecture one can similarly describe the sequence of sights experienced when someone walks through buildings or a landscape or urban environment. If, however, one wishes to go beyond these static markers to describe the perceived dynamics of the time events, one needs notational signs similar to the crescendo and decrescendo indicators in musical scores. In architecture, this calls for concepts such as narrowing and widening, sudden or gradual change, continuity and discontinuity, etc.

The theological question of how an imperfect world could be created by a perfect god is turned around when one asks how the imperfect mind of an artist can create a perfect work.

9 March

While in the hospital, I wondered how long it would take me to lose my usual response to the telephone bell, its alarming appeal, the pleasure of being called upon. Two

129

weeks of time were insufficient. Whenever the phone rang at the nurses' desk near my room, I felt the usual shock, the signal to dash to the receiver. In fact, as I came closer to being released, a returning sense of "being back in circulation" made me feel even more promptly that the bell of life was tolling for me.

10 March

Writers are by no means tied to linear thinking. Michel Butor, who cultivates simultaneity, flash-forwards, and flashbacks in his fiction, speaks in *Répertoire 3* of the way Picasso's works belong together, not merely as a sequence, since "we can no longer arrange them along an ascending straight line, but on a circle, whose center would be the common theme."

17 March

Persons who still need to be weaned of their trust in translations should consider the grave alteration of meaning in the very title of Proust's *A la recherche du temps perdu*. The English *Remembrance of Things Past* suggests a nostalgic dreaming of the good old days, a grandmother in her rocking chair reminiscing with a smile. In the French original, the word *recherche* introduces immediately an active, perhaps frantic sense; and *perdu* is "lost," not "past." The word *perdu,* as Butor explains in one of his essays on Proust, means, first of all, that the past, vanished from memory, is in need of recovery; but it also has the connotation of "wasted time," which the English word "lost" would readily translate.

Before Darwin there was no way of talking about purpose in nature other than the religious: A wise creator had arranged it all for the benefit of his favorite creature, man. Unbelievers objected to such teleology, as did Georg Büchner in his lecture of 1836 on the nerves of the human head. Teleological explanations, he contended, argue in a circle by describing "the effects of the organs as their purposes." To reject this approach meant, however, to describe nature as an artist of the *l'art pour l'art* variety, and in fact Büchner calls the natural creation a manifestation of a primordial Law of Beauty. It took the theory of evolution to give purpose in nature a new lease.

25 March

Students writing dissertations and quite a few authors of scientific papers practice bibliographic name-dropping. They boast of all the great men they have met on paper while revealing at the same time how little they profited from the encounters.

1 April

Being forced to walk more slowly, I find myself transferred from the class of the goal-directed professionals to that of the more leisurely observers of life. Like a tourist I stroll through the urban landscape as though out of pleasurable curiosity. People watching me put me in the category of the unhurried hedonist who is willing to respond to the call of small distractions.

13 April

The portrait photographer for whom I was sitting said at one point, "Just warm it up a bit! You don't have to change your face, just change your mind a little!"

14 May

When discussing in class the reversal of figure and ground, I have often told my students that even Descartes still believed the ventricles of the brain to be the containers of the mental functions. What he took to be mere

131

wrapping turned out to be the tissue of the nervous system itself.

Occasionally I have an inkling of writing in a style of my own. That particular expression, that cadence of the sentence "sounds like me." But those flashes are rare. Otherwise I know only that certain ways of putting things suit me and that for any given instance only *one* wording will do. This, I suppose, is the subjective equivalent of writing in a style of one's own.

18 May

"'Dieu préserve ceux qu'il chérit des lectures inutiles'; c'est la première maxime d'un petit livre de Lavater" (Baudelaire, *Du vin et du hachisch*).*

21 May

Since Mondrian eschewed measurement and determined the shapes of his paintings "by eye," did he make his squares geometrically correct (remember that he did his drawings on graph paper!), or did he compensate for the fact that geometrically correct squares look too tall?

28 May

In Manet's *Execution of the Emperor Maximilian* (Boston Museum of Fine Arts), the emperor is a barely visible, faceless apparition, and the guns of the soldiers are hidden in shadow. What is the rationale for this paradox? Did the painter exploit the effect of uncanny presence that hidden things produce? Or did he challenge traditional history painting by showing that in the real world what we see denies or ignores sometimes what there is?

---

* "Lavater begins a booklet of his with the statement: 'God protects those whom he loves from unnecessary reading.'"

6 June

My doctor tells me that one of his teachers, a German-born professor of medicine, said to his assistants, "I may sometimes be wrong, but I am never in doubt!"

15 June

Writers of radio scripts should take to heart what the psychologist Allan Paivio calls the "conceptual-peg theory." He has found that it is easier to grasp and remember adjectives that follow the noun to which they belong rather than those that precede it. This is so because once the object to which the adjectives apply has been given, they have a perceptual place to settle, whereas in the opposite case they remain suspended until the noun is supplied to them as a perch. More generally, the moral for the radio scriptwriter would be: Give the key concept first, before you deal out the facts depending on it! In painting, the adjectives preceding their noun may be said to be akin to Impressionist vision, which also puts the perceptual qualities ahead of the carrier object. First come the colors of the tree, then comes the tree!

22 June

Can "black art" be understood by whites? Such a question can be asked only by someone who does not know how partial is all understanding. Do we understand African art or Greek art? Do we understand Matisse or the work of our next-door neighbor?

3 July

Heredity is the dark corner to which one relegates what one cannot explain otherwise. It is easy to assert that the basic structure of language is wired into the nervous system, just as it was easy to say that the basic principles of perceptual organization are transmitted by specific inherited mechanisms or as acquisitions of the past. The day will come when linguists will realize that to understand language, one must first consider the makeup of the sensory world that shapes it. One does not have to bother with heredity to explain why all languages distinguish things from actions. It is a distinction conveyed by elementary experience to everybody, long before they learn how to talk.

A linguist asserts in an article that relational words like "and" connote nothing. How could it escape him that in the world of experience, relations are every bit as real and important as the things they connect?

11 July

As I am translating my *Visual Thinking,* my thoughts in German look at times somewhat too simple, too unsophisticated. Has my linguistic limitation led me in the course of these thirty years to adapt the level of subtlety of my reasoning to that of the words at my disposal in English? Or is the mentality that created the English language less *nuancé* than the German, and is it for this reason that English intellectuals like to make fun of the overrefined speculations of the German mind? In much Anglo-Saxon reasoning there is a sober factuality, most nutritious as long as staple foods are what one needs. But then, of course, there is also Milton, and there is Shakespeare.

13 July

The only criterion controlling the composition of Jean Arp's *Constellations of Three Forms* is their equilibrium in space. The three units fit no superordinated whole. That is why they lend themselves to rearrangements. They look as though they could move to anywhere, but balance anchors each to its place nevertheless.

24 July

When it comes to villains, the great writers, to whom we attribute the greatest wisdom, contradict our psychological conviction that evil is not inherent in the person's nature but is merely a response to unfavorable conditions. The great villains have no anamnesis to speak of. Mephistopheles and Tartuffe are devils by nature. So is Fagin, and of Hawthorne it may be said that his Protestant bad conscience makes his wrongdoers go sour by a process of almost biological fermentation. Shakespeare hints at what made Richard III, Macbeth, or Iago grow malignant, but the etiology is obscured by the unmodified blackness of their presence. Perhaps this is the reason for what looks like unsubtle psychology. Such is the weight of evil that its causes do not matter. Shakespeare's villains do not repent, nor does Oedipus; they merely receive what is coming to them.

2 August

Even when Walt Disney had become the head of a large film production company, he insisted on recording the voice of Mickey Mouse himself because he could not find anybody with the right nuance of squeakiness. Is this not the story of all of us? Just now I am spending months of my time on translating my *Visual Thinking* into German because I did not trust anybody to give my text the right note of squeakiness.

Schopenhauer speaking about noise: "Demzufolge lebt der denkende Geist mit dem Auge in ewigem Frieden, mit dem Ohr in ewigem Krieg" (*Über die Sinne*).*

* "Hence, the thoughtful mind lives in eternal peace with the eye but is eternally at war with the ear."

6 August

A radiologist tells me that they have viewing patterns,
which vary from practitioner to practitioner. The patterns
serve to guarantee that each plate is examined systematically, so that nothing will be overlooked. The main spot
suspected of being the culprit tends to monopolize attention. He told me that he scans first the outer rim of the
body, then proceeds to the various organs systematically;
also that by now any abnormality attracts his glance almost automatically. I told him of my similar experience
with proofreading.

13 August

It is difficult not to be disconcerted when the television
cameramen scrutinize you as an object, especially when
they are standing so close that the absence of social grace
is particularly shocking. There you sit under the lights,
concentrating on "making your point," arousing a feeling, while the man at the machine disengages himself
without apology or remorse. Being shielded from all im-
pingement, he is in a position of godlike dominance; he
dwells above your concerns and is even empowered to interfere with your doings because his function has priority
over yours. I am reminded of the movie cameraman described in Pirandello's *Quaderni di Serafino Gubbio Opera-
tore*. Gubbio "takes" whatever human passions are displayed in front of his camera, his mind absorbed with
obtaining the proper image and adapting the speed of his
crank to that of the action before him. Photographing the
deadly motions of a stalking tiger, he observes, "My
hand impassibly obeyed the measure I imposed on the
movement, faster, more slowly, very slow, as though my
will power had descended—firmly, lucidly, inflexibly—to
the pulse of my wrist and was there in charge all by itself,
leaving my brain free to think, my heart free to feel."

14 August

Francis Galton, trying to capture the generality of a concept or type in a picture, superposed the photographs of individuals sharing the same trait. To understand why he obtained nothing better than the cloudy blur of a face, one may compare his procedure with that of the so-called scattergram, by which one plots the results of experiments statistically. The scattergram marks each finding as a dot within the space that represents the range of possible results. If the results are positive, the totality of the dots suggests a clustering, encouraging the experimenter to make the generality explicit by drawing, with more or less justification, the lines or outlines indicated by the bunching of the data. These interpolated lines are structurally clear-cut abstractions representing the underlying pattern of forces; whereas in the Galton pictures we are given the mere scattergram with all the vagueness of the raw data and none of the precision of a possible conclusion.

19 August

Aristotle codified the conviction that tragedy must deal with powerful persons—for the reason, I assume, that only the rulers have the power to express their passions through action that is sufficiently consequential and unhampered to satisfy the dramatic need for valid symbols. The struggle with the daily obstacles of life was reserved to comedy, which excused the limited range of its presentations by describing them as ridiculous. Such humor acknowledges the daily troubles as being small when they are viewed from the vantage point of a higher station. The social drama of the nineteenth century and its resonances in our own time endeavored to show tragedy within the middle-class and proletarian existence. It either succeeded—by proving that limited circumstances do not prevent the depth of human passion (Ibsen, Strindberg, some Hauptmann)—or it shrank to merely sociopolitical accusation and complaint, replacing the drama of the human mind with the inconveniences of poverty and petty malice. Only in the novels of Kafka, it seems to me, does the misery of precarious social circumstances acquire the status of the great tragic symbols. The incomprehensibility of modern society qualifies as a metaphor for the inscrutable nature of human existence and divine control.

1 September

Thomas Mann's *Doktor Faustus* is not a historical novel even though it refers to times and persons known to the reader as having actually existed. Historical novels invite the reader to believe that the story took place as told, whereas Mann employs what he calls his montage principle by presenting his narrator as an invented figure. The combination of the obviously historical with the obviously invented creates a hybrid ontology. To maintain this double reality, historical figures are named but not described or permitted to act, since this would fictionalize them.

"Les ouvrages classiques ne peuvent être bien faits que par ceux qui ont blanchi sous le harnois. C'est le milieu et la fin qui éclaircissent les ténèbres du commencement" (Diderot, *Le neveu de Rameau*).*

2 September

Thomas Mann, in his book on the genesis of *Doktor Faustus,* raises the curious question of whether style is still possible today. Commenting on fiction written by his

---

* "Classical works can be done well only by those who have grown old in the harness. The middle and the end clarify the obscurity of the beginning."

friend Bruno Frank he notes: "Mir merkwürdig aber: Er benutzt den humanistischen Erzähl-Stil Zeitbloms vollkommen ernst, als seinen eigenen. Ich kenne im Stilistischen eigentlich nur noch die Parodie. Darin nahe bei Joyce."* In fact, one of the reasons why he has the Leverkühn story told by a rather academic professor is that of not having to use "his own" style; also, Leverkühn and one of his teachers use a sixteenth-century mode of German speech—Hans Sachs, Luther—which reads as artificial and bothersome. Actually, enough of Mann's own style is present in the *Faustus* to show that it is as beautiful and pertinent as ever, even when he shapes the professorial style by means of his own. What strikes me as remarkable is that he had come to doubt his own language so much as to have attempted to disguise it—owing perhaps, partly, to his distance from where German is spoken as a matter of course. He was writing the novel in California.

18 September

Protest against federal invasions of privacy has made a psychologist warn that the value of privacy is not simply to be taken for granted. Characteristically, however, he thinks of privacy mainly as a hiding of things we would not like others to know about ourselves, things to be ashamed of, etc. But the notion that anything that need not be hidden might as well be revealed strikes me as childish. It leads, for example, to tasteless and tiresome "confessions," literary and otherwise. The maxim should not be Tell all unless there is reason to withhold it! but Tell only what is worth telling! Society, just like the biological organism, does not profit from too much osmosis.

* "What is remarkable to me is that he uses Zeitblom's humanistic style of narration in all seriousness as his own. To myself, style really has become nothing but parody. This is near to Joyce."

13 November

[I am preparing to talk to a psychiatrist who studies the psychological effect of disfiguring facial burns.] If the viewer could only be made to see the abhorrent face as the effect of the fire rather than as a property of the person! What he sees is not a disfigured face but a monstrous one. If only the viewer could switch off the gestalt perception and see a normal face partially destroyed rather than the features of a fiend!

15 November

Titian's late painting *The Rape of Europa* does not tell a piquant anecdote but the story of an old man's lot. The bull is not running away with his prey but is standing in the water and looking at the beholder with melancholy eyes. The masculinity of the bull is tragically burdened with the feminine; the old Zeus is stricken with the leftovers of his addiction. In his late work, the painter looks through the story to the very core of the human fate. He also acknowledges the nature of the art of painting by interpreting a happening as a state of being.

30 November

A young architect who enjoys the slapdash deconstructionism of his generation writes that it would be quite wrong to view the mechanism of the solar system as though it were at rest: "The sun, far from standing still, races through the universe at a speed of . . . ," and consequently the paths of the planets are not the simple ellipses conceived by the shortsighted. He behaves as though to understand the clockwork of his watch he would have to consider its daily journey around the axis of the earth. How will he design his buildings without confining the influence of their environment to a fairly parochial range?

13 December

I have always believed that the art work of patients will be more effective therapeutically when they are able to express their state of mind with the sensory immediacy an artist gives to his shapes and colors. But now that I have seen the large series of drawings made by Jackson Pollock during his own psychiatric treatment, I realize that the ability of the professional artist does not provide a favorable condition for art therapy either. He cannot let his private impulses dominate his drawings or paintings, because he is always governed by the artist's task of depicting the human condition in general. If he could overcome this deep-seated obligation, it would perhaps help his analyst, but it would be his undoing as an artist.

17 December

A student proposed to show various functions and meanings of a work of art by comparing Michelangelo's three *David*s in Florence. The original in the Accademia appears outside of time and space as a monument to a great artist, carrying whatever expression one may find in the individual youthful figure. In front of the Palazzo Vecchio, its original location, the *David* stands, according to Vasari, as an embodiment of the belligerent boldness and strength of the young republic, admonishing the city government to show courage and justice. On the Piazzale Michelangelo, surrounded by cars, vendors, cafés, and hundreds of tourists taking in the famous sight from the hill, another cast of the figure stands, demoted to a standard attraction and landmark and cheapened as a commercially exploited symbol, no better than the other reproductions sold in all sizes as souvenirs.

18 December

When Jupiter assumes the appearance of Amphitryon to deceive the commander's wife, Alcmene accepts him as

141

not only divinely beautiful but also as more truly Amphitryon than her real husband. In Heinrich von Kleist's version of the play she says:

> Ich hätte für sein Bild ihn halten können,
> Für sein Gemälde, sieh, von Künstlerhand,
> Dem Leben treu, ins Göttliche verzeichnet.*

(Act 2, sc. 4)

By preferring the divine version of her husband to himself, she really makes the correct decision, in that the image embodies most perfectly the qualities for which she chose and accepted him. I could not help being reminded of another paradigm to the effect that art is truer than nature, the ethological experiment with a shorebird, the female plover, who prefers an artificially perfected version of her egg to the one she actually laid. (For years I gave a lecture on art entitled "The Plover's Egg.")

* "I could have taken him for my husband's picture, a portrait of him, you see, done by the hand of an artist, true to life but transcribed into the divine."

✿ 1971

18 January

When we look back at the teapots and lamps designed at
the Bauhaus, we realize that the simplicity of their shapes
did not derive primarily from the demands of practical
function, as we had been made to believe, but from a stylistic preference for stark geometry. Something similar
may be true for manufacture in general. Recently
a specialist pointed out that the centric symmetry of the
usual tool handles is not well suited to the kinetic require-
ments of the human hand and wrist. It rather derives
from the practical convenience of making simple symmetrical shapes on the lathe or from molds and perhaps
from a general human preference for regular shapes.

21 January

The Boston Museum has a Narcissus tapestry from about
1500 that depicts the mirror image in the well with as
much tangible concreteness as the gazing youth himself.
To our modern eyes, this absolves Narcissus from the sin
of self-adulation. He has every reason to look with attention and perhaps affection at the doppelgänger, that miraculous duplication of his own self. I am reminded of

what Rilke says about Cézanne's "grosse und unbestech-
liche Sachlichkeit" in portraying himself: ". . . durch den
Umstand bestätigt, dass er sich selbst, ohne im entfern-
testen seinen Ausdruck auszulegen oder überlegen anzu-
sehen, mit so viel demütiger Objektivität wiederholte,
mit dem Glauben und der sachlich interessierten Teil-
nahme eines Hundes, der sich im Spiegel sieht und denkt:
da ist noch ein Hund."*

16 February

Blake says in *The Marriage of Heaven and Hell* that "the
tygers of wrath are wiser than the horses of instruction."

10 April

When I was told that I had to go to the hospital for two
weeks, I got from the library four books I had wanted to
read: Jung's reminiscences, Malraux's memoirs, Benjamin's *Berlin Chronicle,* and Stifter's novel *Der Nachsommer.*
Only when I saw the books stacked on my table did I notice how much they had in common—two books of
memoirs by old men, nostalgic remembrances of a German exile, and a story on the season after the season. The
unconscious makes its choices even when the conscious
mind is in no mood for retrospection.

22 April

"Le soir de la vie apporte avec lui sa lampe," says Malraux
in his *Antimémoires.**

---

* "[Cézanne's] great and incorruptible factualness . . . confirmed by
the way he rendered himself with such humble objectivity, without
interpreting his expression or viewing it with superiority in the least,
but with the trust and the factually interested involvement of a dog
who sees himself in the mirror and thinks: There is another dog."
* "The evening of life carries its own lamp with it."

144

24 April

A woman called a radio station to ask whether she had
to reset her clocks from standard time to daylight saving
time at exactly two o'clock in the morning. The mind
tends to grasp phenomena by their contours. It is the
borderline, the moment of change, the New Year's cele-
bration at midnight, the birthday, the crossing of the
dateline—the contour being the only precise part of a
shape on which one can put one's finger. In painting also
there is the stylistic difference between what Delacroix
describes as *prendre par le milieu* and *prendre par la ligne*.
Taking things by their contours is the psychologically
earlier procedure.

2 May

Leaving my home country in the 1930s, I faced the op-
tion of going the Latin or the Anglo-Saxon way. How
much of my own choice was involved in taking the latter
course I do not know. The practicality of the English language has made me develop the part of my nature that
concerns sensory observation, enjoyment of the tangible
life, the humor of situations. Had I led a French life, it
would have meant the refinement of the intellect, systematic philosophy, the wit of formulation. I like to think
that in espousing the one, I have not entirely missed the
other; but when I read a piece of clever French, I feel the
pleasure of exercising a somewhat atrophied pair of
wings.

15 May

Someone remembered that when my book *Film als
Kunst* was published in Germany with a jacket design by
Gyorgy Kepes, it was shown to Mies van der Rohe, who
took off his glasses and said, "Das ist ein guter Mann!"

145

Obviously he was talking about the designer, for after all it is the jacket that makes the book.

31 May

In early pictorial representation, overlaps are avoided. Objects are seen separately, next to each other, each in its own completeness. Something similar is going on in the imagination, for example, in one's images of historical sequence. I find it hard to realize that the work of Manet overlaps that of Cézanne by twenty years. I keep slipping back into the structurally more comfortable belief that the later artist began only after the earlier had finished.

16 July

It is again my season for making poor drawings and wood carvings. What encourages me is that what I produce looks so much worse than the work of even the meanest amateur that it may hold a germ of the real thing after all.

20 July

One of those psychiatrists who listen with the third ear and keep the other two closed.

16 August

At a cocktail party I meet a retired businessman from Virginia, his face crisscrossed like a butcher's bench by the misuse of body and mind. He wears a shirt from Guatemala with a longtailed bird embroidered on pockets and sleeves. The bird, he tells me, was sacred to the Maya, who surrendered to the Spaniards upon its death. More thoroughly undone than by mere death, the bird is now one of the many symbols whose presence has outlived their meaning. What remains is a calligraphic transcription of nature as a "conversation piece" for the decoration of a corroded man.

21 August

Once again the children remind us how much our formalistic logic has damaged our thinking. The Italian psychologist Mosconi, wanting to find out how children interpret the concept *diverso,* presented them with six pictures, five of animals—a lion, an elephant, a horse, etc.—and one of a boat. He asked which picture was "the most different" from that of a sheep, which he also showed. An educated adult would have selected the boat, but almost none of the children did. To them, nothing can be compared but what has a common base, making the comparison sensible. Nothing can be called different but what in some ways could also be called the same.

23 August

It has been a boon to the landscape painters that cumulus clouds look so heavy. They have helped to add visual weight to the upper half of pictures that would look badly unbalanced otherwise.

31 August

One learns little about the history of "taste" by finding out which art objects people liked and bought and lived with and which they rejected. One has to know what kind of need those objects fulfilled. Was it an appreciation of great art that made the people of Siena join their bishop to celebrate the completion of Duccio's altar painting? If respectable American institutions must place a sculpture by Henry Moore in front of their administration buildings, are they promoters of the arts? Does the sculpture contribute to prestige and status, and if so, by which of the work's properties? Is it the fame of the artist, the purchase price, the sculpture's affirmation of vital strength and wholesome nature, its modernity, its lack of offensiveness? When it comes to the popular arts—film, television, music, novels—what matters first is not whether the stuff is good or bad but what needs it fulfills and how it fulfills them. This introduces the matter of aesthetic quality eventually, but at its proper place: as a means to an end. Certain needs can be met only by bad art—dishonesty or thoughtlessness, for example.

7 September

The truest letters I have written, the ones into which my nature seemed to pour, letters of thoughts for which I had little rational justification and which were formulated before I had time to judge them, were love letters. Most of them will never be collected; I am sure that though they were once laid aside to be kept, they were later dropped on the way by the young women for whom letters were not literary matter but means of life, received and enjoyed and then abandoned, as flowers are welcomed and forgotten.

12 September

There is so much of Spinoza in Einstein's remark to his assistant, Ernst Straus: "What really interests me is whether God had any choice in the creation of the world." Did Einstein actually read Spinoza, or did he voice the traditional Jewish concern with the law—the rigor of the law, so evident in the Old Testament, the obsession with legal definitions, the equating of God and the law in Spinoza? Correspondingly, there is the Jewish rebellion against the law, the Hiob complex producing the revolutionaries and oppositionists. Jews cannot ignore the law; they must teach, preserve, or fight it. Did God have a choice, left open by the laws of nature? Spinoza said no and was thrown out of the synagogue.

15 October

In yoga meditation the key points of the body serve as
way stations for the stepwise elevation of attention from
the ground to the seat of the spirit. The mind passes
through the levels of the human condition, represented
by their organic functions and seats. The ascent climaxes
in the cupola of the skull, to which the mind looks up as
though to that of the Pantheon, then returns to its own
location between the eyes. After exploring the range of
its own disposition, it attempts to interact with the outer
world through giving and taking, exhaling and inhaling.

25 October

I remember warning my students against William James's
advice—contained, I believe, in his chapter on habit—to
automatize "mechanical" routines of the day as much as
possible to keep the mind free for the "higher" occupa-
tions. Such a split would promote alienation from the elements of living. One's way of treating the foundation
shows up at the pinnacle.

13 November

Many of those who clamor for democracy are happiest
under an enlightened authoritarian regime that relieves
them of decision making and administrative labors while
leaving them free to complain about bad government.
The democracy of the United States is composed of
thousands of local autocratic regimes in cities, schools,
companies, and families.

21 November

From the beginning, the language of the dialogue in film
was inferior to that of the image. This became painfully
evident when the words began to be spoken. While the

screen image profited from a refined pictorial tradition,
the talk stayed at the level of popular fiction.

26 November

Happenings in time must be translated into sequences in
space, because only in space can they be surveyed synop-
tically. In the Book of Daniel, the coming of four succes-
sive kingdoms is prophesied when Nebuchadnezzar
dreams of a statue with a golden head, arms and breast of
silver, belly and thighs of brass, and legs of iron with feet
of iron and clay. Of course, an arrow has to be built into
the spatial model, otherwise the linear succession of the
events will be overlooked and the model will mislead. In
the literary description of the dream image, the text of
the Bible leads the reader sequentially from head to toes.

28 November

Upright figures cut pictorial space into vertical ribbons.
Some artists feel the need to reestablish continuity by
crossing the vertical shapes with horizontals. In Dürer's
engraving of Adam and Eve the two figures and the tree
trunks are the warp of the weave. Space is tied together
horizontally by the arms, the snake, the cat crossing the
tree, the cat's tail behind Eve's leg, etc. The painter has
learned from the weaver.

1 December

When in *King Lear* the king as well as Gloucester denounce their children on the flimsiest evidence, this happens not because Shakespeare sacrifices good psychology
to constructing a plot in which faulty accusation and innocence clash spectacularly. Tragic misjudgments have
been favored in literature since the Old Testament, and
they can be understood only if we remember that a writ-

er's story is not a special event but a particular embodiment of a general human condition. Lear errs because he symbolizes man's lack of wisdom. Human foolishness could not be made evident unless the viewer or reader were allowed to know better.

4 December

I do not profit much from the offerings of "minimal" art, but the other day I was struck by a "sculpture" made by Donald Judd, who had attached a stack of boxes to a wall with an open space between each box. Since the lowest box is at about knee level and the highest perhaps ten feet above the floor, the boxes present themselves in different perspectives. The box at eye level is seen head-on, the higher ones reveal their bottoms increasingly, and the lower ones are seen from the top. This makes the column fan out vertically in both directions. The eye level of the viewer determines the center of the display, so that as one bends down, the center lowers itself correspondingly. I had never seen a similar effect. In paintings the perspective is rigidly fixed. A building is too tall to offer a similar range of aspects, and although sculpture changes with the position of the viewer, it does not restructure itself so mechanically at the command of that position. The Judd piece made me feel as though I were directly moving the piece with my glance—not a profound experience but one worth having.

5 December

From a documentary film on Argentine peasants I learned that a man who paints and carves religious images is called an *imaginero,* Spanish for "image maker." He is not called an artist, and in fact he produces his images with the same attitude with which he tailors for himself a pair of trousers or repairs an old harmonium.

151

12 December

A linguistic structure without words would be like a skeleton without bones. Therefore, underlying actual speech there must be either a set of basic normative sentences—which strikes me as unlikely—or a speech-inducing structure that is not verbal at all but consists of images—images of objects, percepts of actions and attitudes, such as asking, looking for, demanding. Before the child can adopt explicit interrogative words (the so-called *wh-*words) what is there in his mind? *Wh* in the abstract? That is obviously absurd. He experiences "questioning," expressed by the raised pitch of the voice. Gradually, as the structure of the underlying nonverbal experience differentiates, language articulates questions more precisely: Who? Where? What? But the deep structure, the well of speech, remains as nonverbal as it was in the beginning.

🌿 1972

The chorus in Haydn's *Creation* was like the chorus of
singers in white robes, carrying palm leaves, in Dürer's
woodcut illustrating the seventh chapter of Revelation.
The blades of the palms rise in visual unison around the
heads of the devoted choristers—an abstract upsurge of
harmony.

When the dentist says: "Tell me when it hurts!" I feel like
Wittgenstein as I answer in my mind: "I can tell you this
only if I know whether you are asking because you need
my sensation as a signal that your drill is approaching the
live nerve or because you do not wish to make me suffer
more than inevitable. Depending on what you mean, I
shall be your fellow explorer or a victim prepared to call
for mercy. Accordingly, I shall either watch out keenly
for even the slightest sensation or try to ignore as much
of it as I can."

5 January

There is no surer way for a writer to reveal his lack of
education than by festooning his pages with the standard

quotations from the great sources. When I read that the world is too much with us, or that the unexamined life is not worth living, or that Euclid looked on beauty bare, I conclude that the writer was brought up on freshman survey courses and never made it beyond them; and I shut his book.

18 February

Cubist shapes resemble the film technique of montage developed at roughly the same time. In Cubist painting, the surface of an object such as the human body is pieced together from small units, which penetrate each other as though every one of the angular shingles were unaware of its neighbors. They have no borders but bleed into emptiness. Only their overall configuration fits a unified volume. Similarly, the units of classical film montage create a continuous sequence through the discontinuity of the individual joints. Each shot is endless in time and space, a mere sample clipped from an ongoing event. They join by mutual interruption, so that the whole is a tissue of small contradictions. This makes for the symbolism of this uniquely modern way of conceiving of wholes.

27 February

Someone told a friend that a man would visit the university to lecture on visual thinking. "Visual thinking?" responded the friend. "There can be no such thing!" But she pondered the matter and amended, "It is true, though, that when I wake up in the morning, I cannot think as long as I don't wear my glasses."

Motion picture theaters, just like airplanes, ought to provide oxygen masks dropping automatically on the seated customer in case of emergency. When a film clogs the vital outlets of experience, the masks would restore the *spi-*

raculum vitae by which the first man was transformed from a lump of clay into the carrier of a living soul.

5 March

When our daughter Margaret was a child, she bought for me with her pennies a birthday plant from the dime store. Grown into a large bush, it flowers every few years. For a day or two, drops of nectar glisten on the small blossoms like the pearls of earrings and fill the living room with the lascivious perfume of oriental harems. How did this mute emanation of exotic vice come from the hands of the child, and how can it draw inspiration from its sober confinement on the third floor?

19 March

Concerning national character. A London publisher prepared a British edition of an American writer's book on American and British usage of the English language. When the author received the galley proofs from England, he discovered that the printer had adapted the text throughout to British spelling. This led to sentences such as: "Where the Englishman writes *colour,* the American prefers to write *colour.*"

13 April

An art historian gave a talk at a lectern, from which he directed the slides by remote control. So accustomed was he to working with a projectionist that he kept saying, "Next slide, please!" and then executed his own command by pressing the button.

Looked at from afar, the moon is a ball of matter surrounded on all sides by empty space. But when the astronauts approached it, there must have been a perceptual change, gradual or sudden, to the way we as inhabitants experience our earth—a solid base, extending forever as a flat plane, with no empty cosmic space underneath.

22 April

Psychologists are still taught that the "constancy of shape" straightens out distortions created by foreshortening. Actually, that mechanism is probably limited to very simple shapes. We do see a tabletop as rectangular and a flower pot as round, regardless of the angle of vision. But if you bend a piece of cardboard to form a Z, you will see it change its shape wildly, depending on from where you are looking. Much abstract sculpture, such as that by Anthony Caro or Mark di Suvero, derives its life from this wealth of projections.

26 April

As one gets older, it happens that in the morning one fails to remember the airplane trip to be taken in a few hours or the lecture scheduled for the afternoon. Memory does return in time, but the suspicion remains that in the end dying will consist in simply forgetting to live.

30 April

Some of the early centaurs, for instance, those on Etruscan amphorae and also some archaic Greek bronze figurines, consist of a complete man with the horse's body and hind legs attached to his buttocks. The front legs and feet are human, and there are two sets of genitals, one on the man and one on the horse. It is an unconvincing creature—a complete human being with an animal supplement. There is redundancy and duplication. By comparison, the classical centaur carries conviction: he is not a composite but a genuine individual. Two incomplete,

mutually dependent beings grow out of each other without a break.

2 May

As holography is perfected, it begins to exhibit the terrifying rigor mortis of all new advances toward illusion. I
look at the life-size portrait of the inventor, Dennis Ga-
bor. He stands before me in full volume. As I move from
the left to the right, I see a part of his shirt that was hidden before by his jacket, and the reflections on his eye-
glasses change. I see his head first from the left, then
from the right. So complete is the illusion of the man's
three-dimensional presence that his immobility makes
him a frightening corpse. The strength of the spell makes
me ungratefully aware of what is missing. Instead of an
image of a live man, I see a real ghost faking life. It will
take a while before this new advance toward realism loses
the power of seeming to be reality. It happened before
with the motion picture, the stereoscope, the sound film.

5 May

A patron of an American university, an admirer of the
arts, had Italian workmen in the Carrara quarries carve a
life-size statue after a photograph of the movie actress Sophia Loren. It represents a woman clutching her face in
grief. Put up in the administration building of the university, it has been called by the faculty "Tenure Denied."

30 May

During Mary's absence I have taken over the duty of
watering the plants in the apartment, and I find that the
dislike I had for one of them because it depressed me
with its ailing appearance is changing to affection. I move
it to a location favorable to its need for shade, I water it

carefully and trim off the dried leaves, and I am reminded of my lifelong conviction that a powerful means of arousing love for someone or something is to do things for that person or object. Teachers and doctors are aware of it. The Freudians can do no better than call it countertransference. I would even be willing to believe that self-love is so strong because the self is the person for whom one does the most.

31 May

A television-nurtured child, asked where her mother was, is said to have replied, "Mama is watching a book."

8 June

We see our fellow men as animated by a soul, and therefore the organs of the body are perceived not in their physical but in their mental functions. The eyes are not a pair of roving cameras but a mind exploring, fearing, desiring. The mouth is not an orifice for the ingestion of food but a mind smiling, frowning, shaping words. The hands are a mind pointing, refuting, handling, exploring. It is almost impossible for a normal man to see a woman's breasts as mammalian glands attached to the body. They are a sweeping double prow, a mind reaching forward in exuberance (*ex uberis*). The penis is unique in the independence of its initiative. Unlike hands and feet, it is not an instrument guided by the mind in the head but has a mind of its own, confined to one urge and intention. Hence the silliness of its single-minded, subhumanly simple behavior.

7 July

In his *Analyse der Empfindungen,* Ernst Mach objects to the linear conception of causality as deriving from a

"primitive, pharmaceutical way of looking at the world,"
according to which "einer Dosis Ursache *folgt* eine Dosis
Wirkung." Instead, he maintains, since all phenomena depend on one another, "alle genau und klar erkannten Ab-
hängigkeiten lassen sich als gegenseitige Simultanbezie-
hungen ansehen."* This struck me forcefully, because in
my analysis of a symbol of interaction I had suggested
that interaction cannot be described adequately as a combination of linear sequences, but I had failed to see that
this objection applies to causality quite in general.

8 July

A silver-gray rainy day, lake and sky the same color.
I love this weather not only because the gray background—favored by Cézanne as *gris clair*—gives the
greens of the vegetation a deep intensity but also because
a blue sky and radiant sun display a strength and beauty
not easy to live up to. They are like "a glamorous
blonde"—who am I to cope with such splendor? But in
the silent oriental tranquillity of the gray landscape the
small figure of an old sage is not out of place.

13 July

The profile contour of a duck's head on a faithfully
shaped wooden decoy—what a beautiful but intricate
line! It is symmetrical neither in the horizontal nor in the
vertical dimension, but it skirts both symmetries, and it
goes out of its way to merge explicitly with the outline of
the body. How difficult to draw is this graceful line, how
hard to remember, and yet how immediately convincing
and "right."

* "A dose of *cause* is followed by a dose of *effect*. . . . When depen-
dencies are precisely and clearly comprehended, they can all be viewed
as mutually simultaneous relations."

17 July

A dead fly in the bathtub seemingly rushing forward
under its own impulse, although merely propelled by a
small stream of invisible water . . . this, if you want to be
one-sided about it, is man's freedom.

19 July

Nothing is more humbling than to look with a strong
magnifying glass at an insect so tiny that the naked eye
sees only the barest speck and to discover that nevertheless it is sculpted and articulated and striped with the
same care and imagination as a zebra. Apparently it does
not matter to nature whether or not a creature is within
our range of vision, and the suspicion arises that even the
zebra was not designed for our benefit.

22 July

Considering the state of medicine in past ages, it is a
good guess that most great works of art, philosophy,
and science were produced by persons in physical distress. Voltaire spent the greater part of his life working in
bed, reports Vauvenargues. "Presque tous les jours il
souffrait des entrailles."*

24 July

I sympathize with the Arab chiefs who, according to
Saint-Exupéry, saw in the waterfalls and fountains of
France the supreme proof of European power. As I turn
on the garden hose, I cannot help feeling that to trust in
the inexhaustibility of the water supply is to challenge nature. It seems like a sinful provocation.

* "Almost every day he suffered from intestinal pains."

160

30 July

With all the insects around, I often cannot tell the difference between the flying bugs in the room and the rapidly moving floaters in my eyes. This establishes a continuum of the objective and the subjective world, which softens, in a domestic sort of way, the dichotomy between the I and the It.

9 August

From building a fire one can learn something about artistic composition. If you use only small kindling and large logs, the fire will quickly eat up the small pieces but will not become strong enough to attack the large ones. You must supply a scale of sizes from the smallest to the largest. The human eye also will not make its way into a painting or building unless a continuum of shapes leads from the small to the large, from the large to the small.

15 August

> The pearls of crystal
> Balancing at the tips of
> Our morning grasses.

> Scarlet tanager
> Burning on the morning tree
> To get himself dry.

18 August

In carving a wooden head, I had much trouble trying to understand the particular curve of the surface that leads from the concavity next to the saddle of the nose to the convex swing between eyebrow and eye, until I remembered how the eyeball is embedded in the ocular cavity. Knowing what is underneath is very revealing.

The birds hold the monopoly of beautiful natural sound. Below them is the machine shop of the buzzing insects, above them the melancholy howling of the mammals. Man had to invent artificial sound to produce something pleasant for the ears.

21 September

In the days of Franz Kafka human degradation was sufficiently symbolized by the transformation of a man into an insect. By now, a middle-class man aspires to becoming a piece of furniture. To feel proud of a memo pad with the imprint "From the desk of Joe Miller" is like being dissatisfied with being a live organism. Instead of thinking of himself as an individual lending his talents to a business, Joe Miller wants to be the voice of a permanent fixture, anchored physically, economically, and socially to the corporation. The desk speaks with the wooden authority of an object. Its permanence is beyond the coming and going of human beings, whose contracts elapse without notice.

3 October

Verbal usage expresses a difference between American and European reasoning. It took me years to realize that the American pronoun "one" does not stand for a generality but for an unspecified individual. Hence, for example, "What one makes, he knows." The very opposite is true for European languages, which, rather than eschew generality, turn concreteness into abstractness. The French elevates the individual by the use of the majestic "On verra" to express "We shall see." Similarly, in German, "Man wird ja sehen!" The Italian language replaces the impersonal pronoun with the reflexive—"Si fa ma non si dice," saying literally, "It's being done but not talked about." Again the generality rules.

162

Some popular quotations smell of airless closets. They exhale the stale imagination of the intellectual lower middle class. "Suspension of disbelief" has become one of them. Dressed up as a scintillating double negation, it serves the pedestrian notion of art as illusion.

There is something almost mediumistic about the unexpected telephone call of an old friend. A voice of the past makes a disembodied appearance.

8 October

When an infant reaches for a ball that is too far away to be grasped, the psychologist concludes that the baby is unable to estimate the distance correctly. But when Orpheus turns around and extends his arms longingly toward Eurydice receding toward Hades, are we to assume that he judges the distance incorrectly?

19 October

A painting comes with a date—we say, "This is early sixteenth century." In photography, such chronological differences, although discernible, are mostly still considered unessential. More characteristically, the subject matter of a photograph comes with a date—we say, "This is Churchill when he was young," or "This is San Francisco in 1906!" In both media it is the date of origin that counts. *The Surrender of Breda* is of 1634–35, when Velásquez painted it, not of ten years earlier when the ceremony took place. It is the brain of the painter that generated the picture, not the physical event itself, as would be the case with a historical photograph.

8 November

More attention should be paid to gestures. I observed a man who accompanied everything he said with the gesture of propitiation used by conductors to make the orchestra play more softly. As his flattened palms pressed downward, he seemed not to attack but to subdue his adversaries; and there was an ominous resemblance with the kind of machine that squashes slowly but definitively.

9 November

The lion cage smell
Of Eucalyptus trees
California.

19 November

Why do the distortions of Joan Miró's figures make them look humorous while those of a Giacometti never do and those of Picasso only rarely? In a Giacometti the distortion overlays the entire figure equally and thereby transposes it untouched into a world of different dimensions. The Miró creatures are unevenly sized. They may sprout one huge hand or foot or a grotesquely stretched neck; they are disfigured within their own structure. Ablebodied victims of circumstance are tragic; humorous victims owe their trouble to their own bad shape.

13 December

A scientific approach has a style of its own, often comparable to that of the arts of the period. When the great psychologist Ewald Hering said at the beginning of his book on the theory of the light sense that our visual world consists solely of differently shaped color patches and that perceived objects are nothing but colors of various kinds and forms, he was convinced that he was making a strictly objective, scientific statement. Yet he was obviously speaking as an Impressionist.

164

25 December

It is good to live in a country where all are immigrants, even the sparrows. Elsewhere the newcomer remains a bloody foreigner all his life. The natives accept him if they like to feel charitable, and he pays by disguising his mind with the new country's garb. In the United States the newcomer is simply the latest arrival: "You arrived from Europe last year? My grandfather came to this country from Poland." Bless you, America!

✣ 1973

In a film about the early nineteenth century a stagecoach traveling along a country road was photographed from an airplane. The anachronism might not have been notice-able, had it not been for the characteristic swaying and sweeping of the plane's motion, which transformed the neutrally recording camera into an individual observer— an out-of-place member of the cast.

The churches and the English departments are converting to a cult of the movies. Considering how little of general interest some of them were doing before, this may be just as well. Some philosophers and art historians are tempted to do the same, and for the same reason.

30 January

We have barely recovered from Jung's archetypes, only to have our good sense attacked by Chomsky's linguists as-serting that the structures of language are inherent in the human germ plasm. Instead of acknowledging that the world of experience around us has a structure of its own,

167

we prefer to take the easy way out by calling that observed structure a piece of inbuilt equipment.

31 January

An identical mechanism seems to operate in two totally different realms of human behavior. I have shown that the literary metaphor brings about the union of two incompatible images by raising the statement to a level of abstraction that draws out their common elements. The same is true for stereoscopy in vision. The two images fuse by what they have in common, thereby rising from flatness to three-dimensionality.

9 February

Thinking back to what pictures there were in my parents' living room, I remember Rembrandt's painting of the Mennonite preacher Anslo comforting a widow (in the Berlin Museum) and a *Madonna Enthroned* by Andrea del Sarto. Such was the secularization of religious art and of families like ours that only now, half a century later, I notice for the first time the curious disparity between the Christian art on the walls and the Jewish background of my family. Freethinking though my father was, he might have felt uncomfortable if someone had made him aware of the discrepancy. What these paintings meant to us, I can hardly tell: the kindly, dignified face of the preacher, the ideal beauty of the Virgin, the middle-class cultural devotion to traditional art—all of this was, I am sure, almost subliminal. Like all good servants, the pictures performed their duties inconspicuously.

In the work of his last five years or so, the sculptor Wilhelm Lehmbruck tended to omit the arms of his figures. He amputated them from their torsos or hid much of them. The arms of a sculptural figure are like the subplots of the drama. They expand and ramify the principal

theme embodied in the compact trunk or oppose that
main theme by the counterpoint of secondary action.
Perhaps in those last years Lehmbruck could no longer
tolerate such interaction with externals. In a bust of a
brooding thinker, a bent hand, devoid of arm, presses
against the chest as though the incubus had to be defined
as residing within the mind, not attacking it from the
outside.

12 February

Our belief in immortality is supported by the uniqueness
of the individual: so special and irreplaceable a person, we
say, could not disappear without leaving a hole in our
world; and, in fact, people continue to remain in memory
in direct relation to how special they were. Actually,
however, in a broader sense the opposite also is true. It is
the generality of nature that counteracts the coming and
going of time. There will always be summer and winter,
dogs and trees, love and despair, so that in spite of the
turnover everything essential remains. If the world consisted only of differences, nothing would last but change.
Notice here how much we are inclined to understand existence as essence. Anything that possesses essence claims
existence, and nothing devoid of essence can be said
to be.

9 March

Some particulars are so loaded with universality that they
clamor to be used as metaphors. Jean-Louis Barrault says
in a book of his that it is impossible to fry an egg properly. The yolk requires more heat than the white. How
true for situations where the whole is hard to deal with
because different parts call for different treatment.

12 April

In the silence of early morning, a few minutes before I
have to get up, a jet plane rises from the airport and nois-

ily crosses my bedroom window. I have no difficulty taking its appearance as a cosmic signal, meant for me. Astrology is hard to resist. Any conspicuous constellation not tied to any other evident purpose is compellingly perceived as a personal message.

21 April

Members of persecuted races possess a special vigilance that must greatly sharpen their sense of observation; but it may also distort what they see.

25 April

As one walks alongside the shelves in the bookstore, the books make their silent advances like prostitutes leaning on windowsills—some fresh, some old, but all at their best appearance.

5 May

Balzac tells us: "Nous ne savons pas quand les femmes comprendront qu'un défaut leur donne d'immenses avantages! . . . L'homme ou la femme parfaits sont les êtres les plus nuls" (Traité de la vie élégante).*

22 June

One fiery lily
In the carpet of bracken
Feu rouge of Corot.

---

* "Who knows when women will understand that a flaw is immensely to their advantage! . . . A perfect man or woman is the maximum of nonentity."

· 1973 ·

27 June

"On ne se doute pas des plaisirs que nous enlèvent les journaux. Ils nous ôtent la virginité de tout" (Théophile Gautier, *Mademoiselle de Maupin*).*

28 June

My library and other possessions had convinced me that one cannot truly own anything unless one knows all the items it contains. I should have been disabused of this trust by the many things that, unknown to me, inhabit my mind and my body. But it took our plot of woods, full of trees I have hardly met and all the life around them, to teach me the disturbing truth.

30 June

One would think that evolution would have taken the itch out of the sting of mosquitoes long ago. What good does the sip of blood do to the survival of the insect when a second later it is squashed by the victim alerted by pain?

2 July

I read that Delacroix complained about the "meaningless gesture" of the woman stepping out of the water in Courbet's *Baigneuses* of Montpellier. It took me a moment to see what Delacroix had seen. To me, the woman just happened to raise her arm, which was enough to justify the gesture if it suited the picture. Perhaps the School of Realism first introduced gestures that authenticate the setting rather than serve the plot.

---

* "We do not realize of what pleasures we are deprived by the newspapers. They rob us of the virginity of everything."

171

4 July

When the dentist asked me to "favor" the molar for
which he was preparing a crown, I, ignorant of the
expression, assumed that he wanted me to chew with that
tooth more than with the others. It had not occurred to
me that somebody or something could be shown preference by being kept from working.

Giorgio De Chirico's *Memorie della mia vita* is the only
truly unintelligent book by an artist I have ever read.
How can one be a good artist without being intelligent all
around? I have known of intelligent artists producing unintelligent art. Auguste Rodin comes close to being one
of them; Roy Lichtenstein is a recent example. But I have
never seen a stupid person doing intelligent art. Another
look at De Chirico's work is in order.

8 July

A friend gave me an old group photograph of gestalt
psychologists taken at a professional meeting. Köhler,
Lewin, Katz, Michotte, Heider—they all face the camera.
Wertheimer is the only one looking at his colleagues,
watching how they behave when they have their picture
taken. He was always the psychologist.

9 July

I wish I could do with my writings what some painters
do with their pictures: keep them forever displayed on
my walls. That way, as I caught a glimpse of one of
them, I'd be able to scratch out an unnecessary adjective
here, replace a noun there. It pains me to see badly expressed things printed irreparably with my name.

15 July

A man testifying on finding his three brothers murdered
in their home: "It was just like on television—I went

downstairs and there they were, lying in a pool of blood."

25 July

Wittgenstein treats a word like a chemical substance of unknown properties. He places it in a sentence as though he were dipping it into a solution and watches the result. But he seems to have felt no urge to go beyond noting down what he observes.

27 July

My calendar is eating time while I am not looking. Not having consulted it for a while, I find that it has swallowed whole days behind my back.

30 July

A good translator is wary of automatically using the same word available in both languages. Hamlet's use of *philosophy* ("There are more things in heaven and earth than are dreamt of in your philosophy") is translated in August Wilhelm Schlegel's beautiful German version as *Schulweisheit,* meaning "what passes for wisdom in school."

2 August

"Bitte keinen, dass er von dir spräche, nicht einmal verächtlich. Und wenn die Zeit geht und du merkst, wie dein Name herumkommt unter den Leuten, nimm ihn nicht ernster als alles, was du in ihrem Munde findest. Denk: er ist schlecht geworden, und tu ihn ab. Nimm einen andern an, irgendeinen, damit Gott dich rufen kann in der Nacht. Und verbirg ihn vor allen" (Rainer Maria Rilke, *Aufzeichnungen des Malte Laurids Brigge*).*

---

* "Do not beg anybody to speak about you, not even contemptuously. And when the time comes and you discover your name mak-

13 August

Did Miranda think Ferdinand beautiful because he was
the first young man she had ever seen or in spite of it?
Does beauty reveal itself by its self-evident harmony?
Surely this must be intended, for a Ferdinand not really
beautiful but only considered that way by an ignorant girl
for lack of comparison would destroy the whole architecture of the play.

15 August

The funnel's convergence in Dante's *Inferno* is not merely
a matter of spatial narrowing but a dynamic increase of
pressure. The progression from top to bottom is a gradual squeezing, a slow strangling, until all freedom of motion is gone and the agony has become supreme:

> Così discesi del cerchio primaio
> Giù nel secondo, che men luogo cinghia
> E tanto più dolor, che pugne a guaio.*

(*Inferno* 6.1)

27 August

When I have written too much, I find that my words begin to look intolerably familiar. They remind me of the
extras in the pageant of the *Meistersinger,* who from be-

---

ing the rounds among people, do not take it more seriously than
whatever else you find in their talk. Think: It has gone bad—and give
it up. Take on another one, any name, so that God can call you in the
night. And hide it from everybody."
* From the first circle I thus descended down
  Into the second, which less space admits,
  And so much more pain that it stings to groan.

(Trans. Dante Gabriel Rossetti)

hind the scene of the opera stage run back to the front to proudly parade again as though they were appearing for the first time.

18 September

In his film *Ukigasa,* the director Ozu tends to separate action from speaking. Instead of treating speech as an outflow of action, he keeps his actors at rest when they talk, often having them face the camera. It is as though the body's activity had to be suspended when the mind takes over to speak. This is a way of remedying the dilemma of the talking film—the disruption of the visual expression of the body on the screen by the mechanics of the speech muscles.

30 September

G. C. Argan tells me that upon arriving at a railway station in India, he was informed that the train he intended to take would be twenty-two hours late. But if you like, they told him, you can take yesterday's train, which we expect to arrive any minute now!

3 October

Every established religion supplies secular thinking and language with a wealth of metaphors, especially for the kind of humor resulting from the contrast between the virtuous dignity of the church and the mundane or even obscene practices of the common man. Balzac called the sex of his mistress his prebend.

28 October

It is easy to see that when two ribbon shapes cross at a right angle, the area of the crossing will be a square. But can you visualize what happens when two barrel vaults

175

cross one another, forming a groin vault? Can you truly understand why in that case the two shapes have no surface in common but only two curved edges? Find the level of complexity at which you can no longer visualize with ease, and start exercising your mental imagery from there.

In E. A. Poe's story "The Sphinx" a man mistakes an insect climbing a spider's thread near his eye for a monster climbing a bare hill across the Hudson River. The insect is supposed to be "about the sixteenth of an inch in its extreme length, and also about the sixteenth of an inch distant from the pupil of my eye." The invention is ingenious, and Poe plays metaphorically with misjudgments caused by wrong estimates of distance, but the story itself does not work. Details of so small an insect would not be visible, and no eye can focus at a distance of one-sixteenth of an inch. Instead, Poe overlaid two mental images, the enlarged insect with the death's head on its breast and the distant landscape. They can combine in the mind but not in optical space.

1 November

In early styles of art, when artists are uninhibited by the demands of realistic correctness, the size of objects is determined by their function in the visual statement. For similar reasons the cinema controls sizes by varying the distance between the camera and the objects. A hand reaching for a gun assumes the size of a crowd of people surrounding a building. This free handling of size can be understood as being justified by the changes in distance from the object, but in actual experience the awareness of such a change of distance plays a negligible role. Nothing bounces back and forth. Rather, the experience is governed by the ancient and persistent visual logic of giving each thing the size it needs and deserves.

176

4 December

A most Italian anecdote comes from an American family that spent a year in Florence. The attention of their native maid was attracted by an edition of the *Divine Comedy* that they had brought from Rome. "Do they know Dante in Rome also?" she wanted to know. Being assured that Dante was known not only in the whole of Italy but abroad and indeed in America, she seemed much moved: "Che comforto per i suoi genitori!"—What a satisfaction for his parents!

9 December

I dreamed that I was asked to recite poems and was given for that purpose a tin cup containing pieces of hard candy, red raspberry shapes and white lemon ones. I said it would be difficult for me to read from this material because I would not know in what order the pieces came. The dream derived from my recent interest in concrete poetry, in which words become things and the sequence of verbal discourse is largely dissolved.

20 December

In those disquieting hours when I try to take hold of a subject on which I have decided to write, I often think of the old-fashioned butcher, dressing and trimming the meat, cleaning it, cutting away the inedible, until the red freshness lies bare. Similarly, in trying to approach my subject, I must cut my way through the dead stuff, the obvious, the trite and uninspiring, until I touch the quick of the theme. It finally reveals itself, alive, surprising, tempting; and as the subject awakens, I myself am revived in the ability to respond.

🌿 1974

15 January

How many bathers have been painted in the nineteenth and twentieth centuries, and how little do they resemble what is seen on the beaches! In a Dutch painting of a tavern, people clearly behave the way they did at the time, and even Degas's laundresses still labor and yawn like laundresses. But when Malevich paints two floor polishers, he is obviously concerned with the grotesque pantomime of the two figures pushing their pads with their naked feet—and this just a few years before the Russian Revolution.

18 January

The exercises of "conceptual" artists resemble the thought experiments of scientists. But why, to meditate on the circular path pursued by a point on Earth during the twenty-four hours of the day, does the artist need to mark the spot with a ballpoint pen on a wall at an actual street corner in Los Angeles? Is it because having abandoned the tangible objects of the studio, even the conceptual artist needs something to hold on to, something geographic, to be touched with eyes and hands?

179

20 January

I was interested, seeing a middle-aged man with respectable hat and umbrella stand near the curb of Forty-second Street in New York and urinate openly on the sidewalk. Although he looked quite real physically, the improbability of his behavior sufficed to transform him into one of those debonair *bonhommes* that populate Surrealist dreamscapes.

28 January

In dreams we know who a person is with whom we are dealing even though he or she may not resemble that person in the least. It is the only case of pure connotation I can think of.

13 February

Pictures in a picture—it is like someone speaking French in a French novel taking place among the natives of Italy or Sweden.

15 March

Since a young woman was murdered in the park I liked so much, I no longer walk through it. I have made it into a monument that I observe by avoiding. Lucus a non lucendo.

30 March

Even though the proverbial savage has to learn how to "read" photographs, this does not make the viewing of pictures entirely a matter of convention and inculcation. What must be acquired is the perceptual attitude deriving from the knowledge that the texture of a surface can be a picture, and a three-dimensional one at that.

9 April

On the north portal of Chartres a sculptor shows God creating the birds and seeing Adam in his mind. Adam stands next to and slightly behind his Creator and is as physically present as the man in whose mind he dwells as a mere image. Seven hundred years later in novels and films of our time, we also see reminiscences, fears, and fantasies presented with the same concreteness as the scenes taking place in actuality. There is, however, a difference in principle between the early and the late conception. The Romanesque artist has not yet worked out a means of distinguishing between mental image and actual perception, perhaps in part because of the powerful reality granted to visions by priests, soothsayers, and dreamers. The modern artist, on the other hand, abandons all the tricks by which he could make the distinction visible because he no longer wishes to attribute greater concreteness to the physical world than to the mental.

27 May

Carol, the good teacher, was told by three of her high school girls that they wanted to put on a performance of the Judgment of Paris. This was approved, but soon the girls came back to report that they could not agree on who should play Aphrodite. Carol refused to arbitrate. "After all, if Zeus was unwilling to pass judgment, who am I . . . ?" (And by the way, if Paris had given the golden apple to Athena, Greece would have been destroyed by the Trojans and the history of the West would have been unrecognizably different.)

6 June

A teacher's self-esteem is most wholesomely tempered when he discovers what kind of persons his students admire besides him.

29 June

One has to get used to architectural plans being readable from all sides, just as buildings can be approached from any direction. A painter's sketch must be viewed right side up because it is the preliminary embodiment of a work that takes its final form as a picture. The architect's picture has no finality in itself; it is only an expedient description of objects to be erected in physical space.

"Il faut être un peu persécuté" (Henri Matisse).*

8 July

The need for poetry in its broadest sense was demonstrated when cosmic space was explored by technicians. In addition to reporting hard and fast "data," they attempted stammeringly to describe what it was like to step on the moon and see the Earth from afar. Inevitably their descriptions were as noncommunicative as the greetings scribbled by tourists on their picture postcards. They did not make us "be there." It takes an artist to occupy a new world for the human mind. Think of what we could have conquered if the space agency had been civilized enough to send Marianne Moore to the moon!

11 July

Realistic detail in the arts calls for as much justification as its omission. When George Grosz in a drawing of a scene of capital punishment marked the trademark of the Solingen steelworks on the blade of the executioner's axe, he meant to indicate that the person executed was a victim of capitalist society.

* "One must be a bit persecuted."

12 July

The plays that shocked audiences at the beginning of our century as unspeakably realistic tragedies are now appreciated as black comedy. Frank Wedekind's *Erdgeist,* which in comparison with his earlier great *Frühlings Erwachen* now reads like a Punch-and-Judy show, has made literary history, whereas Shaw's *Pygmalion,* an immensely better play treating the same plot of the flower girl who makes good in society, only entertains us. Quite fittingly, Lulu became an opera by Alban Berg whereas Eliza Doolittle ended in the musical *My Fair Lady.*

23 July

The character representing the novelist's own self tends to be sensitive and observant but devoid of that activating core that distinguishes a truly functioning and active person from a mere set of traits. Compare the diaphanous web that is Flaubert's Frédéric in *L'Education sentimentale* in comparison with the substantiality of, say, his Jacques Arnoux! And when Robert Musil calls his hero a *Mann ohne Eigenschaften,* perhaps his diagnosis is wrong. Perhaps all his Ulrich possesses are *Eigenschaften.*

26 July

Under certain conditions our normal three-dimensional visual space seems to collapse into projective flatness. Someone told me that under the influence of a painkilling drug, he saw from his hospital bed a wall clock halved by the bed curtain. He expressed his astonishment to his wife: "What a screwy idea to make a half clock, of no use to anybody!" I myself have experienced occasionally during the brief moment of awakening that near and far objects were telescoped into an indecipherable image and that it took me an effort to pick them apart and unfold the world of space.

7 August

Every thing has a size level at which it reveals itself. The dabs of color of which divisionist paintings are composed lose their nature and function when viewed from too close by. But each of the white dots of which the umbrella of Queen Anne's lace is composed discloses under the magnifying glass a beautiful flower, a star of white petals surrounding a phallic pistil in the grand style of Bernini.

17 August

However limited a range of products may be, its best specimens will be considered insuperably excellent. Even the lowest ceiling can become the sky. A film critic, faced with the mediocrity of the year's crop, can preserve his job only by praising the least intolerable novelties as masterworks; and on the faculty of even the smallest college there rules a Voltaire or Matisse uncontested.

Years ago, a student of mine conducted an experiment in which she asked a fellow student to select from a number of photographs of herself the one she thought resembled her most. The girl's best friend was asked to do the same, that is, to pick the portrait she thought resembled her friend most closely. The result was quite clear-cut. The friend chose a picture doing justice to the characteristic features of the particular girl, whereas she herself picked the one closest to a noncommittal, well-proportioned normalcy. This is likely to be generally true—look at the picture chosen by the president of the USA as his official portrait. The same does not seem to hold for the self-portraits of artists. The artist faces himself as subject matter, and that may make a difference.

In the seventeenth century, the language itself was still
poetical, as one can tell by the King James Version, which
was not written by poets but by scholars. The offensively
dry translations of the Bible in our own time show that
today it would take an Ezra Pound, a specialist in poetry,
to match the feat of the old scholars.

2 November

Seurat once defined painting as the hollowing of a surface. That is indeed what it was since the early Renaissance developed the box space. Digging a burrow is an
explorer's activity, and one could perversely say that the
traditional painter shapes his trees or figures by only
stopping briefly on his way to infinite distance, palpating
the obstacles, and then moving on past them. In the nineteenth century the hollow began to become shallower,
and finally the Cubists made their images bulge forward
rather than recede. By then some painters had begun to
abandon their canvases and defect to sculpture. The
sculptor is not captured by negative space, even when he
carves. He makes things one can walk around. The ex-
plorers are being replaced by the makers.

3 November

The Faustian quest is, by its nature, endless. There is
something ridiculously inappropriate about the great
searcher being picked up at the end by the Devil or saved
by the Eternal Feminine. His aspiration deserves neither
punishment nor reward. Therefore it seemed to me logical that Flaubert left his *Bouvard et Pécuchet* a fragment.
But since in the age of general education the pursuit of
universal knowledge is bound to become a comedy, it
also made sense for Flaubert to plan that at the end of his
novel the two retired employees should return, disabused,

to the work they had been accustomed to do at the office, namely, the copying of documents by hand. It is no longer the Devil but mechanization that insists on the fulfillment of the pact after the victims of enlightenment have had their fling.

17 November

When the accused and the witnesses testify in Kurosawa's *Rashomon,* they face the camera head-on. The police commissioner interrogating them is neither seen nor heard, and the flat, symmetrical space on the screen looks self-contained. This makes each testifier appear to be addressing only his own conscience. Every one of them is alone and without awareness of the different stories told by the others. They are chillingly isolated, however intimately they had once been intertwined.

18 November

Several times every day, the inhabitants of the apartment above us drop on their bare floor an object of the size and metallic sound of a knitting needle. Since that is all we know about them, we have formed an image of needle-droppers, some rare species of porcupine shedding an occasional quill, or adherents of a secret sect offering needles to propitiate their gods or preparing needles to kill their enemies by voodoo magic.

2 December

An outsider is privileged to take metaphors literally and thereby discover nonexisting worlds of great poetry. When on the front page of the paper I saw the headline *Jets Upset Dolphins,* I pictured airplanes swooping down to the ocean and disturbing the peaceful ecology of the sea animals. This Homeric image was dispersed only when I began to read, did not understand a word, and realized that the message came from the world of sports, totally alien to me.

6 December

The "mobile home" owners, those human snails settling down and striking roots—animals metamorphosed into plants. First the shell travels with the person, then the person hugs the soil with the house.

❦ 1975

1 January

In the portrait sketches drawn by artists at court trials the
defendants and accusers look disturbingly private, like
the neighbors next door. This is so because as parties to
a legal case they have a claim to public appearance only as
embodiments, types of evil or violence, madness or
scornful justice. The only court artist I can remember
succeeding in revealing the public symbol in the private
triviality was David Low, in his depictions of the Nazi
leaders at the Nuremberg trials.

2 January

The most astonishing thing about dreams is that they
contain surprises. While you are driving along the road,
you are suddenly faced with a steep incline, and you decide to turn back. To make something happen and then
be surprised by it—this means that there are two independent agencies at work, one that thinks up the story
and another that is faced by it.

12 January

"Car l'homme de génie ne peut donner naissance à des
oeuvres qui ne mourront pas qu'en les créant à l'image
non de l'être mortel qu'il est, mais de l'exemplaire d'humanité qu'il porte en lui. Ses pensées lui sont, en quelque
sorte, prêtées pendant sa vie, dont elles sont les com-
pagnes. A sa mort, elles font retour à l'humanité et l'en-
seignent" (Marcel Proust, *En mémoire des églises assassi-
nées*).*

31 January

Being astonished by the discovery that Marcel Proust was
still alive when I graduated from school, I thought that it
would be fruitful to investigate the mistakes people make
in recalling the birth and death dates of historical figures.
Probably any reasonably intelligent person does not
simply memorize dates like telephone numbers but sees
historical periods as sensible sequences of styles, ideas, or
events and adjusts the chronology accordingly. Proust is
for me a voice from before my time. One cannot poke
one's nose through a painting one wants to see.

17 February

Who makes us read numbers as being turned to the left?
It is quite possible to read a *3* as a *B* without a back or as
a pair of breasts. When turned toward the right, a *3* becomes a different shape, just as Tinbergen's figure of a
goose looks like a hawk when read in the opposite direction. All objects have this double character. A brush
points from its wooden back toward the bristles, the op-

---

* "For a great mind can give birth to immortal works only if he does
not create them in the image of the mortal being he is himself but in
that of the model of humanity he holds within him. His thoughts are
granted him as some sort of a loan during his life, of which they are
the companions. When he dies, they return to humanity and enlighten
it."

posite direction being "against the grain." A bottle points toward its opening while a bowl reads both ways. Thus the change of character observed when Rubin's goblet/ faces shift direction is only a special case of the dynamic ambiguity of all shapes. Philosophers spellbound by the duck/rabbit figure fail to see that they are dealing with an individual instance of a common principle.

7 March

The first thing to learn about art is to take its statements literally. When Vermeer shows the painter's model frontally and the painter himself from the back, we are not permitted to consider that this situation would change if we moved forward or the painter turned around. Rather, the model is there to be looked at as the dominant item while the painter joins us in being mere onlookers. Rembrandt or Velásquez do the opposite when they have us face the painter as the principal subject.

20 March

Not much will be learned about mental imagery from experiments in which subjects are presented with a sentence isolated from any context and not involving any demand for thought. In and by itself, the sentence "Mr. Taylor is not a tailor" calls for no help from imagery and therefore will produce little but stray results of no interest. But if you ask me, "Would Mr. Taylor make a good tailor?" a whole host of perceivable traits will emerge from my memories of Mr. Taylor and from what I have known about tailoring and will go to work on a solution to the problem.

7 April

When I draw a map of our town, I find it natural to place south on top and north at the bottom because we live in the north of the city and it is from that vantage point that I look at it. Were the ancient Chinese maps, which also have south on top, drawn by people in the north of the country?

5 May

Since very little of my own work is manual, I can be deeply moved by watching the devoted attention of a housewife bent on folding napkins, a dentist preparing a filling, a gardener setting out plants. It is a feeling of envy and pity, like the affection one has for a child seen earnestly at work.

6 May

Across the river a building is being wrecked with a thundering clamor. Searching for a target as though endowed with eyes and a will, the gaping maw moves toward a wall, takes it between its jaws, and breaks it like a piece of a candy bar. In a heavy plunge it destroys the handiwork of bygone builders by the mere impact of its weight, and it carries off a huge steel beam as a trophy. The machine seems terrifyingly unchecked, left to the initiative of its own brutality. Man is no longer the master of his own house.

27 May

When from our summer house I glanced across the top of the hill, I saw the ark of Noah floating on our lake, a gigantic, archaically simple structure with a gable roof and dark round holes as windows. I then discovered that our neighbor had perched a martin's house on a pole that just cleared our hill and showed up against the water. Fetched back from the distant lake and put in its place in the neighbor's yard, the structure quickly acquired its proper smallness.

28 May

Nature begs the question of why humans and animals yearn to survive. She has bred them that way.

29 May

There is nothing particularly refined about praying for the survival of the soul, because it is mostly for the sake of the survival of the body that people desire that of the mind.

3 June

By the seventeenth century the playing of music is firmly tied to written notation: when Caravaggio presents an angel entertaining the Holy Family on his violin, he shows us a winged creature who possesses eternal youth and beauty but not the ability to play without looking at the sheet music, which in fact Joseph is holding up for him.

Schopenhauer, writing in the early nineteenth century, quoted all languages in the original and bothered at most to supply a translation into Latin for passages from the Greek or Sanskrit. English is the only language he thought in need of a German translation. Thus while he quoted Lao-tzu in French, he accompanied passages from Shakespeare with a German version for the benefit of the illiterate.

16 June

Profiting from the perfidious power of words, the American automobile industry speaks of "full-size" cars to describe the overblown monsters that amaze and amuse our foreign visitors. Once those acromegalic wagons are established as the norm, cars of a more sensible size become minor deviations, toys for the special taste. By such a shift of the norm level, pathology is made into health.

20 June

When I saw in a film on an auction of Pop Art the bronze beer cans of Jasper Johns shoved around by the personnel of the company, I felt that finally they had been returned to a situation they could handle.

Looking down on a branch of a maple tree, one can admire the artful and considerate distribution of the leaves, which barely overlap, giving every individual as much exposure to the light as possible. When it comes to human arrangements, we call it a matter of morality: Giving everybody a decent chance! As though morality were anything but biologically sensible conduct.

28 June

The good kind of ambiguity lets me know that a certain object is one thing as well as another. The bad kind is incapable of telling me whether the object is one thing or another.

10 July

In one of his short stories the novelist Siegfried Lenz hits on a powerful theme to castigate the bad conscience of the Nazi generation among his fellow Germans. He presents the figure of a vagrant who antagonizes everybody by his total clairvoyant recall of past events. For example, being shown someone's house, he comes forward with the name of the former owner, who had been expropriated by the Nazis. What makes the figure of the man particularly compelling is that he does not produce these unwelcome facts willfully but as though driven against his

own wishes by an impulse as mercilessly unavoidable as
the chronicle of history.

25 July

As we drove along the highway, a woman in her car was
waiting at the corner of a side road to let us pass. Her
mouth was open in a large yawn, and since no motion
indicated that the mouth would shut, it looked as though
she, and by implication her car as well, was frozen into
immobility by a spell and would stay at that corner of the
highway forever.

28 July

The mind is reluctant to pick a place in the unstructured
infinity of space or time. A birthday is needed to mark
the passing of time. A dog needs a tree against which to
raise his hind leg, and the pedant looks at his watch and
says, "Tea is indicated."

1 August

The machine reawakens the old fear of the dead coming
alive. The Frankenstein story comes at the beginning of
the Industrial Revolution. Poe's pendulum assumes a
murderous initiative, and in *The Tale of Two Cities* the
guillotine acquires a personality of its own. In our own
time we have the rebellious computer of popular fiction.

3 August

A good editor, under whom I worked, taught me always
to throw away the first page of any manuscript: "It gives
you a fresh, interesting beginning. The author needed to
warm up, the reader does not."

12 August

The writer and the painter face the surface of paper or canvas orthogonally. It seems natural to do the same in sculpture, but actually the head-on view flattens the relief of the wood and hides the path of the chisel's action. Look at your work in profile, and you have a contour to work with, which tells you about the most subtle changes.

3 September

H. W. Fowler says in one of his prefaces, "Define, and your reader gets a silhouette; illustrate, and he has it in the round."

A supremely constructed plot like that of Hugo's *Notre-Dame de Paris* is a choreography of puppets, which move with an almost mathematical perfection. Labeled with their defining properties—evil, virtue, ugliness, lust, in-nocence, beauty—the puppets combine systematically in duets and occasional trios, and the themes deriving from the clashes of their properties supply the action. The end comes by necessity when all combinations are exhausted. The balance of it all seems so lucid that one would expect it to display its perfection if the pattern of its themes were translated into the kind of molecular model used by chemists.

5 September

The photographic illustrations of dictionaries must conform to the task of the entries if they are to define concepts. The picture illustrating the word *lei* shows the wreath of flowers worn by a girl with horn-rimmed glasses. Were she playing the piano, the glasses could

claim a relation to the playing; but accidentals, so vital
to the nature of photography, violate the rules in the
realm of rationality.

14 September

Although I grew up using the metric system, I must admit that there are significant sizes within the range of our
eyes and hands that are not done justice if one describes
them only by multiples of centimeters. To say that something is an inch or a foot long acknowledges basic units
of our human world, which is not that of a beetle or an
elephant.

Among today's writers there is more talent for description than for telling stories. The opposite should be more
natural. Literature began with narration. Perhaps the curious change has come about because goal-directedness
has become so weak in our time. If a person does not feel
that he is going anywhere, what story do you want him
to tell?

20 September

An elderly professor stricken by a heart attack during a
reception at the museum had been placed on the porch
behind the columns in expectation of the ambulance. In
his festive attire, lying in Egyptian symmetry on his
back, he looked like a realistically colored statue that
was being relocated by the sculpture department.

7 October

There is a species of erratic driver that punctuates his
conversation isomorphically with the changing speeds
of his progress on the highway. Driving behind him, one

can tell by his sudden braking that he is saying to his companion, "You must keep in mind, however . . ." only to race suddenly ahead when he assures him, "But I made it clear that under no circumstances . . ."

18 October

Announcers on radio and television teach us that communication no longer needs to be authentic. The neutral voice of the messenger turns the authenticity of the news into hearsay. He who speaks is no longer he who knows. How refreshing to hear a meteorologist's inflection and grammar afflicted by events he has himself experienced. Printed language is expected to be indifferent to what it is conveying; but a human automaton, not speaking anybody's mind, gives the impression that the events of life do not matter. We have come a long way since the bearers of bad news were killed by the royal recipients.

31 October

Why does the distinction between poetry and prose not exist in the visual arts and in music? Is not the choreography of pantomime, opera, and even drama sometimes poetical and sometimes prosaic?

6 November

In the eighteenth century, portrait painting gives the sitter a new alertness. He responds to the moment, his gestures point, argue, explain. This must have helped prepare Europe for the photographic snapshot.

23 November

Why does the bird have to call twice in the second movement of Beethoven's *Pastoral* Symphony? Shall I ever understand the function of repetition in music? Most phrases and themes are repeated, and yet they do not tire us—Why? The answer would tell us much about how music copes with the absence of simultaneity in a medium confined to sequence in time.

2 December

No need for the relativists to feel triumphant when they discover that the Chinese use the color red in traffic lights to signify *go* and green to signify *stop*. By no means does this prove that color has no inherent expression. Red looks highly active in both cultures, but to us it means "Danger! Be alert!" whereas in a Communist setting it means "Be alert! Start moving!" Green has for us the calmness of safety—"Go in peace!"—and for the Chinese—"Rest! Desist from action!" The connotations vary, but the expression of the visual percept is the same.

5 December

The principal objection to the "secondary images" supposedly harbored by some works—for example, the psychoanalytic vulture in Leonardo's *Virgin and Child with Saint Anne*—is that they destroy the unity of the composition. No work of art can be grasped in all its aspects at the same time, but the elements must add up to a visually unified whole. The "negative spaces" of a painting cannot be seen in the same percept as the positive ones, but the mind must be able to fit them together if the whole is to make sense. The vulture could have gotten into Leonardo's picture only by a pathological *coup de force* that would have left the artist's conception in shambles.

16 December

Symmetry comes from the inside out or from the outside in. The wings of a bird grow outward from the central core of the body; but a skull grows inward from two

199

halves meeting in the center. This is why we have pairs
of teeth at the front of both jaws, not central single ones.
The frontal colonnades of most Greek temples move
from the sides inward since they have an even number of
frontal columns. The Temple of Zeus at Agrigento, however, has a central column, a spine, which seems to rein-
force the peak of the pediment unduly and thereby split
the façade in the middle.

28 December

We walked through the woods to the lake on the untouched snow. Then, turning back, we followed the
tracks we had made in coming; and it was as though we
were returning into the past from where we had arrived.
Time itself was moving toward us, visibly reversed and
retraced.

29 December

Afterimages follow obediently with every movement of
my eyes. This reveals them to be of my own making.
Similarly, the scenes I call up in my thoughts do my bid-
ding as they come and go when I want them. Revealed as
images, they differ in principle from the table, the chairs,
the people around me: my looking at them cannot move
them. This cessation of my power draws the line between
the reign of my self and the outer world. Much though
the phenomenologists may dislike it, the world must
come apart and split in two. In fact, this subdivision fur-
thers the unity of our experience by resolving a structural
dilemma.

The advocates of visual thinking have never had an easy
time. Condillac already writes in his *Treatise on the Sensations:* "When a philosopher surmises that all knowledge
might have its origin in the senses, all the intellects [*es-
prits*] rebel right away against an opinion that seems to

them so strange. What color is the thought, he is asked, if it comes to the soul by vision? How does it taste or smell, etc. That is, one inundates him with a thousand difficulties with all the confidence supplied by a generally accepted prejudice" (pt. 1, chap. 11).

✖ 1976

12 January

In the drawings of Goya I discern the rare case of an artist
whose form does not work out at the level of the micro-
structure. The elements of those drawings, the small lines
and patches, look neither coordinated nor expressive.
They are often downright ugly. Only at the grander scale
of composition do his statements become readable and,
indeed, beautiful.

16 January

There must be a definite overall mood to any situation.
I wake up from a dream with nothing left of its content
but that mood, of which I can recognize only its general
tone, a sense of well-being or discomfort. If this is true
for dreams, it should be true for waking situations as
well, although the mood is harder to detach from them.

14 February

Has our sense of passing time changed since our clocks
have ceased to tick? Clocks can still be seen but no longer

heard. Have our homes and offices become timeless acoustically—places where nothing requires rewinding?

22 February

The Balinese, I am told, determine geographic directions on their island by relation to a centrally located volcanic mountain. Once again, the so-called primitives put us to shame. Our own Cartesian grid, forced upon us by practical considerations, is nothing better than a neutral network, where no one place is better than the next. Our north and south poles are desolate locations of purely geometrical and physical distinction. Compare this with orienting one's life toward a holy peak, a center outside one's own humble habitat, putting man in his small objective place as one among the many, all subserviently grouped around the high dominant.

9 March

Footprints have a morphology all their own. By size they correspond roughly to that of the animals to which they belong, but there is little resemblance between the body of a deer and the double-pronged wedge of its footprint. And what does the triangle of a bird's webbed foot or the soft rosette of a dog's paw have in common with its owner? To be sure, the raccoon's devious intelligence reflects itself in the delicately shaped pattern of its tracks, and no animal other than man leaves an imprint as complex in its swinging curves. Compare this with the dumbness of the traces left by inorganic tools, the lifeless groove of a wheel, the absurd holes poked by a walking cane.

16 March

How African is the Bishop of Hippo! What strikes me in Augustine's *Confessions* is how entirely open is the play of

the passions, how devoid of the protective crust of more
sophisticated conduct. The upsurge of the instincts, the
desperate attempts to control them and to be "good," the
frustration and the anger, the guilt feelings, the fear of his
mother, and the boundless affection for his friends—it is
all as touchingly naked as it is in a child. The "confessions" do not seem to derive primarily from a moral obligation. They pour forth like a spring of uninhibited
water. The refined clerics of Milan must have looked
at him with the envious smile we have for Othello.

What am I to make of the fact that 95 per cent of my civilization passes me by and I seem to be the better for it? I
have not the slightest knowledge of sports, television
programs, popular music, or Broadway shows, and it
would never occur to me to read any of the novels praised
in the *New York Times Book Review*. As long as I can protect myself from the occasional noise by which these
things clutter my peace, I thrive happily on the conviction that for the good life the few best things are barely
good enough.

20 March

Inevitably, when a minority has been repressed, it will
behave impertinently after emancipation. This is an in-
convenience the majority has to put up with as a punishment for its past sins. The pendulum cannot reach a state
of equilibrium right away.

Looking up at the façade of our building, I could hardly
believe that the partition between our bedroom and my
study is only a few inches thick. From the inside, how
unrelated are the two small worlds, how unaware of each
other—friendly neighbors only when I step from the one
room into the other.

21 March

Great artists and thinkers assume in our imagination the
measured speech of their work. This becomes more evident the farther they move away from us. I can hear Matisse or Cézanne chatter in lively French or Einstein con-
verse in German. But who can imagine Leonardo or
Michelangelo talking in the sort of Italian now spoken
in the streets of Florence? Or Rembrandt or Spinoza in
Dutch? This is why historical movies will never work.
The detached language of the drama would sound unnatural, and an easy vernacular would not suit our reveren-
tial distance from their characters.

22 June

There is a deplorable tendency among performers to play
eighteenth-century music too fast. Insensitive to expression other than that of the Romantics, they try to remedy
by speed what they perceive as a lack of content in the
score. But their virtuosity empties rather than fills the
music. It produces an undignified, mechanical haste, not
unlike the panic of automobiles and pedestrians in pixi-
lated movies.

Art history is subject to a seismography, which registers
tremors upsetting the usual calm and joyful relations between the artist and the world he depicts. A shock wave
in the sixteenth century produced the distortions of the
Mannerists and the monsters of Bosch and Brueghel.
Around 1800 we have the nightmares of Blake, Fuseli,
and Sergel and a century or so later those of the Surreal-
ists. These upsets are quite different from the revolutions
initiating changes of style. Rather than revitalizing the
arts, they shake them for a while at their foundations.
Why and when do such quakes occur? Can the historians
do better than measure their strength on the Richter
scale?

Heredity grows nightmares in the nineteenth century. In Hawthorne's *House of Seven Gables* or in Zola's *Docteur Pascal* the blemishes of past generations burden the present one like a curse. Compared with the Ibsen ghosts haunting the attics, the original sin of the Bible looks comfortably remote.

4 July

Architects cannot sincerely cling to traditional symbols when their culture ceases to back those symbols up. If a church looks like a countinghouse, the architect may deserve praise for his insight rather than blame for his insensitivity.

25 July

The art critic, like the monkey of Master Peter, the puppeteer in *Don Quixote,* can talk only about the past and the present. He cannot predict the future.

26 July

Finding the door of my study closed, I cannot shake off the psychotic notion that I am sitting in there at my desk working as I usually am when the door is closed. Hesitant to face my double, I have to master a bit of courage before I turn the door knob.

29 July

Psychiatrists interested in delusions might want to study Cervantes' subtle handling of their subject. Sometimes Don Quixote's figments prevail. The windmills remain hostile giants. In other episodes the Don recognizes the real situation, which disavows his fantasy—for example, when instead of Dulcinea he meets a smelly peasant woman. Here the expectation is not of his own making

but is fraudulently suggested by Sancho: he believes that
evil magicians have cast a spell on him so that he cannot
share what Sancho pretends to see. Elsewhere he takes reality itself to have been transfigured and therefore to have
become unrecognizable to him. Which of these mechanisms is used under what conditions? Which reality factors evoke and sustain the illusion?

31 July

Have the three primary colors ever been used, as a *hagia
triada,* to symbolize the trinity? My vote would be: the
generative fire of red for the Father/Creator, the transmit-
ting blue for the spirit, and the disembodied light of yellow for the Son.

1 August

"Unbehilflichkeit," writes Theodor Hetzer, "ist ein Kenn-
zeichen nur der grössten Meister und der schöpferisch
ringenden Epochen"*—a profound observation, apt to
warn us against an easy admiration for the elegant
smoothness of a Van Dyck or Holbein. But although that
supreme clumsiness is a privilege of the masters, not all
clumsy artists are masters. It makes all the difference
whether one is handicapped because one is wrestling
with the angel or just because a technical inability prevents hand and eye from making what the artist wants to
make.

2 August

An aspiring art critic compared Robert Smithson's *Spiral
Jetty* in the Great Salt Lake with its "precedents"—Stone-
henge and the Egyptian pyramids. It was a devastating

---

* "Clumsiness distinguishes only the greatest masters and epochs in
the throes of creative struggle."

comparison, because it revealed the difference between the meaningfulness of the ancient monuments and our modern playing with big shapes. The "precedents" reflected the power of an empire in an elementary shape or made man's relation to the universe evident in a circle of boulders. Devoid of such connotations, our shapes are merely gigantic matter, because their appearance does not pronounce ideas. Hence the poverty of our naked whirl or huge wrappers.

3 August

I am grateful for my weak memory, which enables me to start afresh every time I think again about the elements. At each new encounter they seem to me as surprising and puzzlesome as ever, and what I thought of them before presents itself as a discovery to be scrutinized anew. I may not "build" much as I continue through the years, but at least my targets grow no crust.

6 August

Since the artist creates a world of his own with his clay and paint and words, he will also be tempted to shape the live materials of reality itself. But, of course, the social world resists with its own constraints. This accounts for some of the trouble that artists stir up as fathers, husbands, and citizens, and as founders of dream empires. Hitler, in his own miserable way, had something of the attitude of the artist. His plan to exterminate the Jews and other minorities was first of all a visual abstraction: the white race undefiled by darkness. When an artist tries to use the world as his modeling clay, he finds that it lives and crawls and bleeds and fights back.

7 August

The rich brown color that conquers the paintings of the late Titian or the late Rembrandt is not only, as Theodor

Hetzer has it, the broad symbol of the earth as the gene-
trix of all things. It may also be the color synthesis of
darkness and light and may thereby overcome the incom-
patibility of illumination and color that plagued the painter's palette since the fifteenth century. If redness stands
for darkness and yellow for light, the union of red and
yellow in the brown tones of the masters may present the
birth of light from darkness as the pervasive elementary
event, caught in authentic color.

9 August

Although Robert Oppenheimer advised President Tru-
man that a hydrogen bomb, though possible, should
never be built, the president went ahead and had it produced. Has mankind ever refrained from making something that could be made? Make it and then not use it,
perhaps yes; make it and limit its use, yes—but not to
make it at all would seem to be beyond the restraining
power of the human mind. Some most daring exploits or
most dreadful crimes may have been committed just to
quench the irresistible urge to do what can be done.

16 August

People rocking their bodies and limbs at concerts degrade
the music visually. Perhaps the music—say, a Beethoven
quartet—is alive in their minds with all its complexity of
melody, harmony, and rhythm. But in the visual realm
they reduce all that intelligent splendor to the dumbness
of a basic beat.

18 August

When I was forty-seven years old, an old friend of our
family was seventy-four. I figured out that this inversion
of the digits had occurred every eleven years of our lives.
When I was twenty-five, he was fifty-two. Also, accord-

210

ing to the formula $x = 9 (a - b)$, the age difference had to be divisible by nine, and amounted to nine times the difference between the two digits. In our present case: $7 - 4 = 3$, therefore $3 \times 9 = 27$, the age difference.

26 August

Sometimes the splendor of the blue sky, that space-occupying expanse of emptiness, strikes me as pointless. This morning the sky is gray, like drawing paper willing to be filled. And right away the terrestrial world acquires shape and color and forms pictures, ready to be read and recorded.

31 August

The other night a north wind drove the smell of burning wood and peat from a forest fire on the Upper Peninsula two hundred miles across the waters of Lake Michigan to our beach cottage. The messages of anything one sees or hears report veridically that the source is at a distance, perhaps miles away; smells, however, carry their source to wherever they reach a nose. Here we were, in an undisturbed night, with the conflagration surrounding us as a smell and setting our dark trees invisibly on fire. It was like a madman's delusion.

10 September

A striking quotation from one of Flaubert's letters to Louise Colet: "Because I always sense the future, the antithesis of everything is always before my eyes. I have never seen a child without thinking that it would grow old, not a cradle without thinking of a grave." What is the relationship between two distant phases of a scale or development and the antithetical opposition between them? Low and high are differences in degree, but they also face each other as adversaries; so do black and white,

211

and young and old. When do phases of the same scale turn against each other? The main condition must be that quality turns into quantity. "Higher" and "lower" are not antagonists, but high and low are. Different grays may vary only by degree, but black and white are opponents. Next question: Under what circumstances does the one or the other view control a person's *Weltbild?*

12 September

At the time of Gentile da Fabriano, when painters first experimented with perspective, the foreshortening of a shape was not yet obtained by a projective change of aspect but simply by a contraction of the frontal view, which squashes a face as a pretense for turning it.

14 September

Neither the architect nor the painter can produce a flat surface "free of charge" by simply making use of a physically flat plane. Flatness has to be created by explicit perceptual means.

15 September

It is time to become distrustful of stimulation. Educational television programs undertake to "stimulate" the interest of their audience by fleeting bits of science, art, culture. Poeticizing scientists, preferably British, write and lecture to the same effect, the pretense being that their audience, mightily aroused, will now turn to a more substantial study of the topic. What happens instead is that the readers and viewers, enjoying the stimulation but being reluctant to do the work, take the tokens for the real currency and the smattering for true gain.

4 October

In weightless space, astronauts often do not recognize tools floating around them. This alienating effect of foreshortening occurs less in our terrestrial visual experience, because the framework of gravitational space helps us to ascertain in what direction the object is likely to extend. As we look down from a window or along a tabletop, a dominant spatial direction is established to which objects are likely to conform.

The designers of the first Skylab chose to imitate terrestrial conditions by giving the workroom a floor, a ceiling, and walls. The astronauts tried to conform to this framework but became confused when they realized that in weightless space there is no distinguished vertical. Standing upside down on the ceiling, they faced a paradoxical environment. My guess is that the interiors of spaceships should be spherical, with the ceiling equipment of lights, etc., suspended in the center. This would create an isotropic space where all directions would be equal. The only invariant vertical remaining would be that of the astronaut's own body, which would no longer be contradicted by the grid of the environment.

Now that human bodies come to experience atonality in space, we should be able to appreciate the problem faced by musicians when they try to organize tonal relations without reference to a tonic.

20 October

In his travel diary *Meerfahrt mit Don Quixote,* Thomas Mann reports being struck by the unique trick of Cervantes, which I, too, pondered last summer. Writing a second volume of his work fifteen years after the first volume was published, Cervantes makes the first volume a book read by some characters in the second. He thereby turns the story told as a reality in the first volume into a mere narration figuring in a secondary reality, which has taken over from the first. This dizzying performance could be compared with, and clarified by, the practice of

213

painters such as Matisse or Seurat, who showed their own earlier works hanging on the walls of their paintings of interiors.

The startling beauty of natural forms is more readily explained if one remembers that well-shaped things come about more directly than misshapen ones. A butterfly wing or the stripes of the zebra produce pleasantly balanced ornaments more easily than disorderly ones. Only because man has fallen from grace has he come to believe that good form is the ultimate accomplishment.

24 November

Carl Nordenfalk notes that not before the time of Robert Campion did Western painting represent the outdoors as seen through the door or window of an interior. The pictorial device seems to me likely to correspond to the developing use of the picture frame. The frame presents a separate outer world, whose space continues beyond the boundary. This is precisely the conception needed for the notion of an outdoors framed by door or window.

27 November

Schiller in his poem *Die Künstler* called death "den sanften Bogen der Notwendigkeit."*

* "The gentle arc of necessity."

☙ 1977

What better example of the beauty of great scientific conceptions than the "mobile" described in Kepler's second
law of planetary motion! A line drawn from the sun to
the place of the planet on its elliptical path traverses equal
areas of the ellipse in equal times. One must savor the
lively harmony of the ratio that makes the planet slow
down in the exact measure of its increasing distance from
the center of its rotation and speed up as it comes closer.
The mechanical spin is animated by the rhythmical variation of speed and distance, and the variation is held in
balance by the strictly contrapuntal relation between the
two parameters. The elegant simplicity of the ellipse is
dynamized by the eccentricity of its motion. No wonder
Kepler heard the harmony of the spheres.

No bodily metabolism could cope with supplies presented in so disorderly a fashion as those challenging our
intellect. On one evening I read a monograph on the visual aspects of quantum physics, a review of a new translation of the *Genji monogatari,* and a description of Freud's
apartment in Vienna. I like to believe that in less tattered
ages people thought about one thing at a time.

7 January

Four short words from the poems of Eugenio Montale
remain with me firmly as a call signal: "E fu per sempre . . ." They signify the transformation of passing
events into the state of lasting being, when the moth—
wearing the frightening death's-head on its back—
struggles among the papers, blinded by the lamplight. "E
fu per sempre con le cose che chiudono in un giro sicuro
come il giorno . . ." Even more touching is the beginning
of the short poem "Lindau":

> La rondine vi porta
> fili di erba, non vuole che la vita passi.
> Ma tra gli argini, a notte, l'acqua morta
> logora i sassi.*

The erosion of the stone reflects the existing anxiety
about the passing of things. Not by coincidence am I
now concerned with architecture, the most lasting of
tangible thoughts.

10 January

Lying awake last night, I undertook to translate the
Montale poem into German:

> Dorthin die Schwalbe trägt
> Ihre Hälmchen, sie will
> Nicht dass das Leben ende.
> Doch nachts an den Dämmen zersägt
> Das tote Wasser still
> Die steinernen Wände.

---

* "And it was forever among the things that close in a firm orbit like
the day . . ."
   "The swallow carries bits of herbage; it does not want life to cease.
But under the quays at night the dead water grinds the rocks."

"Ladies and Gentlemen" is reverse discrimination. Why should the women come first? But in a sequential medium there can be no coexistence.

14 January

When Bergson speaks of numbers as "des éléments provisoirement indivisibles," he reminds me that the law of differentiation I have formulated for the development of visual form should be applied to concepts in general. Concepts will remain as abstract as the situation permits. Or, differentiation takes place—or ought to take place— only to the extent to which the situation requires it. The atom remains indivisible as long as there is no need to subdivide it.

6 February

At the time of the energy crisis, President Carter advised all government offices to keep the heat at 65°. Since this proved infeasible in many of the buildings, which continued to be overheated in the usual manner, some of the bureaucrats, to comply with the president's directive, turned on the air conditioners. This generated the prescribed temperature by doubling the expenditure of energy as a means of attempting to reduce it.

15 February

In Japan, where they are still civilized enough to respect objects, they celebrate on the eighth of February each year the Hari-kuyo, a Buddhist requiem for the needles broken during the year by the seamsters.

16 February

Those ancient male chauvinists were unwilling to say that Adam was made from a rib of Eve, although that would have been closer to the natural order.

21 February

When I listen to the greatest music—and Beethoven's String Quartet in E-sharp Minor, opus 131, is perhaps the greatest piece of music ever written—I cannot help suspecting that I have been admitted by mistake, since I have no right to attend something so much beyond my capacity. It is as though a careless priest had let me take a peep at the Athena in the cella of the Parthenon.

22 February

The neat finality of the printed page is really the only confirmation a writer receives. Otherwise there are only the friendly noises made by one's acquaintances, the strictures formulated by foolish strangers, and the accidents of applause. One will never know what value there is in those pages, except that they bear the imprimatur of having been set in type.

14 March

I heard somebody say, "You hit the nutshell on the head."

It seems incredible that I should have listened to a concert in Berkeley only last night. Having traveled across the continent in the meantime, I seem to have created a gap in time by having moved in space.

15 March

As I touch the new softness of my leather suitcase, I think of her, two thousand miles away, who rubbed the animating oil into the hide two days ago; and the gentle response of the leather curiously blends with her sudden presence in my senses.

16 April

Karl Kraus wrote in 1911: "According to the census, Vienna has 2,030,834 inhabitants—2,030,833 and me." One does not have to be a monomaniac like Kraus to feel that way. The other day we had an election in Ann Arbor in which our candidate for mayor won by one vote. I doubt that there was anybody among us who did not feel that his vote had made the difference.

Action into timelessness: Two large, black turtles faced each other on a tree trunk in the pond of our woods. Like medieval knights, their necks erect, they stared at each other in complete immobility, while a third turtle—a female?—watched from a short distance. The potential of explosive action charged the silence of the entire landscape with a suspense almost beyond endurance.

Timelessness into action: Marguerite Yourcenar describes in *Souvenirs pieux* the noisy evacuation of a wealthy townhouse, in which the bust of a helmed Minerva, too heavy to be moved, remains standing on its marble base, "indifférente comme toujours aux transactions de vente et d'achat."* The flux of surrounding action transforms timeless immobility into an unwillingness to move.

17 April

Perhaps after years of deafness the purely sensuous timbres of the various instruments are what is least remembered by a composer or, at least, what is likely to lose importance in his imagery of sounds. There remain the highly abstracted qualities of tonal relations and rhythms, so prominent in the late Beethoven.

* "Indifferent as always to the transactions of sale and purchase."

219

2 May

I often envy people in whose business there can be an objective distinction between right and wrong. The man who succeeded in capping the spewing oil well in the Atlantic Ocean is also an expert in fighting oil fires, and he served on a bomb disposal unit during the war. "With bombs and fires you get only one mistake," he said.

2 June

Alton Becker reports in a paper on the Javanese shadow plays that every *wayang* has two separate audiences, a nonessential one consisting of the people and an essential one, namely, the spirits, demons, gods, and ancestors, to whom the puppeteer addresses himself in Old Javanese and Sanskrit, unintelligible to the popular listeners. In a very real sense, any artist anywhere speaks in a language largely unintelligible to his public, except for the few spirits and demons who happen to be the experts.

25 June

If you believe in a Creator, will you admire him for being a nimble enough mechanic to place thousands of genes on each chromosome of a microscopic animal; or will you rather think of him as a zoom creature not tied to any size range and therefore equally able to work in what we call the large and the small?

30 June

It astonishes me to see theorists quote commercial dictionaries for definitions of concepts in their own fields: "Webster defines . . ." How can they fail to realize that they are not quoting Holy Scripture but are relying on an authority likely to know less about the matter than they

220

themselves are supposed to know? It is the expert who has to instruct the dictionaries, not the other way around.

11 August

Not by coincidence perhaps is André Gide obsessed with the problem of the *acte gratuit* in *Les Caves du Vatican,* a story so ineptly conceived that the characters break into incoherent pieces as one tries to follow them from page to page. The attempts to dismantle the course of time in some modern novels, plays, or films may not be unrelated to their authors' inability to tell a story.

12 August

The beach is strewn with plastic things rejected by the waves—pink rabbits, green toy boats, combs, and bottles. They deface our landscape because their shoddy materials offend us with fake imitations of form. The legitimate tenants of the beach—stones, wood, ropes, boats—owe their shapes to the forces of nature and human hands, whereas the plastic baubles were squeezed into their shape by the indifferent molds of machines. Their curves were never bent, and no tools have sharpened their edges. They are frightening zombies.

The monarch butterflies, rallying for their migration to Mexico, are all over our trees, as though someone had torn up rusty brown paper and with a mischievous joy tossed the scraps into the wind.

19 August

Viewing the past is like waiting in the station for a train that arrives with myself on board. Upon its arrival, the me on the train and the me in the station click together. The future, on the contrary, is a train taking off without me, while I am trying to capture a seat on it.

221

4 September

What is the point of hooting in the dark? Perhaps the owl, devoid of activity and company, uses its voice as its cogito. "I hoot, therefore I am."

25 September

A small house with its organs, ducts, and sensors is so much like a living organism that it makes one feel like an intestinal worm profiting from the facilities but also compelled to adapt to the idiosyncrasies of the host.

23 October

The erosion of language. A young man called my hotel room to accompany me to my lecture. I told him I would meet him in the lobby in two minutes. "Terrific," was his reply. What words shall we have left when some day the Earth collides with a meteor?

30 October

I was quite certain I had observed in Nagasaki that the place to which the Dutch traders were confined during the Edo period was a small island connected with the mainland only by a long causeway. The map I just looked at convinces me that there neither is nor ever was such a large stretch of water in between. At most, the Dutch settlement was separated from the town by a small bridge. The social isolation of the foreigners must have translated itself in my mind into a geographic detachment.

18 November

The archaic smile is not limited to the statues of antiquity. Gottfried Keller writes in *Der Narr auf Manegg:*

· 1977 ·

"Auch prangten an den Wänden einige Familienbildnisse, welche wegen zu schlechter Arbeit aus den Wohnräumen verbannt worden. Ihre Gesichter lächelten alle ohne andre Ursache, als weil die Maler die Mundwinkel mit ange-wöhntem, eisernem Schnörkel so zu formen gezwungen waren. Diese grundlose Heiterkeit der verjährten Gesell-schaft machte fast einen unheimlichen Eindruck."*

28 November

The so-called random distribution is actually the very special and rare condition of offering the same opportu-nity to each element. Only because each element is given the same chance can such a distribution be used statisti-cally for a comparison with other situations where partic-ular causal factors are suspected of creating an uneven pattern.

3 December

The shapeless and mostly muscular expression of Rodin's figures invites the worship of people who "feel" rather than see. Certainly it brought out the worst in Rilke.

6 December

On the Sistine ceiling God is gradually transfigured from a Renaissance citizen of the Earth—the dignified ruler meeting Eve on the common ground—to the divine Cre-ator. When he faces Adam, he does so still on the mortal man's own level, but now the two appear in separate compartments. Even further on, the Lord is raised to the

---

* "Brandished on the walls, there were also some family portraits, which because of their poor quality had been banished from the living quarters. Their faces were all smiling, for no other reason than that the painters had been forced to shape the corners of the mouths that way with an accustomed wrought-iron flourish. This unfounded hi-larity of the overaged company made an almost uncanny impression."

clouds, removed to the realm of the spirit, perhaps by demand of the Counter-Reformation.

8 December

The automobile has ruined the reputation of snow. A snowfall is now a scourge, a catastrophic emergency. Because of those unfortunate wheels, people are losing the sense of the beautiful, silencing cover, the smoothing of edges, the angelic purity. And what became of the pleasure of lifting the white load on the shovel and letting it dustily disperse in the wind while the lungs inhale the clean cold?

13 December

I have made and collected slides—by now more than twenty-five hundred—over three decades as illustrations for the principles and arguments I discuss in my lectures. Lately I find that my procedure has almost reversed. Now the images are primary. I pick a group of slides and arrange them on my viewing board like a bouquet of flowers. My lecture becomes a comment on the pictures appearing on the screen. This approach bestows upon the images the natural dominance they claim perceptually.

14 February

Somebody notes that Leonardo in his famous anatomical drawing of the human embryo drew the uterus "falsely spherical" because of his sense of "divine proportionality." Relate this to the preference for spherical shape in the Renaissance, described by Panofsky in his essay on Galileo, but keep also in mind that natural shapes are simplified toward elementary geometry when the more accurate shape is not known, left unobserved, or neglected as unimportant, or when it distracts from the essential.

There is no way for an artist to combine successfully the narrowly ribald with the narrowly virtuous. Puvis de Chavannes's pornographic violence in his private caricatures is as one-sided as the anemically angelic classicism in his paintings. Two deficient halves make no whole even though they may seem to complement each other.

15 February

Heinrich Mann's novel *Professor Unrat,* which I recently read, made me revise my view of *The Blue Angel,* Joseph

von Sternberg's famous film. For more than forty years
I had admired the film almost automatically, in consensus
with the other devotees of the cinema. The novel on
which the film is based made me realize that the very
visual and musical delights of the film keep it within the
confines of the entertainment industry, that is, of what
is pretty, comical, and romantically heartrending. The
film's Lola is beautiful, but Mann's Künstlerin Fröhlich
is a run-down whore. And whereas Mann's doomed
schoolteacher is a ghostly derelict, Emil Jannings's mas-
terly clown is nevertheless no more than a skillful character act. A high polish of inoffensive smoothness makes
the drama palatable and the temptress attractive.

Not that the novel impresses me as a work of art so
superior as to tarnish the film. Taken by itself, the novel
is not successful. It presents the demonic power of the female, recalling the stylized figures of Zola's *Nana* or the
superhuman villains of Balzac. But whereas in the French
writers the presentation remains consistently stylized,
Mann's dialogue is "true to life." It is as though the
expressionist characters of a Nolde or Kokoschka were
to speak conversational German. The sense of style is no
longer intact. If one compares the language of *Unrat*
with, say, that of Wedekind's *Frühlings Erwachen,* a play of
the same generation and similar subject, the difference in
quality is evident.

In Gauguin's painting *Mahana no atua* (*The Day of the
God*) [in the Art Institute of Chicago] there are two symmetrical figures, inverted in rotation somewhat like Day
and Night in the Medici chapel.

19 February

What accounts for the surrealistic transfiguration of
Bramante's Tempietto that I experience in San Pietro in
Montorio? As I enter the courtyard to which the circular
structure is narrowly confined, I am met by an apparition

somewhat like the ghostly architecture of De Chirico, although not sinister but noble. Does this happen simply because there is something unreal about a whole building standing like a mere fountain or oversized tabernacle (which in fact it is) in the center of a courtyard? Or is it its smallness as a building that makes it look like a mere model and, as such, like something belonging someplace else? Or is it the perfection of shape that raises the Tempietto beyond all matter of stone, function, and habitation to the level of an incorporeal image?

21 February

The raised foreleg of Marcus Aurelius's horse on the Capitoline Square, where the monument now stands, was poised originally on the head of a defeated enemy. This alters the visual dynamics of the leg: it presses downward when the figure of the barbarian is added; it lifts up if there is no such target.

Some architects and sculptors have demanded that the shapes invented by the artist should correspond to the physical qualities of the material: marble should be treated as marble, wood as wood. Actually, the opposite principle is more important. The shapes imposed by the artist define the nature of the material of which the buildings or statues seem to be made. Depending on the particular curved or straight edges and planes, smoothness or roughness, compactness or featheriness, the perceived material assumes qualities of flexibility or rigidity, firmness or fibrousness. Borromini's brick walls bend with the elasticity of a steel blade—the character imposed by the shape is more compelling than the evidence of the material texture.

It is essential, therefore, that the architect keep the elements of his buildings from behaving in a contradictory manner. A wall should not be flexible and rigid at the same time. However, different elements, though built of patently similar material, can successfully display different "timbres." Sometimes Borromini attaches firmly cubic windows to an elegantly curved wall.

23 February

In a Baroque denial of weight, the cupola of San Carlo alle Quattro Fontane does not seem to rest on the four pendentives but instead, paradoxically, on the vertices of the four arches. It is held up by hollows.

The distance between the two base points at the springing of an arch is influenced perceptually by the length of the path run through by the curve. This creates the sense of a larger distance compressed into a smaller one.

26 February

Under the high ceiling of our Roman bedroom every sound is mixed with air to such an extent that at night when Mary turns around in her bed, I hear the muffled noise of a distant avalanche in the mountains.

The retired general in charge of San Carlino told me about the sacristy: "All furnishings were designed by Borromini, the altar, the chairs, with the exception of the radiators."

One of the nice things about Rome is that one never knows exactly what time it is. No two clocks ever agree. One perceives the moment through a soft focus, in which the edges of all duties and commitments are happily cushioned.

6 March

As the tiny figure of the pope approached the altar under Bernini's baldachin and the lights came on in the golden vaults, a cosmic roar, like a biblical flood, filled the gigantic hollow of Saint Peter's Church. Originating nowhere and everywhere, it was the applause of the crowds, divested of its human origin by the resonance and by the loudspeakers amplifying it from all corners.

7 March

In the skyline of the Italian landscape, two elements alternate in endless variation: the pointed spindle of the cypress and the umbrella of the pine—the spire and the cupola. The two elements combine in irrational rhythms, monotonous perhaps in their binarity but inexhaustible in their combinations.

27 March

Does the theological rivalry between Christ and the Virgin Mary reverberate as late as the seventeenth century? In Caravaggio's *Madonna dei Palafrenieri* it is the mother who squashes the serpent with her foot, but it is the foot of the child that either initiates the action by pressing down on the mother's foot or is prevented (by the mother's interposed foot) from doing the squashing himself. There is also some ambiguity in the gesture of the child's right hand, which may be seen as his defense against being held up and halfheartedly restrained by his mother.

6 April

A trompe l'oeil picture does not show the object "as such." It serves the stylistic purposes of certain civilizations but would be useless to others. Remember here that an insect looks different to an entomologist, a frog, a housewife, an infant, an exterminator.

8 April

The Italian postal system upsets the temporal sequence of events in the manner known from the novels of the Nouvelle Vague. You receive a letter announcing a friend's forthcoming arrival in Rome three weeks after the reunion took place.

When we talked to a Roman lady about the close ties in Italian families, she nodded assent, "Yes, we like to hear the voice of our family." Clearly, by using the word *voce* in the singular, she intended to refer not to anybody's voice in particular but to that fluffy tissue of sound that fills a Mediterranean house from morning to midnight.

10 April

I stood with captured attention before the Torso of the Belvedere in the Vatican while the cascades of tourists, like the damned in Dante's Hell, forced their way along the walls of the corridor in the midst of which the demoted marble stands. In the Sistine Chapel, a recorded voice trumpets in three languages every five minutes as though out of the thundercloud: "Be silent! Respect the sanctity of the chapel! Do not use flash!" No Cocteau or Fellini could invent a more frivolous takeoff on religious veneration.

13 April

The notorious inefficiency of a typical Italian transaction is explained, I believe, by the constant intertwining of all social relations, which requires that every activity involve the participation of everybody around. Watch in a bank how an employee, intent on one of his laborious manipulations, is approached by a colleague about some other matter, or indeed just for conversation, and is deflected from what he is doing, so that the operation turns into an intricate and extensive assembly of unrelated elements, leading to a precarious outcome. I watched the cashier drift into a leisurely talk with the policeman stationed

next to him for the protection of the money while the
customers were patiently waiting in line.

18 April

There can be only one Madonna, but every place needs
one of its own. According to an old tradition in the Na-
ples area, the Madonnas in Campania are six sisters: the
Madonna del Carmine, the Madonna of the Hens, the
Madonna of Montevergine, the Madonna of the Arch,
the Madonna Annunziata, and the Madonna of Piedi-
grotta. According to Roberto de Simone's notes to his
folk opera *La Gatta Cenerentola,* a seventh sister was
added, the peace Madonna of Giugliano, called the Gypsy
Madonna because of her dark complexion. De Simone
notes that this legend seems to derive from an ancient
cult of sister goddesses, associated with the seasons and
later transferred to that of the Madonna. In still another
story, six pagan sisters were outdone by the seventh, who
was a virgin. This ancient theme, vacillating between the
Madonna and the Cinderella, tangles also with the problem of identity vs. multiplicity.

No two views of the whole are ever successfully coordinated in a work of art. That is why I do not believe that,
as someone has maintained, there are in Bernini's sculpture—for example, in the *David* or *Apollo and Daphne*—
several valid views of equal importance. Such a coordination would create an insoluble contradiction. More likely,
there is one principal view, which dominates a hierarchy
of views. Each of those aspects enriches the "orchestra-
tion" of the theme, namely, the principal view. I am reminded of my contention that when several media are
combined—for example, spoken dialogue and the mobile
image in the cinema—one of them should rule the composition.

Gestures are used to convey expression in two different
ways. They may carry a standardized symbolic meaning,
for example, the raised fingers of the oath or victory sign;
or they may carry nothing but spontaneous individual action, such as that of Degas's fatigued washerwoman
stretching her arms while yawning. Laying one's hand on
another person's shoulder may be only a friendly gesture
or the legal acceptance of him as a member of the clan.
Thumbs down or the raised fist of the Communist belong to the gestural vocabulary of symbols. There may
be archaic styles of art in which only symbolic gestures
occur and naturalistic ones in which they never do.

Even when sculptures avoid all vertical and horizontal
elements, they cannot be said to be "atonal." The weights
and masses are likely to be distributed around the center
of the sculpture in such a way that the whole composition
is balanced around a virtual spine. For example, in the
Discobolos or the Niobide in the Museo delle Terme all
contours and surfaces deviate from the spatial framework
but play around it as a melody plays around its tonic.

I noticed a curious perspective phenomenon in the or-
chard murals from the House of Livia now in the Museo
delle Terme. Figure 5a, representing an enclosure for a
tree, shows a symmetrical indentation when seen from
in front. If this were an actual physical piece of fence and
were looked at obliquely from the left, it would look like
Figure 5b, foreshortened at the left, longer at the right.
If, however, one looks obliquely at the picture, as in Figure 5c, one notices the opposite effect: the left side face,
closer to the viewer, looks larger, the right one is more
foreshortened. One sees a distorted shape that has lost its
symmetry.

I noted earlier that Rodin's sculpture seems to rely mostly
on muscular anatomy, gesture, and pantomime but ne-
glects visually organized expression, which alone

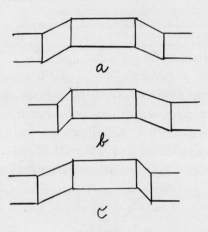

Figure 5

makes art legible. Would it be heretical to observe that a
similar defect can be found occasionally in Rodin's great
master, Michelangelo? I find that I get lost in the garments of the early *Pietà* in Saint Peter's or in the beard
of the *Moses*.

6 May

When God created Adam from a lump of clay, he made
a graven image and thereby violated the second of the
Commandments he gave man afterward. Had he cared to
give him a good example, as a teacher should, he would
not have created him in the first place.

13 June

M. H. Pirenne's photographs of Pozzo's ceiling painting
taken off center at San Ignazio in Rome look indeed aw-
fully distorted. But the other day when I looked at the
ceiling in situ, I found that I could stray quite far away
from the prescribed spot on the floor of the nave without
noticing any distortion worth mentioning. The perceptual constancy of shape, which corrects distortions in
physical space, is much less effective in flat photographs.

15 June

When one discusses the visual expression of windmill wings in their various positions, one needs to consider that they were used as a sign language communicating news to the neighbors. A particular position of the wings indicated not only that the miller was ready or not yet ready for business but also reported about the weather and announced the arrival of important information.

17 June

The English language has no equivalent of *vieillard* or *Greis* to describe an old man as distinguished physically and mentally from other age-groups. The American *senior citizen* is an embarrassing euphemism. A friend of mine has proposed to speak of "the elders."

20 June

Far from "expressing his emotions," a good composer confines his feelings to his private life. When I hear music outpouring joy or suffering, I turn off the radio, irritated by someone inconsiderate enough to importune me with his own business.

23 June

The earliest examples of "writing" in the Middle East seem to have consisted of small clay tokens kept in clay containers. It makes sense that the first conceptual representations would have matched a thing with a thing rather than with a mere sign on a writing surface. Also, instead of being strung up in a defined sequence, those little tokens were simply thrown together in their pot. The next step is the linear order, the precursor of the sentence. In fact, some of those tokens do have holes suitable for stringing.

234

24 June

In the neighbor's cottage, the raccoon reached cautiously through the balcony door. Then, noticing us two strangers, he looked with deep earnestness first at my face and then at Mary's, and, reassured, he took the peanut from the floor with his two hands, solemnly as a priest grasps the chalice.

25 June

What is my particular relation to my sister, the only surviving member of my family? It is not so much the memory of our life together in the past—I remember little of that. Nor do I have much of a sense of belonging to the same kind—we do not seem to be that similar. It is rather that she is the only person whose undeserved and unconditional loyalty I am willing to take for granted. Even in a marriage, every day of togetherness ought to be earned. One never quite deserves what one receives, and one ought to be consciously grateful for the ever-renewed gift.

Suddenly in the midst of our scrubby dunes a single orange wood lily unfolded from nowhere, unforeseen, undeserved—an *acte gratuit* if there ever was one.

1 July

When in the nineteenth century the expressive forms of music were interpreted by the Romantics as manifestations of the composer's mood, the traditional sudden changes from movement to movement, from the playful to the tragic, became unconvincing and almost ludicrous. They began to sound as though the composer were not being honest but just frivolously pretending.

It is not good for our wisdom that we are so close to the top in the hierarchy of organisms. If we lived parasitically

in the body of some giant creature, related to it the way
an intestinal worm is to the body of its host, how much
easier could it be to form a reasonable notion of our place
in the whole of nature.

3 July

The colorful lures of the fishermen have kept up with the
changing stylistic fashions of the times. By now they are
a flourishing branch of advanced modern sculpture, looking as though they were designed by Miró or Arp. Remarkably, the fish accept these daring abstractions as
bona fide living creatures, whereas so many of our fellow
citizens refuse to put up with modern art.

10 July

For the first time in my life I had a migraine headache.
While my attention was fixed by the aggressive pain
waves, I was taken nevertheless with the phantasmic kin-
esthetic transformation of my skull, which seemed to
bulge asymmetrically on the upper left. Also for the first
time, my experience confirmed that the eyes are a part of
the brain. As the irritation affected them, I could feel my
brain reach out all the way to the surface of my head,
where that inner organ looks out at the world through
the two cavities.

9 August

Architects cannot criticize society by depicting the repulsive effects of our shortcomings, as writers and painters
can do. They can commit sins, but they cannot portray
them. Good architecture displays harmony, unity, order
through patterns that reflect traits of its historical period
and thereby show that the way of life of its time can be a
way of living the good life.

12 August

As I crossed the dune, I saw from behind, walking along the otherwise empty beach, two young women of identically perfect shape. They walked at an even pace, keeping a fixed distance between them but without any sign of being aware of each other. The same woman seemed to be walking there twice. I followed her, or them, with my eyes until they vanished at the horizon. It was straight Surrealist magic, straight Delvaux.

20 August

The *Tale of Genji* refers often to the belief that a person of perfect beauty will die young. Our own culture expresses no such fear consciously. We do not let the cherry blossoms tell us that they are beautiful but will not last. However, we also feel that such beauty does not quite belong: it is not of our kind, and we do not deserve it.

We shall be closer to maturity when our automobile doors, instead of closing with a crashing bang, will close with the exquisite click that locked the covers of our fathers' golden pocket watches. Brutal self-assertion is infantile. Grown-up minds do not slam doors; they do not make scenes.

12 September

Like the behaviorists of old, some psychologists of our own generation are trying to eliminate the mind. The Watsonians denied the existence of anything but external action. The Gibsonians evacuate the mind from its dwelling place by misinterpreting its images as outer reality. The new attempt will abort like the old one, although sometimes even untenable principles make people stumble into useful results.

18 September

Someone wanting to study the effects of wine on the human disposition would not obtain reliable results if the wine were diluted with water or sweetened with sugar. Yet the adepts of experimental aesthetics use without hesitation mediocre or inferior works to study responses to art.

25 September

The attributes of Utamaro's women are, for the most part, the opposite of what a Western artist would choose to arouse erotic attraction. Their skin is whitish; their bodies and limbs are flat; their eyes and mouths are small; their fingers pudgy. The Western viewer sees a kind of "pale fire," whose charm is that of the *volupté décente* cultivated by the French in the frigid shapes of classicism around 1800. In the eyes of today's Japanese, do or did Utamaro's figures have a similar classicist frigidity, or do they look as heatedly sensuous as did the nudes of Courbet or Bouguereau to their contemporaries?

29 October

Why during long periods of the history of Western painting are the colors red and blue allowed to display their purity while the third primary color, yellow, is conceded a similar role mostly in examples of "primitive" coloring? Perhaps red and blue, and sometimes green, serve as the basic pillars of color composition, whereas yellow yields to the browns and pinks of skin and earth.

If, by the way, Theodor Hetzer is right in noting that two color schemes dominate the history of painting since the high Renaissance, the red-blue theme of Titian and the red-green of Giorgione, then two basic worldviews must have vied with each other. According to one of them, the world is run by two fundamental powers as independent of each other as the two primaries red and blue, yet in balance; according to the other, the two powers are complementaries like red and green, needing each other to create a more unified whole.

22 November

What we call white is presumably nothing but the color of the illumination that happens to be provided by the principal source of light in our terrestrial setting. It would be a strange coincidence if the particular makeup of our sunlight happened to be the one that created an achromatic effect in our perceptual receptors. More probably the color prevailing in an environment acquires the neutrality of an unspecific experience.

27 November

When scientists stand "on the shoulders of giants," they form a totem pole on which each is placed higher than the one below him, a little closer to the truth. But in the arts, when Cézanne succeeds Poussin, he is not therefore closer to the truth. In the arts, the giants stand in a circle around the truth and scrutinize it, each from his own angle.

1 December

As my memory weakens, I find myself sometimes resorting to unusual, "original" expressions simply because the more appropriate common word has slipped my mind. This can work well, but it can also make for unwarranted indirectness. I would rather be able to determine my wording by free choice than by the bricolage of expediency.

3 December

In literature, all dimensions of space carry symbolism: a direct or a crooked path, narrowness or vastness, the wall between Pyramus and Thisbe, the place "where three roads cross" at which Oedipus kills his father. Those spatial props are not arbitrary; they symbolize human predicaments such as the freedom of choice, the obstacles to love, the inevitability of fate. Here belongs also the *Rashomon* effect of various perspectives offering different views of the same fact, similar to Hokusai's thirty-six views of Mount Fuji.

10 December

By choosing square-shaped canvases for some of his late paintings, Monet shows his indifference to the anisotropy of space. He may have wanted to minimize the gravitational pull on his compositions. The pictures float.

22 December

John Teal says in his book on the Sargasso Sea that "damaging rays pass through transparent animals unchanged because radiation reacts with an object only to the degree it is absorbed by the object." On the same day, I am reading Fechner's witty essay on the anatomy of the angels, whose shape is spherical and transparent, showing their superiority.

24 December

When discussing aesthetics, I avoid the word *taste,* because its use encourages a verbal shell game where one smuggles objective validity into one's own preferences while at the same time softening one's own absolute judgments by making them sound as though they were only personal. The "man of taste" is ostensibly a person

in whom by preestablished harmony personal liking co-
incides with the supreme good. There is no craftier way
of fudging a problem.

28 December

An ingenious student of mine wrote in his examination
paper that central perspective was invented by the ancient
Egyptians. They used it to establish the vanishing point
at the top of their pyramids, toward which all edges converge. Live and learn!

I woke up late. I had a lot of dreaming to do. That takes
time.

🌿 1979

1 January

The crossed beams riding on the thatched roofs of ancient Japanese sanctuaries such as the Ise Shrine may be said to spell out the dynamics of the pitched roof. The ridge of the roof is, ambiguously, not only a peak but also a crossing.

4 January

Franz Kafka's most uncanny device is the drab sobriety of reasoning and language in his style. One seems to listen to the report of a minor civil servant or shopkeeper talking sensibly about the problems of practical life; it is the mentality of husbandry and insurance. But within the events reported in this deadpan language seethes the tempest of paranoia. Quite different from the Expressionists, who explode colorfully all over the place, Kafka exhibits a gray container, ready to implode from infernal inner tension. The new middle-class civilization makes its entry with Kafka. He is beyond the uninhibited melodrama of the realists: Zola is still Racine, but Kafka reflects a different world. No wonder he identified so readily with small animals, rodents and birds, whose every motion is ac-

243

companied by vigilant circumspection. All those quick glances that go with the scratching and gnawing and pecking, all those constant provisions against mortal danger, are executed with the indifference of an office routine. It is the bourgeois version of the human tragedy.

My father was the youngest of seven children, who had been born in a burst of fertility between 1859 and 1867. His mother, Julie, née Meyer, lived from 1833 or 1834 to 1886; thus she was about twenty-five years old at the birth of her first child and about thirty-three when my father was born. Her husband, my paternal grandfather, Julius Arnheim, lived from 1825 to 1883. He owned, I believe, a small stationery store in Berlin.

Of those seven children, only two married, namely, the oldest and the youngest. The oldest, Max (1859–1894), had one daughter, whom I vaguely remember. The youngest, Georg, my father, had four children. Three of my father's sisters died young, in their twenties or thirties. A brother, Paul (1863–1909), a bachelor, lived to the age of forty-six. The youngest sister, Margarete (born 1862), was a regular visitor at our home. I believe she fell victim to the Nazis in 1938.

My father (1867–1943) died in Oakland, California, of a heart ailment at the age of seventy-six. My mother, Betty, née Gutherz (1879–1966), died of intestinal cancer in Ueberlingen, Germany, where she had spent her last years near my oldest sister, Leni. Her two sisters, Erna and Alice, also died of cancer.

Two of my sisters, Leni and Marie, were married but had no children. My child, Anna Heide, was born in 1934 in Rome to my first wife, Annette, née Siecke, and died there in 1940 of Hodgkin's disease. My second eldest sister, Hilde, married to a physician, died in 1938 of tuberculosis at the age of thirty-one. Her only child, Michael, is a dermatologist in California. He is the only consanguineous child of the four of us.

My second wife, Mary, née Frame, was born in 1918; we were married in 1953. Our daughter, Margaret Nettinga, comes from Mary's first marriage and was born in 1947.

9 January

One cannot use Albert Michotte's experiments on the perception of causality to disprove Hume's contention that causality is based on nothing better than the association between phenomena that follow each other habitually. What Hume denies is the physical reality of the relation between cause and effect. Michotte actually confirms this. He shows that causality is compellingly experienced in cases in which it does not exist physically; but he also shows that in perceptual experience causality is not based simply on association. It depends on factors inherent in the perceptual situation itself, such as relative speed, time intervals, direction of motion, and so forth.

14 January

A cloud can look like a camel, but a camel is unlikely to look like a cloud. This is so because the signifier must be able to stand for the whole category of the signified. The cloud looks like all camels, but no camel looks like all clouds.

15 January

A monkey's ability to use tokens does not prove that he understands the nature of images. Tokens can be used simply as a means to an end, the way one pulls a lever to get a candy bar from a vending machine. The lever is not an image of the candy bar in the same manner in which, say, a black circle stands for the city of Chicago on a map.

22 January

G. T. Fechner asserts in the *Vorschule der Aesthetik* that the use of knife and fork is unknown in Persia. "When a Persian touches a dish of rice," he says, "he can tell by feeling whether or not the rice has been tastily prepared. This goes so far that a Persian shah told a European envoy he could not understand how in Europe people were willing to use knives and forks since taste begins in the fingers."

26 January

Our notion that what is worth seeing is also worth painting is a stylistic idiosyncrasy not shared by most other cultures. When art serves ritual, protective, or symbolic functions, the indiscriminate detailing of matter would make for an inadmissible distraction.

9 February

There are musical performances that should never be recorded without the thundering applause following the final flourish for which they were created. The paradoxical silence we hear instead is a cruel giveaway, although not an undeserved one.

The intense counterpoint in Michelangelo's vestibule of the Laurentian library: the steps moving downward and forward against the visitor who is climbing them in the opposite direction. It is like walking up the descending steps of an escalator—what an introduction to the Baroque age!

24 February

When a painter attaches actual objects to his canvas, a disturbing contradiction results if his painting displays illusory depth. But when that illusion is abandoned and the image limits itself to the texture of the surface, the painting becomes a physical object, to which other such objects can be readily added.

When an airplane flies above a loose layer of clouds through which one sees the ground, the relativity of motion can be nicely observed. Although the clouds may be standing still, they can be seen as passing over the ground, because perspectively they are displacing themselves faster than the ground. But if one perceives clouds and ground as one connected system, the clouds appear to stand still and the system as a whole remains unmoved while the plane flies over it.

9 March

In a letter to a newspaper's investment counselor, someone wrote that since he had bought stocks for ten thousand dollars and then resold them two years later for eight thousand dollars, he now wanted to know who had his missing two thousand dollars. He considered the value of his stocks a property permanently belonging to them, a part of their very substance. When broken off and removed, it had to be someplace else, like a lost hubcap.

18 March

It would be most wholesome if for at least twenty years art historians were forbidden to refer to any derivations. If they were not allowed to account for a work of art mainly by tracing where it comes from, they would have to deal with it in and by itself—which is what they are most needed for.

15 April

What Walter Benjamin calls the aura of an original work does not adhere to just any and every art object. It depends on whether the work emanates the sense of having been generated in an atmosphere of its own. Compare a good early Eskimo carving with a more recent, commercialized, but equally handmade product. Apart from being of higher quality, the older piece carries with it the spirit of the igloo, where it was made; whereas the specimens of "airport art" are outside of space and time, like so many of our own standard industrial products. I am reminded of Antonio Gramsci's observation that even the best recipe does not guarantee authentic yogurt. It takes the smell of the goat and of the Sardinian shepherd to get it right.

26 April

An artist said to me that when a painting is laid on the floor, the painted shapes seem to be physical objects. This goes well with my assertion that the vertical dimension is that of vision, whereas the horizontal plane is the arena of action. It makes sense that in the realm of action all things are of material substance like ourselves, the actors.

30 April

It would be appropriate if we humans, too, would more commonly stop and look at each other as thoroughly as dogs do when they first meet.

12 May

When Aileen's mother's cats misbehaved, she used to say appeasingly, "But they are only human!"

27 May

I overheard somebody saying, "Since I retired, I have been doing more things accidentally than I used to do on purpose."

248

29 May

We resent it when reality is distorted in literature by the author's wishes. Compare Rolfe's *Hadrian VII,* a pet exhibit of psychoanalysts, with Kleist's novella *Michael Kohlhaas.* Rolfe's fantasy of the defrocked priest who becomes pope is indeed childish and pathological, despite much strikingly convincing detail. Kleist's story of the horse trader who after being defrauded and mistreated by a feudal lord starts a civil war and carries his call for justice all the way to the emperor is equally likely to have been inspired by the aggressive needs of its author. But so strong is the true writer's sense of reality that his story, by the power of its own inherent logic, takes off to the climax of a terrifying punishment.

31 May

The glance of the eye finds it hard to turn the corner around the bow of a ship or around the wedge of a flat-iron building. Perhaps this is why Alberti says that acute angles are not permissible in architecture. In sculpture also, when a cleavage splits two adjacent shapes, the eye is prevented from seeing them as parts of a continuous volume.

Is there a difference between early and late Vermeer typical of the distinction between early and late styles in general? Is it in the early paintings that Christ argues actively with Mary and Martha, and the young gentleman fondles the courtesan, and in the late ones that people coexist silently without influencing each other's behavior? In *The Letter,* the mistress and the maid gaze at each other without a word. Exchanging letters, making music, painting from a model are social relations that suit the late style because they are communications that partners engage in separately.

249

4 June

In a newspaper advertisement a critic is quoted as having
said about a certain film that it is "a corker, a walloper, a
rouser, a screecher, and a ton of fun. . . . If all movies
were as thrilling, I would happily spend all my time in
the movies." If now I think of the lowliest creatures
around me, the cockroaches or the dandelions, and I ask
whose way of life, interests, and values are closer to my
own—theirs or those of the monster who wrote those
words, could there be any doubt?

29 June

A metaphysical quandary. The telephone rang, and a
young boy's voice asked, "Is Joey there?" I told him he
had the wrong number, but he repeated, "Is Joey there?"
I explained, less patiently, that the number he had reached
was not the one he wanted. Unperturbed, he insisted. I
could have satisfied him by telling him that no, Joey was
not there. But that would have been a gross misstate-
ment, supported only by the lame excuse that Joey was
in fact not present at the place about which the caller inquired. Actually, Joey was neither there nor not there,
thereby violating the rule of the excluded third. I confess
that I hung up—chickening out, you might say.

2 July

Imagine the Trappist abstinence from speech extended to
the very thought of words. It is remarkable how well you
would get along with such total aphasia once you lived in
a place where you could not talk to anybody anyway. All
the things of the world would still be available to your
senses, and you could deal with them as intelligently as
usual. There would be memories, wish-dreams, learning,
and creative imagination. There would be a sensitive
awareness in the company of your equals, with no deaf-

250

and–dumb communication to disturb it. The world
would be limited to what could reach you and what you
could reach. You might be better off.

4 July

Kuleshov notes that when one looks at the painting of a
chair, one sees a chair; but when one looks at a photograph containing the painting, one sees a painted chair. If
this is so, it shows that in looking at paintings one enters
their medium and drops it from the percept as a constant
factor, whereas in the photograph the painterly medium
becomes a part of what is represented and therefore stays
on in the percept.

Departments of comparative literature are often particularly lively. They owe this virtue to a condition that
should be adopted by many more academic disciplines.
A department of comparative philosophy would have to
expel much of the stuffy pedantry that is avoided in comparative psychology and comparative zoology. Think
what a department of comparative arts would do for the
average art school! More power to comparison!

21 July

When a mosquito sucks blood only to be swatted to
death immediately afterward, its investment would seem
hardly worth the trouble. But is not our own life, in the
words of Prince Genji, "as brief as the time of the morning dew"?

24 July

Permanent features of existence identify themselves by
occurring more than once. A bird's call or a gust of wind
is likely to be repeated. But the crash of a falling tree or a
scream in the street are unique events—dated, recorded,

and likely to change the state of affairs. They are history. Here again, the *Tale of Genji:* "Unchanged a thousand years, the voice of the cuckoo."

4 August

I cannot get much interested in the average person's responses to art, which are so devotedly recorded by some experimentalists in the psychology of art. It is one thing to ask a person which of two lines looks longer, because any person is as competent an observer as the next. The adequate viewing of a work of art, however, is a special accomplishment requiring sensitivity and skill. As long as research is concerned with art rather than with the social psychology of everyman's taste, the most skilled and gifted viewers are barely good enough to supply reliable data.

11 August

When I play the violin by myself, making sure that the windows are closed and nobody can listen, I often produce music that does not exist but is music nevertheless. I may play an allegro as an andante because my technique is not up to the required speed. Or I may simplify a piece to make it manageable; and all the way through I treat the violin part of a sonata or concerto as though it were the complete composition. This practice, although deplorable, does work because a good structure can be subjected to all sorts of transformations yet remain structure. You hear a different thing but one making a sense of its own.

21 August

Alice tells me about a small headlamp, worn on the forehead, which focuses on a narrow area but, as one moves around, gives one the impression of being in a fully lighted room—a nice example of the integrative power of perception. We know that shapes complete themselves through the partial views they project. An object is seen as a whole most convincingly when one moves around it. Here now the same effect is shown with lighting.

10 September

More and more often we replace moral conduct with physical constraint. A small street nearby has been plagued by cars racing through it at a dangerous speed. Now the city has installed ridges at hundred-foot intervals across the pavement, which forces everybody to drive at a snail's pace. Instead of ethics we have bumps.

25 September

When their masters have gone to bed, the instruments, for their own amusement, play Brahms. That kind of music flows out of the strings all by itself.

An Eskimo woman who has learned to practice the arts confirms Michelangelo's famous dictum. She thinks sculpting is easier than drawing: "I always find it very hard to think of what I am going to draw. It is easier when I am just chopping a stone, because what I am going to make is already there—I just chop the pieces off."

The uncanny effect of knowledge upon pictures. The newspaper printed the photograph of the head of a smiling woman. After the story has told me that this woman has just been decapitated by a revengeful lover, her easy smile freezes into a ghostly apparition. Now the head, cropped by the photographer, is truly cut off, like the talking head of the horse Fallada in the fairy tale.

20 October

All through the early and middle years of life the earth is nothing but a flat plane one rolls across with ease, like a ball. In the late years, that base underfoot changes into a relief of hills and valleys. One climbs with keyed-up breath and enjoys trundling down. The handicaps of old age oddly enrich existence.

30 October

Has it been observed that a common type of hypochondria is a variety of paranoia? Instead of being pursued by human enemies, the sufferer is beleaguered by germs, chemicals, dust particles, and fumes, which gang up on him with the same malicious intent that is feared and fought by paranoiacs. One ought to investigate the causes that make certain individuals transfer their fear of people to a fear of things.

7 November

Rodin's *Burghers of Calais* is perhaps the first monumental acknowledgment of the bourgeoisie as an agent of history. In essential ways this monument deviates from the tradition: instead of an individual hero it tells of a heroic group; and instead of victory it celebrates the courage of sacrifice and surrender. The citizens of Calais, still guided by feudal values, were bothered by Rodin's original intention to mount the historical scene as a spectacle of despair. Even in the final version there remained the problem, still unresolved, of the team of their forefathers represented as a half-dozen individualities sprawling in all directions. The halfhearted concession to collectivity is reflected in the controversy about the compositional shape of the group. Rodin insisted on arranging his figures in a cube, whereas the citizens of Calais pleaded for the "more graceful" conic shape of the traditional hierarchy. Even the revolutions of the twentieth century have not done too well with the artistic image of man en masse.

3 December

The other day when I looked at Picasso's *Guernica,* perhaps for the last time before it goes to Spain, I suddenly discovered an essential feature that had escaped me all these decades. The triangular group in the center is distinguished from the lateral scenes—the bull with the wailing mother on the left and the woman falling from the window on the right—by being transfigured through transparency. Shapes overlap without occluding one another and are dematerialized by edges of falling lights and shadows. The light at the top seems to thin the bodies of the central scene and to change them accordingly into a mere apparition. This aptly reinforces the function of the lamp as the bringer of truth. And perhaps just to remind us that the vision reflects brutal reality, the corner themes retain their stark, opaque presence.

12 December

The perspective trickeries of the Baroque should not be interpreted as intended deceptions. The playful shifts back and forth between what things are made to seem and what they actually are constitute the relevant statement.

14 December

Styles of art seem to run through three phases. At first, works in a new style are rejected as being unnatural. In a second period, when the style truly conforms with its culture, the works look like nature itself. Still later, they lose their naturalism and are recognized as conceptions of abstract beauty. They turn out to be works of art.

❧ 1980

Nothing more ghostly could happen than if an animal
suddenly showed a smile on its face. It would indicate
that a human mind had been lurking in the creature, with
the whole arsenal of irony, judgment, and the awareness
of our frailties. We have long suspected that the cat is
judging us. Its smile would be the terrifying proof. Think
also of the opposite case of persons without facial expression, like the dwarf in *The Tin Drum*. There, terror is
produced by a body deserted by its soul.

15 April

The particular blend of heaviness and lightness in Mies
van der Rohe's architecture shows in the I beams he likes
to use as supports of his buildings and to attach to his façades. Seen from in front, the I beams look massive and
powerful, but from the side the hollow channel framed
by narrow edges looks almost delicate.

4 May

Even the deepest tragedy looks inadequate when watched
from a sufficient distance. We can smile at Madame Bo-

vary when she is upset by the loss of Leon, her miserable little clerk. But only God can smile at Oedipus and Hamlet.

5 May

The question is not, Why did Cézanne not use correct perspective? but, Why should he have? The tradition of naturalistic representation has made us forget that every pictorial device calls for justification—including the conformation to nature.

14 May

When the psychologist John M. Kennedy shows that the blind have no difficulty using lines to depict objects in drawing, he confirms my conviction that lines are not discovered in the visual world and then copied in drawing. Lines are all but nonexistent in the visual world, nor do they occur in the world of touch. Rather, they translate into a two-dimensional language the surfaces of the objects in the three-dimensional world of sight and touch. The fact that the blind use contours is no more surprising than that the sighted do, nor is it less so.

3 June

> Is it she breathing
> Or are the waves of the lake
> Moving in the dark?

10 June

When I was modeling a small female figure, I found that it needed some kind of a spiral wrapping around it as a counterpoint to the symmetry of the body. I tried a garment but was distracted by its hanging. The shape I needed required the firmness of a snake—and so I found

258

myself modeling an Eve! I am not suggesting that the ancient myths invented their images to accommodate their arts, but there surely exists an interplay between the themes picked by artists from the ancient stories and the morphology of body stances on which sculptors and painters depend. The *Venus pudica,* for example, is a study in the counterpoint between body and arm.

12 June

For the Middle Ages and the Renaissance, antiquity lay at a remote distance in time, no more connected by a workable bridge than was our own distance from the moon before we first set foot on it. There was no sense of the continuity of history. A similar lack of continuity existed in a different area, the depth dimension of painted space. But the gap between foreground action and background landscape was most conspicuously overcome by central perspective already in the fifteenth century.

13 June

When one opens the door for the cat, the animal stops precariously between in and out, surveying the prospect before submitting to it. This intelligent circumspection compares favorably with the rashness of our own exits and entries.

20 July

It may take a Frenchman to impose with impunity the strict logic of the mind upon the raw material of experience. German literature is better off when it is composed with a rich looseness, a kind of uninhibited effluence. The free rhythms of Hölderlin's poetry surpass his early rhymed poems, and although Goethe constructed the *Wahlverwandtschaften* like a magnificent piece of engineering, that novel is less German than the crowded medita-

259

tions of *Wilhelm Meisters Wanderjahre*. Dürer loses his exuberance when he tries to compose in the Italian manner. Most recently, Günter Grass in his giant novel *Der Butt* has the seven deadly sins gush forth with an authenticity that rivals Grimmelshausen's great chronicle of the Thirty Years' War. But when Grass tries to tie all this luxuriance together by collapsing whole galleries of historical figures into a single woman and a single man, the reader falters, grasping for a trellis that does not hold.

5 August

Stendhal can create a powerful shock by merely reporting on a sequence of events in clock time. The prince has been told that if he insists on going to bed with the duchess, she will leave his court forever. "Chassé par la duchesse indignée, il osa reparaître tout tremblant et fort malheureux à dix heures moins trois minutes. A dix heures et demi, la duchesse montait en voiture et partait pour Bologne."*

15 August

As I read Kenneth Clark's book *The Nude,* I am amazed at his expertise on the correct proportions of the human body. This head is too small, we are told, and the distance between those breasts and the navel is too large. I look and, sure enough, he is right, there are those deviations, which I, too, might notice in a live body. But never have these things impressed me in a successful work of art: I do get bothered when proportions are incongruous, but the dimensions of a figure by El Greco seem to me as correct as the voluminous lumps of the prehistoric Venus of Willendorf, even though I have looked at man-made

---

* "Chased away by the indignant duchess, he dared to reappear, all trembling and most unhappy, at three minutes to ten. At half past ten, the duchess got into her carriage and departed for Bologna."

figures all my life and have made some myself. Might
there be a generational difference by which the standards
of anatomical correctness are finally yielding to those of
art?

5 September

Let us play the game of placing the great men on the
dates at which they should have lived. Many of them, of
course, came too early: Michelangelo, Rembrandt, Spinoza, Hölderlin. But Bach was a little late. Freud should
have been with the rationalists of the Enlightenment, and
Jung belongs among the Romantic worshippers of the
unconscious.

17 September

Thomas Mann in a lecture at Princeton in 1938: "Ein
abgetanes, zurückliegendes Werk wird mehr und mehr zu
etwas von ihm [the author] Abgelösten, Fremden, worin
und worüber andere mit der Zeit viel besser Bescheid
wissen als er. Man hat überhaupt nötig, an sich erinnert
zu werden. . . . Es hat seine Reize, sich von der Kritik
über sich selbst aufklären zu lassen. 'Possible que j'ai eu
tant d'esprit?' Ich bin Ihnen sehr verbunden, dass Sie
mich so freundlich an mich selbst erinnert haben."*

20 September

Our culture has sobered considerably since the 1920s,
when the actors on the Expressionist theater stage threw

* "A work of the past that an author is done with becomes more and
more something detached from him, something alien, about which, as
time goes by, others are much better informed than he is himself. . . .
There is something alluring about being enlightened about oneself by
the critics. 'Is it possible that I was that brilliant?' I am much obliged
to you for having reminded me of myself in so friendly a manner."

up their arms to convey ecstasy and entreaty. Those human-size V shapes had simmered down to Churchill's raised two fingers of victory when World War II came to an end. Since then, the V in its diminished size continues to hold its place as an accepted newcomer to the repertoire of symbols.

21 September

In the great love stories, consummation is either denied or occurs only when the story is at an end. In Stendhal's *La Chartreuse de Parme,* perhaps the greatest of them all, the intensity of passion and the pain of denial are at their purest when Fabrice and Clelia, kept apart in their prison towers, can communicate from window to window only by sign language. The sense of sight is the principal vehicle of the great passions. By the time the couple tumbles into bed, the poet has gone elsewhere.

1 October

It almost looks as though Picasso worked out a particular style for the representation of each of his women—a style that went beyond portrait resemblance. A cool smoothness seems to have gone well with one of them, a lusty trumpeting of primary colors and vigorous shapes with another, a classicist calm with a third.

In comparing the various forms of Cubism, it is helpful to distinguish paintings whose shape could be reconstructed in a coherently carpentered wooden model from others where the elements penetrate one another "blindly." To obtain the latter effect, Picasso omits the edges that would define the overlappings of units in consistent space.

Very few of Picasso's deviations from correct anatomy are to be understood as intentionally monstrous distortions. Picasso does use visual violence in scenes of slaughter, but when he depicts women, he uses deviation to explore the endless variations of shape relation, size, and spatial orientation. Those images are not denunciations of the body and the spirit inhabiting it but rather celebrations of their inexhaustible wealth.

To Picasso, a horse is a woman, attacked, mounted, victimized, and often beautiful. Its partner is the bull.

He often creates a struggle between the contours and the planes or volumes they are supposed to enclose. For example, in the *Embrace* of 1925, the contours become independent objects, producing calligraphic ornaments that transform the picture space into a kind of wrought-iron grid. Some late works of disturbing complexity are composed of two incomplete pictures, one made of colorful objects, the other of black strokes and curves—leaving the viewer with the task of making one whole out of two imperfect ones.

Still lifes, with their arrangements of incongruous objects, are the forerunners of Cubism. The modern mind has been taught to discover discrepancy in what used to be considered harmonious wholes. For the Cubist, the more gracefully symmetrical the model—be it a guitar or a nude—the stronger the temptation to reveal the precariousness of its equilibrium.

The full-frontal face and the straight profile are too definitive to be usable as phases of a stroboscopic flip. Hence when Picasso in his *Woman with Sculpture* of 1925 places a pink frontal face uncompromisingly upon a black profile, we are enjoined to see the two as one simultaneously. The painter refrains from using aspects that are transitional and therefore amenable to fading smoothly into each other.

263

11 October

If proof were needed to show that celibacy distorts a person's view of human sexuality, it would be offered by Pope John Paul II's recent assertion that "a man must not use his wife, her femininity, to fulfill his instinctive desire" because "concupiscience diminishes the richness of the perennial attraction of persons for interpersonal communion. Through such a reduction, the other person becomes the mere object for satisfying a sexual need." It is only logical that a man in whose own experience sexual desire is detached from the experience of marital companionship will think of the two as necessarily separate.

12 October

How remarkably well we get along with our cats, considering that they live in a totally different world. To them, a shoe is an object with provocatively fluttering laces, and an automobile is an underpass or shelter between wheels. And night should be day. Given such profound differences, how do we manage to communicate as well as we do?

Translations interfere with understanding and evaluation everywhere, even when they are done competently and carefully. I am looking at Willard R. Trask's translation of Erich Auerbach's *Mimesis,* one of the most beautifully written texts of German criticism in our century. The very first line of the English version catches my eye: "Readers of the *Odyssey* will remember the well-prepared and touching scene in book 19, when Odysseus . . ." Well-prepared? Like a tasty dish? A trite acknowledgment of Homer being a good writer? Can the reader help doubting the intelligence of the author he is about to read? But "well-prepared" is a mistranslation. Auerbach has *wohlvorbereitet*. Not the scene is well-prepared, but the reader is well-prepared for it. Instead of dispensing gratuitous praise, Auerbach defines, with a single adjective, the scene's position in its context. The quick flash of this observation puts the reader on his guard. The translation does the opposite.

17 October

What I said about the finality of frontal face and profile adds also to the style of Georges Seurat. In his *Sunday Afternoon on the Grande Jatte* he holds most figures of his crowd to these two basic positions. He thereby strengthens the abstract geometry of his Parisians, who stand among the trees like stone monuments.

22 October

People who ask me to do something for them speak of my "busy schedule" as though they knew all about my calendar. "I hope that in spite of your busy schedule . . ." I can see why they would expect me to be busy. But the assumption that I run by a timetable like a trolley bus is something I resent—precisely because the assumption is almost correct.

11 November

I watch the shadow of the airplane racing across the fields and highways and towns. What a panic the monstrous metal bird would create if it actually chased through the world below at such a speed! It goes to show that incompatibles will get along with one another as long as there is enough space between them.

Educators and philosophers make much ado about what physiologists are discovering on the different functions of the brain hemispheres, as though we needed such bodily confirmation to know that the mind relies equally on its analytical and its more intuitive capacities. But perhaps

the symmetry of the two lobes supplies the conceptual
image needed to convert the many who still believe in the
uncontestable supremacy of the intellect.

18 November

I did not know that beginning with Carolingian architecture and throughout the Romanesque and Gothic periods
the square of the crossing served as the module for the
grid of the ground plan of churches. This practice gives
additional strength to the central importance of the crossing. And yet the meeting of nave and transept, the very
heart of the cross-shaped plan, is used more often than
not as a mere transition to the sanctuary in the choir.

27 November

Isak Dinesen writes in *Carnival* that "at whatever place—
throat, arm, waist, or knee—you cut her slim body
through with a sharp knife, you would have got a perfectly circular transverse incision." A few pages later she
talks about the brilliant painter whose face looked like the
posterior of a baby, so that his students "had developed a
theory that there had been a shifting about in his anatomy, and that he had an eminently radiant and expressive
face at the other place."

14 December

There is a precedent to the disturbance that speech
wrought in the talking film when it broke the expressive
melody of visible acting. Eduard Hanslick complains that
Wagner's *Gesamtkunstwerk* violates the music with words.
He objects to "the displacement of the melody of song by
declamatory recitation, enervating monotony, and mea-
sureless expansion."

🌿 1981

3 January

Notice on the toilets in restrooms on Japan Airlines: "Do Not Throw Foreign Articles!"

7 January

It is like a Surrealist montage: you are lying in a hospital bed peacefully reading during the most private hour of your morning, while outside in the corridor a stream of chattering people rolls past your room without giving you more than an occasional glance through the offensively open door.

20 January

At some fairly recent time in literature it became legitimate to tell a story as a report on what someone is observing and thinking. Before that date—and who was the first writer to do what Proust does?—such a report had to be legitimated as a story told by one character to other characters in the book, for example, Odysseus telling his adventures at the court of the Phaiakians or Aeneas telling the story of the Trojan War. In Proust, the universe of lit-

267

erary discourse has switched from a physical world of
bodies to the mental world of a perceiver and thinker. Is
this a delayed adoption of the ontological switch performed in Descartes's *Meditations?*

11 February

If it is true that a good artist has no choice—that is, that
for any particular task his outlook prescribes one and
only one solution—then architects might seem to be condemned to make fatal compromises, because they have to
adapt their own solution to fit someone else's needs. Actually, a good architect incorporates the client's needs in
his task by asking, "What is my solution to the problem
of building a home for Mr. Soandso?" The client thus
assumes the same role that the subject matter has in
painting.

16 March

With a hatred generated by the instinct of self-preser-
vation, I have fought the conception of the world as a
purely subjective construct, the notion that we perceive
not the "real" world but only the "shapeless, unformular-
izable world of chaotic sensations." It is a poison that
strangles us and dissolves the ground under our feet. The
destructive doctrine is stated with unsurpassable cleverness in part 3 of Nietzsche's *Der Wille zur Macht.* There it
is: the object is nothing but the effect of one subject upon
another; truth is nothing but usefulness; the similarity of
things is nothing but a subjective imposition to make
classification possible; there are no things and there is
nothing lasting, only an indivisible flow of changes; Eu-
clidian space is nothing but the idiosyncrasy of a certain
species of animals; and so forth. When this poisonous
Continental doctrine is grafted upon Anglo-Saxon empir-
icism, the creed of those fairly sober skeptics becomes
truly virulent.

31 March

After my teacher's death I took from his desk the tobacco
pipe on which he used to gnaw when he worked. If that
pipe looked flawless, it would not exert its spell. The
rubbed and tooth-marked stem confirms the "aura" created by my memories. Together with the framed photograph of him that I keep on my desk before me when I
write, it serves as an amulet, protecting the integrity of
the spirit he helped to nurture.

12 April

Gaston Bachelard's observation on the water in the cave
looking like black stone took me back to the Byzantine
Church of San Vitale in Ravenna, that jewel box of gold
and colorful mosaics covering the walls and high vaults,
resplendent with sunlight. In the dark recesses of that
spectacular hall, however, water had flooded the floor
and stood there stagnant, yes, like black, shiny basalt, deprived of its liquidity, while, paradoxically, the brilliant
reflections on the walls freed the glass and stone of their
hardness and gave them a mercurial twinkle.

24 April

One of the reasons why I classify myself as a writer is
that a scientist writes only when he has results to communicate and often even then only reluctantly. For me,
the urge to write and the pleasure of doing it is so fundamental that I become unhappy when I am not writing,
and therefore I am forever in search of ideas and observations with which to feed my addiction.

10 May

Sign in a Japanese hotel room: "Explanation how to open
the window is attached at the window flames. Please do
not try it! Fire alarm to be sounded."

13 May

Sometimes it astonishes me that the world operates all by
itself. In the morning the light comes on outside on time,
and spring turns on the leaves and flowers without my
throwing any switches, just like the furnace in the basement gives heat when it is needed. I am tempted to believe that we have already achieved a fully automated environment.

31 May

I started a new notebook with the epigraph "Simplex
Sigillum Veri." Yes, simplicity is the seal of truth.

In modeling as well as in drawing it is good to start from
the inner core of the object and develop it, moving outward, toward its last reaches. In carving, on the contrary,
one moves from the outside in. The sculptor encircles the
piece of wood like a boxer skipping around his opponent
to probe for an opening, for a place close enough to the
surface to allow a direct entry; and from there he works
inward.

The cat Toby never moves his eyes laterally. He moves his
head instead and faces his every target frontally and full
face. He is capable of tricks and can even deceive us at
times, but no deviousness ever crosses his mind. Or at
least it never crosses his face. Imagine the effect of a cat
peering askance like a movie villain! Never shifty-eyed,
Toby's impact is so direct that the meeting of our eyes
amounts to a breach of good manners. I look away, and
Toby himself can stand his straightforwardness only for
a few seconds.

2 June

There exists an erroneous notion to the effect that only
particular objects are sharply circumscribed, whereas ab-

stractions are of necessity vague and imprecise. On the
contrary, any abstraction, no matter at what level, needs
precision in order to be usable. A tree seen out of focus
by a myope is of little help; only when seen sharply can
a tree at a distance serve as an abstraction for trees seen
nearby. The distance makes details drop out but replaces
them with the correspondingly greater prominence of the
larger structure. On the other hand, we put an undeserved trust into what we call the individual case, which
actually is nothing but the level of abstraction beyond
which we cannot individualize, except with special help.
Look through a magnifying glass, and you will see a
much more specific object, compared with which the
thing you saw with your naked eyes is an abstraction, a
generalization capable of covering lots of possible, more
specific individuals.

3 June

In his *Counterfeiters* of 1925, André Gide has one of his
most corroded youngsters boast of having put a mous-
tache on the Mona Lisa. Since Marcel Duchamp performed the same questionable feat in 1919, is Gide suggesting that he wants Duchamp to be counted among his
counterfeiters? Remember that in the Romance languages, *to sophisticate* means, more commonly than in
English, "to corrupt the genuine."

5 June

I have met at least two persons who never learned to
smile. Like an infant when he first attempts it, they suddenly contort their face as though they had slapped a
grinning mask on their unmoved features. I have no reason to doubt that either man is kindly and warmhearted;
but both may have missed the crucial moment in their
first development at which a particular muscular skill is
either acquired or lost forever.

13 June

Stendhal says in *La Vie de Henri Brulard* that it took him quite long to develop a character of his own. He thinks this is the reason for his inability to remember people's facial expression. "Until I was twenty-five, and in fact often even now, I have needed to hold on to myself with both hands so as not to be at the mercy of the sensations produced by the objects and to be able to judge them reasonably by means of my experience."

18 June

The mean-minded never abandon the secret hope that the achievements of the giants may turn out to be not as disturbingly great as they are made out to be. Hence the gleeful joy when forgeries succeed in deceiving the experts. If greatness is indistinguishable from imitation, mediocrity has nothing to fear.

I cannot get used to the idea that a person who so clearly embodied a particular way of being human can simply vanish from the earth. Since he so clearly *is,* how can he not be? In this sense, every individual is an endangered species.

Identical twins frighten us not because the same person is shown to exist twice but, on the contrary, because the twin gives us the uncanny impression that one person we know has been deprived of some of his nature and fitted with alien responses and memories. It is more like a sudden change or loss of personality, which endangers our trust in things being and remaining what they are.

Nobody would be willing to say that if astronomers cannot tell whether a certain object they see is a single star blinking or a double star, then the difference does not exist or does not matter. In the arts there are people ready to believe that if a difference cannot be discerned by the experts, it does not exist.

The work of art does not necessarily stop at what the naked eye can see. If a magnifying glass reveals subtleties of stroke or relation not visible otherwise, they may belong to the work nevertheless. Graphologists use magnification legitimately to trace refinements of motor behavior, the difference between hesitation and decisiveness, trembling or firmness.

Since a building does not have to be put together by the architect's own hands if it is to count as his genuine creation, I doubt that all painting and sculpture has to be entirely the artist's own handiwork to qualify as an original. The purists claim that a Mondrian redone by someone with a ruler and primary pigments would lack that decisive something. Would it? Now that so much art is fabricated by mechanical procedures, would it not be more intelligent to try to distinguish between what is of the essence and what are mere accidentals?

20 June

It does not occur to us that the works of the great thinkers and artists of antiquity were products by which they made their living. When Pliny tells us that the heirs of Aristotle auctioned seventy terra-cotta bowls from his estate, we find it hard to reconcile the name of the man to whom we owe the *Poetics* and *Metaphysics* with that of a self-employed professor running a well-equipped home. His name stands for a syndrome of traits we have extracted from his works and molded into a person, not for an Athenian citizen of the fourth century B.C.

1 July

A hundred wood lilies on the slope are little more than a sprinkle of red animation in the eyes of an Impressionist.

But a single lily, looked at from close by, becomes a revelation of medieval design.

4 July

Michel Tournier suggests that every person has an "essential age," which he keeps all his life, so that he is "too
young" until he reaches that age and "too old" afterward.
In my case, I believe that the dynamics of my life has
been influenced at any time by my being not yet or no
longer sixty years old.

One should blush at the thought that in writings about
the art of our century, the most frequently cited work is
probably Duchamp's urinal, that is, a joke. The inability
to realize that artists, and particularly the French, sometimes joke or play has handicapped American art criticism. To stare gravely at certain minor Picassos is to con-
found one's standards. And the main trouble with
Magritte is that he does not smile when a smile would be
the only saving grace. As to Duchamp, one should have
given him credit for tilting the urinal from its intended
position and thereby demonstrating that an object, as
Ernst Mach was the first to point out, alters its visual nature when its orientation in space is changed.

11 July

I learned a lesson about civilized eating from the old tempura chef in Tokyo, who prepared morsel after morsel in
our presence, passing them one by one across the table to
each of us so that whole minutes went by between bites.
After initially feeling some Western impatience, I came to
enjoy the peaceful rhythm, which changed the feeding
into a quiet accompaniment to the meeting of friends in
conversation. As a pun-loving friend of mine said, "O
tempura, O mores."

18 July

Tournier speaks of the transformation of the *symbole* into the *diabole,* which occurs when the symbol takes over and carries instead of being carried. The Nazi swastika was one of those emancipated symbols. Tournier warns: "Rappelez-vous la Passion de Jésus. De longues heures, Jésus a porté sa croix. Puis c'est sa croix qui l'a porté. Alors le voile du temple s'est déchiré et le soleil s'est étaint. Lorsque le symbole dévore la chose symbolisée, lorsque le crucifixe devient crucifié, lorsqu'une inversion maligne bouleverse la phorie, la fin du temps est proche."*

25 July

Looking is moving through space. For a fleeting moment I thought that today I could not look out at the lake from our window because the deck in front of that window is freshly painted and I must not step on it.

2 August

Although every one of these trees belongs to us, I explained to the Italian visitor, we hardly ever walk in the wooded plot behind the cottage. The driveway cuts through it, and we enjoy looking at the green splendor and appreciate being protected by it from the road. In Europe, every square foot of ground is cultivated, and one can walk wherever one wishes under the trees on a nicely cleared bed of needles or leaves. In the United

---

* "Remember the Passion of Christ. For long hours, Jesus carried his cross. Thereafter it was the cross that carried him. Then the veil of the temple rent in twain and the sun went out. When the symbol swallows the symbolized, when the crossbearer is crucified, when an evil inversion overthrows the *phorie,* the end of time is near."

States, woods and forests are parts of the vast areas that have not been taken over by man. Until need and greed encroach further upon them, these virgin territories occupy our essentially empty continent. We can cut paths through them, but we do not own them.

8 August

The eager searchers who hope to find the secret of beauty in mathematical proportions expect that the golden section or some other ratio will offer them a recipe for how to design a successful building or painting. Actually, all that such measurements can do for the artist is to sharpen relations he has selected intuitively. If he wants to find the middle of a canvas or façade, a yardstick can help; but it is the artist, not the yardstick that indicated the middle as the proper answer to a compositional question. Le Corbusier's *modulor* never made a success of anybody who lacked the genius of its inventor.

13 August

Sensory analogies cut without hesitation across the zoning categories of practical reason. A fellow tenant of ours used to boast that she had the largest apartment in the building and that it had two balconies. Since she was herself an ample figure, I used to call her, among friends, the lady with the two balconies. Poor man's poetry.

17 August

I cannot understand why children yell and scream. If there ever was a period in my own past when I practiced screaming as a way of life, I have forgotten it—owing, no doubt, to the "childhood amnesia" to which Ernest Schachtel has attributed our selective memory. Are children suffering from a perpetuation of the primordial scream? Or is the expression of joie de vivre, which in

276

songbirds makes for such melodious twitter, reduced in our own species to the level of dogs and terns? Surely Michel Tournier's Abel Tiffauges must have been disoriented by his repressed temptations when he recorded the noises of the school yard and listened to them with rapture.

20 August

In ancient Japan when a mother had lost her teeth and could no longer eat properly, she was carried by her son to the top of a mountain to die of exposure. Those are said to have been barbarous times, but how much more barbarous are our own repositories of decrepitude! Unfortunately, we cannot be trusted to tell what kind of life is worth living and what is not.

22 August

Sometimes the difference of the sound alone determines the difference of meaning in the same word as it is pronounced in two languages. Compare the English *delicious* with the French *délicieux*. The squishiness of the English word assigns it to things moist and sensuous, to the material pleasures of touch and tongue. In the French word the vowels coil around the consonants with the gracefulness of a violin scroll. The English word applies to desserts; the French one, to a lovely dancer.

30 August

Delacroix says of one of Courbet's *baigneuses:* "Elle fait un geste qui n'exprime rien."* I remember observing that in the nineteenth century the gestural language of dramatic expression is joined by everyday gestures like leaning,

---

* "She makes a gesture that expresses nothing."

yawning, etc., which by traditional standards do indeed express nothing.

A friend, back from Egypt, confesses that he felt repelled by the gigantic sphinxes of the temple areas. He may have seen them as sculpture whereas their large size may perhaps warrant that they be looked at like the more summary shapes of architecture. In such large figures the detail curves of an eye or mouth would become unsurveyable, as though perceived from too close; one should view them rather like columns and arches. In fact, the caryatids of the Erechtheum are prevented by their lovely femininity from properly fulfilling their function as supports. Lacking the bland loyalty of columns, they might step off their base at any moment and let the roof crash to the ground.

1 September

How long ago were we first afflicted by the notion that the "incompleteness" of certain works of art is remedied by the beholder, who supplies what is missing? Even Delacroix is willing to say that perhaps the sketch of a work is attractive only because everybody completes it at his own pleasure. Obviously, no such filling in has ever been practiced by anybody unless the light was so bad that he saw what he was not seeing. The assertion implies a naturalistic criterion for completeness and is likely therefore to be a product of the Renaissance.

Those who believe that central perspective reproduces the natural and objective look of perceptual space would do well to leaf through a history of Japanese painting: they would experience there the shock of coming suddenly across the first paintings done in imitation of European perspective—the violent funneling of space toward a single vanishing point, the panicky squeezing of a world that had reposed for all those centuries in the unhurried expanse of tranquil parallels. To arouse in ourselves some of the anguish experienced by the artists who bravely accepted and imitated the imported nightmares of distortion is the best way I can think of to cure us of this bit of Western provincialism.

The dracaena in my study fills its space with enviable ease. It quietly spreads in all directions, proving that space exists only when it is organized. Each shiny blade slides from the stem and moves without effort, continuing to rise for a short while and then curving downward by its own free grace. The leaves are so sharply honed that they cut the air without friction. As the stem grows, new leaves appear on the top of the umbrella, and the oldest ones dry up and fall. Sometime in the future perhaps the little tree will have risen beyond me, performing its kingly spread for my protection.

20 October

Michael Fried describes absorption as a characteristic feature of French painting in the eighteenth century. I wonder whether those images of absorption are the secularized version of an originally religious attitude. During the Renaissance, religious art begins to turn from the telling of Bible stories to the description of a devout state of mind, a state of absorption and meditation. This shift toward the psychological response is evident in Rembrandt; when, a century later, Chardin or Greuze shows a child deeply absorbed in blowing soap bubbles or studying a lesson, the mental stance is still the same but the subject of attention has changed.

7 December

Why is there no such thing as a discordant color whereas there are discordant chords in music? Is it because the

279

components can be discerned in the music but not in a visual mixture?

Kitsch often indulges in unbridled passion by an equally unrestrained exploitation of color and shape. Just as schmaltzy music makes the strings quiver, the shapes of shameless painting or sculpture bulge and the colors drip with sweetness.

8 December

The so-called creationists are faced with the dilemma that science has built a system in which no place is left for a supernatural power. They relegate God to the position of a featherbedding bystander.

❧ 1982

4 January

When the alexandrine verse of the French poetic tradition breaks into two equal halves of three feet each, it creates a symmetry that blocks the continuity of the sequence. It endows the two halves with the same weight and the same function. The blank verse of the German classics reduces the six iambic feet to the odd number of five, which bridges the hole in the middle with a kind of keystone. Therefore the French verse stands heavily, like a symmetrical façade, whereas the blank verse flows. Compare Racine—"Toy qui connois mon coeur depuis que je respire"—with Schiller—"Lebt wohl, ihr Berge, ihr geliebten Triften!"*

It is not prudishness or lack of courage that makes a good film director avoid the explicit performance of physical acts such as sex or violence. Art calls for expression, not for documentation. The labor of the sexual act looks ridiculous or even incomprehensible; it recalls the saw of the carpenter or a power drill breaking up the pavement.

---

* "You who have known my heart as long as I have breathed."
"Farewell, you mountains, you beloved pastures."

By giving love the appearance of physical mechanics, a picture meets Henri Bergson's formula for the comic. A similar objection holds for violence and indeed for any purely physical occupation. An actor concentrating too much on the exact technical motions needed to pick a lock, prepare a meal, or perform an appendectomy may fail to transform a practical chore into symbolic expression, that is, into art.

The invention of nuclear weapons has made war into a kamikaze action. You can kill your neighbor only by killing yourself.

10 January

If beauty is understood as the means of displaying an artistic statement clearly and powerfully, it is in fact an ethical quality, and Plato did well not to distinguish it in principle from the moral good.

15 January

Physicists speak of "conditional elementarity" to indicate the level at which, for the purpose of a given discourse, they are willing to treat a phenomenon as not further divisible. In the arts also, the level of abstraction in an artist's style determines whether a figure is presented as an elementary unit or a complex of interacting forces. In a medieval mystery play or even in a Boccaccio story, each character stands for a single attitude. Compare this with what happens to the miser or lover or murderer in the psychological novel of the nineteenth century. Or think of the hierarchy of divisibility in a play, where subsidiary figures behave like elementary particles whereas the principal characters unfold a whole range of impulses.

18 January

"Painterly" paintings used in windows look like projected lantern slides, not like stained glass. This is so because in true stained glass every unit of the composition must look itself like a little window, charged with the function of letting the light pass and modifying it in the process.

1 February

A handshake feels limp, almost nonexistent, in a dream. So does most, and perhaps all, touch. Is it that dreams are sustained by vision and hearing only and fail to reproduce the sensations of the other senses?

6 February

In the past, writers of theory did not hesitate to invent emblematic characters as carriers of concepts. Thus Lessing, at the beginning of the *Laocoon,* presents the amateur, the philosopher, and the art critic in a "historical" sequence. This device affects the argument with a touch of fraudulent authenticity, unless we understand that we are reading parables. Even in our own time, my teachers in psychology enjoyed inventing dialogues and episodes without indicating explicitly when they were reporting facts and when they were telling stories. By no means did this "falsify the data." It turned systems of ideas into scenarios.

12 February

The cat Toby fills a gap in our domestic conversation. Embarrassing though it may be to confess it, one of us has him speak in a squeaky voice and the other answers. In these utterances he displays a distinct personality of his own, a brash and blunt expression of complaints and selfish demands. It is a mood lacking otherwise in our behavior and giving voice perhaps to what otherwise would remain unsaid.

Lessing predicting Heidegger: "Aus ein paar angenommenen Worterklärungen in der schönsten Ordnung alles,

was wir nur wollen, herzuleiten, darauf verstehen wir
uns, trotz einer Nation in der Welt."*

15 February

Before the body dies, the mind's awareness of the world
pales and fades out. Similarly, as our civilization proceeds
to destroy itself, it loses reality in its thinking. If after the
final disaster something remains of our books and someone is there to look at them, he will come across the
writings of philosophers who denied the objective existence of the world. This will make him understand that
the nihilism of our thinkers and the physical destruction
by war, pollution, and selfishness were part and parcel of
the same blight.

5 March

When the artist was shown a painting he had done years
before, he gave it a quick look of recognition but then
walked up to it and touched its paint, as though contact
was needed to let him be sure, "Yes, I made you with my
own hands."

14 March

The bargain-basement romanticism of popular scientists
like Lewis Thomas captures an easy audience with the in-
expensive thrill of mystery. Do not teach students the
facts, he urges, teach them how much is still in the dark
and how little we know—as though the unknown by itself holds any attraction unless it is experienced as what
lies beyond where our knowledge presently stops. Only
by teaching how much we know do we charge the un-

* "To derive anything we please in the most perfect order from a
few explications of words, that is something we do better than any
other nation."

284

known with the lure of the hidden truth lurking ahead of us. In and by itself, the unknown is just a bare expanse. Also, how gratuitous is the challenge of recommending the poets as a model for the scientists—as though there were less pedantry in the writing and teaching of poetry than there is in the sciences.

17 March

No experience goes to waste. When an Indian guru taught me how to concentrate in meditation on the key spots of my body, I thought I would never use it. But now as I am exercising on a trampoline, I find that by focusing on the toes, the knees, the hips, and the shoulders I control weight and balance more effectively in response to the perceived requests of the joints than I would by thoughtless bouncing.

14 April

Dreams are the prime example of sensory deprivation. When the outer world is shut off and the self is thereby deprived of the interplay with the nonself, dreams are the self's way of replacing what is missing. They are the complementaries of the self, somewhat comparable to the way vision produces, through afterimages, the complementaries of perceived colors, to obtain the necessary balance. The balance between the inside and the outside, the self and the nonself, is supplied by the dreams.

28 May

Since the Cathedral of Barcelona was right opposite my hotel, I entered it several times each day for moments of contemplation. My mind was elevated and purified not by the presence of the divine figures to which the worshipers, kneeling here and there on the benches, appealed in prayer but by the visual sweep of the pilasters that

moved my eyes upward to where they fanned into the
vaults of the high ceiling. My recreation came from the
clean consonance of all shapes, the absence of any entan-
gling smallness, and the dark silence of it all.

In a Rogier van der Weyden painting at the Prado, the
Christ child jumbles the pages of the leather-bound
prayer book with a careless clumsiness fitting his age
but violating the demands of symbolic behavior. Such a
breach of the rules testifies to the happy state of affairs
that let the symbols walk the earth.

30 May

Antonio Gaudí thought in cement, that is, in a fluid medium, even when he built in stone. His shapes flow, drip,
twist, and sprout quite consistently. Nothing in all this
exuberance, which combines the playfulness of Art Nou-
veau with the power of Gothic expression, strikes me as
arbitrary. But the conception does not cover all the elements of his buildings. The construction of the Church
of the Sagrada Familia has been going on for a century,
and even now the builders are busy. The gigantic shell of
the four walls with their façades and towers stands
around the open ground of the interior and therefore can
still be viewed not only from the outside but also from
the inside. There are two discordant features. In some of
the earlier parts, traditional Gothic windows have all the
precise geometry and symmetry avoided in the main texture of the building. The church was started by another
architect, and Gaudí's own style may have needed time to
come into its own. Even more disturbing are the life-size
sculptural figures that inhabit the façades but partake in
no way in the idiom of the architecture. They were cast
from live models and finished with a cheap nineteenth-
century slickness.

  Although a translation of the human form into
Gaudí shapes would have been possible—there are some

chickens and snakes that do much better—the living inhabitants of buildings are what they are and must be
reckoned with. In thinking about Gaudí's necessary con-
cessions to the human body in gravitational space, one realizes that even the most reckless frills and undulations of
the Gothic and the Baroque tolerated without inconsistency enough vertical walls and horizontal planes to let the
human users go safely about their business. But although
Gaudí convinces the eyes of the visitor by the melodious
bulgings and garlands that envelop the balconies, windows, and doors of his apartment buildings and offices in
Barcelona, one searches with some worry for the necessi-
ties of human safety and comfort. In fact, they are not
absent. There are enough solid walls and staircases inside
to make one realize, somewhat ungratefully, that all that
imaginative charm is a holiday costume after all, which
covers the solid anatomy of the building delightfully but
does not overcome the duality of structure and decoration.

In a folkloristic pageant I saw, the music was supplied by
a sturdy gentleman who played a long flute by fingering
the holes with his right hand while adding the bass by
banging on a drum with his left. A few hours later I noticed exactly the same instrumental setup in a musician of
the fifteenth century: he supplied the merry accompaniment to Salome's display of the head of Saint John in a
painting at Barcelona's magnificent museum of Catalo-
nian art. Apparently, the music stays the same through
the ages, just as the atrocities committed by the rulers
vary little.

After its transfer to the Prado, Picasso's *Guernica* is now
displayed in a huge showcase, much like the glass box
that holds Rembrandt's *Night Watch* in the Rijksmuseum
in Amsterdam, and for the same reason. Both paintings
have been attacked with a knife. *Guernica* stands as the
only exhibit in a tall historical hall of the Casón del Buen

Retiro and thereby arrests the visitors as it was never able
to do on the second floor, busy with transients, of New
York's Museum of Modern Art. By having more space
around it, the painting expands into monumentality, and
its figures move more freely. It is also better lit. But although incomparably more powerful at its new location,
the painting chills the visitor by its solitary confinement.
It has never been quite itself since it was removed from
the defining setting of the pavilion for which it was designed; but in the midst of the New York museum it enjoyed at least some nearness to other works. Now the
painting is isolated from the public as well. Encased in
its box, it is something between a slide projection and an
epiphany, that is, something less and something more
than the painting itself. And as I was privileged to lecture
on *Guernica* right in front of the work itself, I got the
sense of a pious legend, in which a humble worshipper of
images is rewarded for his effort by the miraculous apparition of the radiant original itself.

4 June

An unexpected telephone call of an old friend from the
Middle East at five o'clock in the morning—she had mis-
calculated the time difference—reminded me that the discontinuity of space and time is a distinctly modern experience. Unexpected events have always existed, but in
earlier days the unexpected could be counted on to arrive
by way of a space-time continuity. Only through the immediacy of communication by electricity are totally disparate spaces and times disturbingly juxtaposed. In the
arts such juxtaposition of discontinuous and disparate
contents appears for the first time in history, in photo-
montage. Byzantine medallions in the midst of other
scenes were clearly meant to belong to spaces of their
own, and in paintings the apparition of God in the clouds
was miraculous but not spatially paradoxical. In the pho-
tomontage, independent images are shown to share a

common space, just as that long-distance call fit into my all too early morning quite seamlessly.

5 June

Holbein's anamorphic skull in his painting *The Ambassadors* must be looked at from the upper right to be recognized. Symbolically this demand to change our point of view tells us: Head-on you see the two gentlemen in their official splendor, but look at it another way and you will discover the *vanitas* of all things! Everyday vision leaves the deeper truth distorted and thereby hidden.

Uccello in his *Battle of San Romano* makes the debris of war conform to the demands of perspective. He arranges the broken swords on the ground along orthogonals converging toward the vanishing point, and even the corpse must toe the line.

13 June

A fine case of serendipity. I was reading an essay by Karl Popper in which he uses a "cloud" of small gnats as an example of a perfect lack of order: "Each gnat does exactly what he likes, in a lawless or random manner." A cluster of gnats, in other words, would be an entity in which the gestalt factor is zero. But then I read in the current issue of *Scientific American* an article about the "schools" in which roughly one-half of all species of fish travel. Biologists have now shown that in those schools every fish keeps a preferred distance from its neighbor. They never bump into each other, and the group as a whole executes sophisticated maneuvers to outflank predators. To be sure, gnats are not fish, but the sort of coordinated navigation I have seen performed by swarms of small insects makes me wonder whether they are truly without order. Never underestimate nature! And for that matter, who knows, perhaps it is only our myopia that makes us see nothing but disorder in Brownian movement?

But the kind of order that keeps a school of fish together is quite special. It is not the standard type of gestalt, in which the structure of the whole controls the place and function of the parts. Rather, the whole is a conglomerate of local gestalt relations between neighbors. It is homogeneous rather than hierarchic and, in principle, without boundaries. It can be exemplified by swimming magnets that attract and repel one another: the fish are drawn together by what they see and kept apart by the motions of the water they sense kinesthetically. This kind of order is also a favorite of modern artists. Notice the sensitively controlled "random" distribution of windows in Le Corbusier's Ronchamp Chapel or the tissue of shapes in Jackson Pollock's paintings. Socially, here is the solution for those who are willing to adapt to their neighbors but reluctant to submit to control from above.

When the same musical recording is used for a set purpose every day, for example, as the "theme" for a broadcast, the very particulars of the performance that make it sound live and spontaneous become, by their mechanical repetition, the annoying indicators of a frozen product. The ontological relation between performance and recording is quite intricate. The other day while someone was playing a Mozart sonata on the radio, there was a cough in the audience at the sixth measure or so. But when the pianist did the repeat, the cough was not there, and I said to myself, "It was a repeat, but then again it wasn't!"

7 July

The manufacturers of visual aids ought to keep in mind the predicament of E. T. A. Hoffmann's erudite tomcat, Kater Murr, who wanted to learn how to write. Since he seemed to be unable to follow the instructions given in an old manual of penmanship, he began to suspect that the dignified sleeve covering the wrist of the writing hand in the illustration was what he was missing for success. As I noted earlier, visual presentations, to be usable, must observe the law of parsimony by leaving out whatever might distract from what matters.

10 July

The portrait painter Chuck Close has said he chose to work from photographs because that gave him an objective criterion of whether he was doing right or wrong. Actually, the literal copying of photographs should reveal the very opposite of faithfulness to nature. Looked at closely as a model for the painter, the photograph dissolves into irrational shapes that alienate the picture from the objects it represents. The discovery of this new, visually incomprehensible world suits today's fascination with accident. But accident makes for sterility when it leads to masochistic surrender instead of urging the sense of form to find meaning in the amorphous hints at many meanings.

25 July

What are we to conclude when we discover no musical difference in principle between Haydn's depiction of an ordinary thunderstorm in his *Seasons* and Verdi's *Dies Irae* in the requiem telling of the Day of Last Judgment? Words and style aside, the two examples do not seem to differ either in intensity or expression. Are we to say that the range of expression is determined by the medium, not by the subject matter? And if so, does this wipe out, for the artist, the difference between a passing spell of bad weather and the final reckoning? Or is there, in the arts, no such thing as a mere thunderstorm, since the events at the surface always reach to their deepest reverberation, the ordinary always reflecting the extraordinary?

291

26 July

The carvings of the Haida Indians are barely a century old, which made me wonder how they have managed to preserve the uncontaminated power of early art. They look ancient. The best totem poles are as well protected from dilution by modern civilization as the Doric columns of Paestum. Somehow I seem to have assumed that it takes distance in time for art to remain so pure.

27 July

Only a few years after Alexander Baumgarten established the concept of *aesthetics,* the professor of aesthetics had become a stock character, open to ridicule. In E. T. A. Hoffmann's *Kater Murr,* published in 1819, Professor Lothario, angry at the erudite tomcat, is told by a colleague, "Am I to believe that you are jealous of him because he writes verses? Don't you worry, the little gray man can never become a professor of aesthetics. After all, the ancient academic statutes clearly specify that owing to excessive abuse no more professorships are to be granted to asses—a regulation that surely applies to other animals as well, including tomcats."

29 July

The Pointillists displayed the Newtonian revelation that neutral gray comes about as the union of various colors. Although the effect of a straight gray does not vary all that much from the additive mixture of multicolored dots, it makes all the difference for the meaning of the pictorial statement that the drab tranquillity of standard existence is revealed as an accumulation of all the riches.

4 August

Hoffmann's *Kater Murr* is an early example of montage in the novel. The intertwining of two independent stories is realistically motivated by the scholarly tomcat's tearing out pages from the autobiography of the composer Johann Kreisler to use for drying the ink on the pages of his own autobiography as he writes it. Hoffmann pretends that by mistake the two manuscripts were interleaved in the printing. By mere confrontation the resulting twin story presents a humorous contrast between the outpourings of the conceited cat, who fancies himself a poet and thinker but ends up in pathetic frustration, and the truly great musician, whose power over the hearts of men and women remains equally inconclusive. Irony and pessimism create a double tale in which high-flown romantic tragedy is tempered by the smile of persiflage, and caricature is deepened by the resonance of suffering. The two stories disavow each other's reality, but at the same time the one enriches the other by compensating for its limitation.

7 August

I had thought that the kind of unself-conscious grace that Kleist, in his essay on the puppet theater, describes as the prerequisite of art was first discerned and singled out for praise by the Romantics. However, as early as the Renaissance, in Baldesar Castiglione's *Book of the Courtier,* a similar quality of grace is deemed the principal virtue for performance in the arts. To be sure, there is a significant difference between the two conceptions. The Romantics raised the profound problem of intellectual control as a threat to intuitive creation, whereas the Renaissance courtiers were concerned merely with the superficial ease of execution, the avoidance of sweat as not in keeping with the leisurely superiority of the nobleman. This ideal of the relaxed, elegantly skillful amateur survives more nearly in the nineteenth-century English dandy and up to the present day in the dislike that English intellectuals profess for the drudgery of systematic inquiry.

13 August

My first "published" writing was a periodical whose issues, about three pages long, I wrote and mimeographed myself when I was in my early teens. The publication was called *The Universe* and contained noteworthy facts about the solar system and the stars. In a way, everybody starts out by writing about the universe and struggles with the problem of how to reduce his subject to manageable size. Whoever supervises dissertations knows what I am talking about.

"Pauca sunt enim, quae proprie loquimur, plura non proprie, sed agnoscitur quid velimus" (Augustine, *Confessions,* bk. 11).*

30 August

Older people talking to each other would not have to say everything twice if our language had an opening signal like the British "I say," or the Japanese "Anoné" to alert the partner that something is about to be said. The oldsters often fail to understand something the first time it is said, not just because their hearing has gotten weaker but because they have become slower in tuning in on any appeal from the outside.

3 September

Michel Butor's obsessive manner of telling the story of his *L'Emploi du temps* by repeating the same facts over and over again makes reading tiresome, but the device is rewarding nonetheless as still another way, in recent French literature, to avoid showing the passing of time. Instead of letting episode after episode come and go, Butor keeps

* "We say few things correctly, more often we speak incorrectly, but one realizes what we intend to say."

the totality of the facts present before us, although he augments them at each repetition by new elements. At each point, one sees the situation changed without ever witnessing the action itself. It is as though one were looking every evening at a building in progress, noticing its growth but never seeing the builders at work.

29 September

In Grünewald's *Crucifixion,* John the Baptist points with a long index finger at the scene, to which he belongs neither geographically nor historically. He was not present at Christ's death, but he still functions as the herald of his coming. In pictorial space, things are made to coexist for a more important reason than that they occurred together in a story or setting. They are united by the picture's theme, and it is that theme that authorizes the story to serve as subject matter. I am saying, to use another example, that in paintings of the Annunciation, the angel Gabriel and Mary appear in the same room not because such an event did in fact occur; rather, the scene "was made to take place" because the Virgin Birth had to be announced.

3 October

When the human response is multiplied by the thousands and ten thousands, it is distilled back to an elemental nobility of nature. Sitting at my desk on a football afternoon, I hear from the stadium the distant swells of applause like the magnificent roar of a tempest at sea. The repulsive noises of the beer-can boors have been purified by distance to become a remote power with which I can live.

19 October

Picasso uses objets trouvés to explore the relation between things that are mechanically produced and shapes that are invented and molded spontaneously by the artist's mind and hands. Basketry patterns and corrugated paper, nails, plastic toys, and leather shoes stand for the impersonal finality of standardized shapes and textures. To prove that the two species of shapes are not enemies but can complement each other to create a richer world is a playful challenge for an artist not deterred by antinomies. Even live leaves share the fate of being cast in bronze and accept the role of welcome strangers in the realm of Picasso's imagination.

At a modern high school that is intended to do pioneer work in a neighborhood where most youngsters are badly in need of more self-esteem, I was shown the expensively equipped art workshop. When I inquired what the pupils were doing with all this, I was shown brooches, each consisting of a slab of plastic in the shape of a cat. The cat was identical in all the brooches because it had been sliced, sausage-fashion, from a prefabricated stick of plastic. The work of the students consisted in doing the slicing by means of a splendid electric saw and attaching a pin to the insipid animal. In other words, the boys were doing everything except what they needed to be inspired to do.

The doyen of American psychologists, a man of my age, had some advice on how to supplement the fewer good working hours available per day in the late years. If one used to enjoy "complicated puzzles, or chess, or other intellectual games," one should give them up and instead indulge unashamedly in reading detective stories and watching cheap entertainment on television. I myself have never conceived of how anyone could live with impunity at different levels. If you cannot work and play and rest with the same undiluted engagement of all the mind's best abilities, you probably are neglecting them everywhere. Be shallow and half-present in your off-hours,

and the deficiency will show at your desk. Dullness is
indivisible.

20 October

An Israeli said to me that by treating the Arabs so bru-
tally, his country had "lost its point." Indeed, what distinguished Israel from other nations was that it owed its origin to the transformation from martyrdom to a state of
purified saintliness. By now, however, its government has
painfully shown that there is no exception to potential
cruelty and that historical accident alone decides whether
at a given time a given people will be the victim or the
oppressor.

5 November

Study the function of clothing in sculpture and painting.
Clothing can smooth over the articulation of muscle and
bone and thereby interfere with the body's structure and
expression; but it can also reduce the complexity of limbs
to geometric shape so that the anatomy of an arm, simplified by a sleeve into a cylinder, may state the arm's role
more precisely than the naked arm could. It would be rewarding to observe where a good artist lets the limbs
speak and where, and to what end, he modifies and replaces them with clothing.

8 November

In a performance of *The Rake's Progress* by Stravinsky and
Auden, the director Robert Altman and his set designer
gave a stunning rendition of Hogarth's *horror vacui*. Every
inch of the stage floor and of a scaffold at the full height
of the background was crawling with the limbs of human
bedlam. In the midst of this perpetual motion the solo-

ists, like fishermen in a trout stream, waded laboriously through the viscous medium of madness.

9 November

In a recent book on mathematics, Morris Kline makes the curious assertion that mathematics is not always true, by which he means that it does not always match the facts of nature. For example, he says, if in mathematics both *a* and *b* are equal to *c,* they are bound to be equal to each other. This, he says, need not be the case in perceptual experience. Colors *a* and *b* may both look like *c* but not look equal. This is correct, but it does not make mathematics untrue, since mathematics has never pretended to apply to anything but fixed quantities. Perception does not have that limitation.

14 November

Modern art first ran into opposition because it rendered the image of nature more faithfully than earlier art had done, not because it deviated from nature. The Impressionists modified local color, found color in the shadows, and dissolved contours in accordance with what a sunny landscape showed them. What is taken to be true to nature depends, as Gombrich has demonstrated, on what has been adopted by the tradition. As long as art is required to respect the accepted "thingness" of nature, modifications of size, shape, or color are impermissible.

15 November

While the old masters prided themselves on building their paintings from dozens of layers, it became a matter of honesty for painters of the nineteenth century to work *alla prima,* that is, by definitive strokes. To compose a tone from a sequence of translucent glazes came to be considered fakery, the fraudulent pretense of achieving

the mastery of the right touch—similar to what we think
today of the opera tenors who obtain powerful voices
mainly by relying on electric amplification. The German
painter Wilhelm Leibl, a virtuoso of the *alla prima* technique, is reported to have said, with utter contempt, of
a rival, "Das Schwein lasiert!"*

21 November

There is something slightly terrifying about someone
who does not look his age. Rather than be credited with
an asset others lack, he is suspected of being without an
essential human quality, the sensitivity to the afflictions of
human life. He may seem to be modeled of wax and be
preserved by a chilling absence of feeling.

24 November

There is a similarity between the music I derive from
looking at a score and the images formed in my mind
when I read a story. I get to hear little of the sound of
music, but I sense the voices climbing and falling rhyth-
mically in their interaction. The actors of a story do not
appear to me as pictures, but I see them behave gently or
harshly and loom large or sneak along meekly as disembodied hubs of action that play their parts without being
fully present.

4 December

In *The Tempest,* Shakespeare reserves his deepest thoughts
for his last words, the epilogue spoken by Prospero. For
here he reveals that, to him, Prospero's magic is a symbol
of the poet's own power, which has been handed over to
the audience. Only the audience's fancy can release Prospero from the island and give him the freedom he himself

* "That pig even uses glazes!"

could grant to Ariel when he was still the magician. It is in the nature of the spell that the "insubstantial pageant" must fade, to the "despair" of his maker and the undoing of his vision, unless it is kept alive by the ultimate guardian of such figments, the mind of the audience. Unlike the conventional request for applause, the aging poet's last epilogue begs for two contradictory favors: release and survival.

12 December

What drives inept writers to kill their sentences by composing them from strings of nouns although life consists more relevantly of actions than of things? Lawyers, bureaucrats, scientists, and college freshmen—they all need to be disabused of this vice. The cause must be that at an elementary level conceptual thinking is like pointing with the index finger. It is an enumeration that makes action into things, verbs into nouns. Being called upon to be counted petrifies them.

16 December

Many writers proudly tout the many drafts they produce until a piece of work is done. What better demonstration of the toil and struggle it takes to reach the peak! Teachers of writing also seem to urge their students to plan for many drafts. I am suspicious of this procedure. It seems to me to favor a sloppy spontaneity of dashing things down, harmful to the discipline of always trying for the best. I myself always write final versions, although they require much revision sooner or later.

21 December

The caption in the newspaper said, "The mayor took a seat while his budget director explained the new regulations," and the photograph showed just that. It was the first time I had ever seen a caption in the past tense. Photographs always dwell in the limbo between showing what was and showing what is. For paintings, the past tense is inconceivable: *George Washington Crossed the Delaware*. In the newspaper, the change of tense turned the caption into a part of the narrative report and the photo into an illustration of the caption. And yet, a photograph, like any picture, is also a present being.

23 December

To show a human head lying sideways, one has to paint the symmetry of the face perversely across the grain. This involves translating the lateral correspondence of the eyes into an up-and-down relation. There must be a temptation to turn the canvas ninety degrees and do the face in the normal orientation. But I suspect this would not work. Slight deviations from symmetry are needed to show the concession of the face to gravity and keep it from floating in empty space. When the problem is solved successfully, the face will look symmetrical, although if one turns the picture sideways the face will look off-balance.

1 January

Do we marvel sufficiently at the paradoxical situation of a world populated by billions of human beings who want only a peaceful existence but are at the mercy, in each country, of a handful of people who work for the very opposite? I ask myself: Where in the social hierarchy is the cutoff level at which neighborliness switches to hostility? Or is it the case that with each increase in size, human community, by some diabolical law of nature, adds gradually a corresponding admixture of bellicosity, from marriage to family, to village, town, and nation, where the accumulated evil bursts into the open?

2 January

Some people experience detailed mental images of the characters about whom they are reading in a novel. They can supply the hair color of the protagonist and what his lady is wearing; but I suspect that those hallucinators are not the best readers. The impressive life of the figures conjured up by literature seems to me to result from their abstractness, their being reduced to visual formulas of motion, slowness, pudginess, or shiny agility, to splendor

or dullness, or perhaps to a certain tone of voice. Readers
sensitive to this abstract freshness are also the ones most
likely to object to illustrations. I wonder about stories
whose imagery is taken over by powerful illustrations.
Alice in Wonderland, for example, being a play of words
and constructs, has never been able to shake off the tyranny of John Tenniel. Its figures had to borrow a creator
to receive the breath of life.

When novels were still published in newspaper installments, they were subject to the tempo of our daily pur-
suits. The same is true for our narrative comic strips.
From our time perspective, the detective is too precipi-
tous when he tackles the villain in a jiffy, and the curly-
haired heroine makes us impatient when she dawdles on
vacation. Something similar happens in the theater,
whereas in a book, not tied to the speed measure of real
time, the velocity of events varies in accordance with
what is going on.

3 January

In painting, the gradient of perspective is often tempered
by a countergradient of objective sizes. Things nearby
tend to be made larger, but distant things are also more
likely to be buildings, trees, or mountains, much larger
than the human figures and the furnishings of the typical
foreground. This lets the units on the canvas approach an
average size, regardless of the distance depicted.

5 January

The twelve-tone system in music is unlikely to undo the
structural relations inherent in the diatonic scale, which
still rules the minds of listeners. Will the character of the
basic intervals ever be flattened out to leave us with a set
of tones none of which possesses a character of its own
and with a set of relations that will all be equal? And if

such homogeneity were obtainable, how attractive would
be the music it could produce?

One hesitates to compare our own reactionary government with practices of a Mussolini or Hitler. It does make
a considerable difference whether one tortures and mur-
ders people oneself or whether one indirectly supports
the brutal practices of distant regimes, and there is a difference between actually invading other countries and
limiting oneself to preparing for war by armament, provocation, and unwillingness to talk peace. But the historical and political function of fascist regimes does not depend on such gradual differences; it consists in protecting
the privileges of capitalist industry and money monger-
ing by preserving the outer appearance of humanitarian
policy and democratic government. It thereby deflates the
ever-increasing aspiration toward a more sensible conduct
of affairs and maintains a last resistance to progress.

6 January

In paintings the nude human body looks curiously isolated. As a self-contained creature, it fails to acknowledge
visibly its debt to the force of gravity. Each of its elements—the sphere of the head, the cylinders of trunk and
neck, the ovoids of the thighs—are shaped around their
own centers. Especially in painting, those stalking and reclining figures seem homeless in their perfection, unaware of the world they are meant to populate. It takes
the luxurious togas of the Romans and the robes of the
angels to counteract with their rolling falls the upright
pride of man and the flight to heaven. Only in sculpture,
where the body is more isolated and becomes a closed
universe, can the unclothed limbs perform unchallenged.

11 January

A "published poet"—what a tragicomic designation! To
be a poet is a consecration, which is reduced to the state

of practical success when the pathetic adjective assures us that he does better than mail typescripts to his friends or manage an occasional reading. Is this dilemma unique to poets? Nobody speaks of a performed composer, a constructed architect, or an exhibited artist.

17 January

To demonstrate problem-solving by restructuring, I have often used the puzzle of how to convert Figure 6a into Figure 6b by moving no more than three dots. The figure is the ancient *tetractys,* holy to the Pythagoreans because its visual perfection is composed of the four digits 1, 2, 3, and 4, adding up to 10. When viewed in this version of structure, however, namely, as four rows of items, the puzzle cannot be solved. Only if the triangle is restructured as a rosette detachable from the three corners, as in Figure 6c, does the visual form offer the needed subdivision.

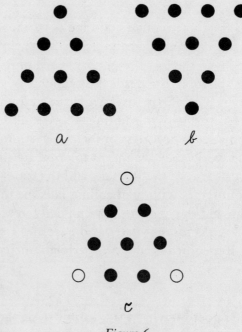

Figure 6

When nature designed the human eye, the law of simplicity suggested that the mouth of the optic nerve be placed
on the central axis of the eyeball. This would have made
for an elegantly symmetrical design, and this is the way
the Arab scholars depicted it in their anatomical drawings; but it also would have put the blind spot precisely in
the center of the retina, the place needed for the fovea,
the focus of sharpest vision. Therefore the solution agreeable to nature and any human designer had to give way to
the makeshift arrangement of having the optic nerve enter the eye obliquely.

25 January

What is the ontological status of a component within a
gestalt? Since its nature is purely relational, it cannot be
ascertained "as such." Obviously, however, it must possess a nature of its own, since there can be no relations to
things that do not exist. The dilemma has to be con-
fronted in any area where gestalt relations occur—physics, economics, and of course perception.

2 February

The problem faced by children in Piaget's conservation
experiment repeats itself in the visual thinking of adults.
The child has to cope with the interaction between two
spatial dimensions, the height of containers vs. their
girth. A musicologist friend of mine told me that her students had little trouble understanding either melodic sequence or the harmony of a chord, but they found the
musical synthesis of horizontal and vertical hard to grasp.
A similar difficulty arises for architects when they have to
visualize the interaction between ground plan and elevation. It is like playing ticktacktoe in three dimensions.

21 February

The figures in narrative paintings often do not look in
the direction prescribed by the physical situation. In

Rembrandt's *Anatomy of Dr. Tulp* not one of the seven
doctors looks at the muscle exposed by the professor, not
even the closest doctor, who leans so eagerly over the
corpse. The deviation of the depicted glance from the figure's optical line of sight is practiced routinely by painters
pretending to show figures that look at something or
somebody. They do this for the good reason that the eyes
would have to be shown cast down or turned away to
look in the right direction. This would hide the eyes'
expression of attention, awe, or concentration, which is
more important for the pictorial message than the correct
rendering of spatial relations.

23 February

Might one maintain that at their highest level of excellence, the art works of different cultures resemble one another astonishingly? At a recent exhibition of five-
hundred-year-old bronze heads from Nigeria, I was
struck by their classical beauty, which reminded me not
only of Greek sculpture but equally of the best Egyptian
work, and indeed of Japanese and Chinese statues of the
great periods. Add to this the best of Romanesque sculpture, and you begin to suspect that the conceptions of art
at their peak shed the accidentals of their styles and even
their racial particulars and show a purity whose geometric simplicity, perfect proportion, and serenity of expression reveal something like the Platonic *eidos* of the human
countenance.

28 February

In a new book on cosmology I read that the thought of
the running-down universe "calls for regret or resigna-
tion or fatalism." Does it really? It is a response that
strikes me as childish and certainly foreign to my own
thinking. I have never shared the notion that the value
of what we are and do depends on the length of our sur-

vival, on something continuing beyond ourselves, so that the coming to an end would mean that it has been all for nothing. A flower blooms happily for nothing, so did Greece and Rome. And never would I want to exchange a good ending for the nightmare of an excessively long stay.

6 March

When the painting is finished, the artist vanishes from the canvas. Until then, the brushstrokes, not yet bound by the composition, call for an outer cause. They show that they have been put there by someone. But once caught by the rhythm of the whole, they no longer owe their presence to anybody. The picture admits our eyes but nobody's hands.

A new optical illusion (Figure 7). The top line is divided in two equal parts, but its left segment looks larger because it partakes in the size of the larger truncated triangle.

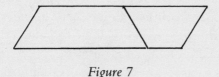

Figure 7

21 March

To an uninstructed person the tones of the musical scale sound as though they were at equal distance from one another, although of course the half steps are half the size of the whole-tone intervals. Does this mean that under certain conditions when the structure of a situation is perceived, the inhomogeneities are attributed to that structure while its elements are perceived as equal? Are there visual examples, perhaps in depth gradients, brightness gradients, etc.?

26 March

Would it be foolishly inappropriate in front of a Jackson Pollock painting to be reminded of the medieval description of the universe or God as a sphere whose circumference is nowhere and whose center is everywhere?

Although Walter Benjamin's essay on the work of art in the age of reproducibility deserves its reputation, it confuses the reader by failing to make some indispensable distinctions. Benjamin does not note the difference between reproduction and the multiplicity of originals. Reproduction often deprives us of qualities possessed only by the original. But, and this is also overlooked, even the poorest reproduction may possess an "aura," because the aura is not an objective property but one given to the work by the user. A valuable painting may possess no aura for the person who dusts or wraps it and often not even for the dealer who sells it, whereas the cheapest print of a Raphael Madonna in the bedroom of an Italian peasant has all the magic of an icon. Cheapening afflicts reproduction and original alike when, in the conception of the user, the art object is reduced to a merchandise for consumption and its value is determined by its price. Then again, an art form that produces a multiplicity of originals—graphics, books, photographs, films—is unlikely to suffer from an absence of aura, simply because the work exists more than once. Each print or copy can have the full aura of an original. An actor on a movie screen is not a reproduced human being but a visual creature in its own right. I remember in the olden days at the opening nights of films the actors taking curtain calls and our letdown in seeing the magic, gigantic black-and-white shadow on the screen deprived of its superhuman abstractness when a pink-faced, smiling pedestrian of our own size appeared to take a bow.

310

30 March

While listening to one of our most successful painters lecturing on his work, I could not help noticing the pathetic discrepancy between a brilliant visual talent and a totally empty mind. His paintings shown on the screen were attractive to look at, but they said trivialities about trivial things. What was missing in the man was not education. Some of the greatest painters had probably less education than he. But there was a lack of spontaneous concern with the essentials of life, the concern with birth and death, awe and loveliness, danger and security, abundance and austerity, harmony and horror. How much talent is wasted by hollow men and women in the arts, in literature, and in the music of today!

1 April

There are people complaining mistakenly about "circular thinking" when someone tries to account for the interaction of gestalt factors. "In a melody the rhythm influences the structure of the sequence of pitches, and vice versa." Both causal statements are correct, and both hold at the same time. A petitio principii can occur only within one logical chain, not in the relation between two. Every interaction can be described in both directions.

4 April

In the modes of medieval music the distribution of the half steps in the scale is such that in several of the modes there is no clear structural reference to a tonic; accordingly, one might surmise that there was less insistence then on closed pieces of music with a pronounced beginning and ending than is the case now. Music was more like chanting, heard for a while but not framed like a picture.

311

10 April

Since all things in this world can be viewed symbolically and there is no limit to the "depth" of meaning to which the symbolization can be carried by a carefree viewer, artists have an easy way of creating images susceptible to being interpreted as profound revelations. A spinning bicycle wheel can be pronounced an initiation to the cosmos, which is all right as long as the artist is not credited for more than it takes to make a bicycle wheel spin.

12 April

An early attack on the doctrine that art duplicates nature comes in Diderot's dialogue on the actor, in which he forcefully argues that a performance engendered by genuine passion would look ridiculous on the stage and that what looks natural on the stage must be an image calculated by the actor. Diderot speaks of a "paradox"—which it is, as long as the difference between art and nature is ignored.

13 June

Suddenly on the empty blue of the lake there appeared the straight line of a message in Morse code—a procession of ten brilliantly white and slowly moving swans. The straightness of the line, the identity of the sign ten times repeated in the calligraphic shape of each bird's body like an Arabic letter written in series seemed an epiphany of human rationality on the background of nature. Yet, there was nothing rigid about the sequence, nothing artificial in the rhythm of the intervals, which, more musical than metric, behaved like a phrase that slowly changed as the birds in their progress across the lake altered their distances slightly but freely.

312

In Michelangelo's incomplete sculptures there is a range
from rough and sometimes flat overall shapes to shiny,
articulatedly modulated and detailed ones. He proceeds
on a hierarchic scale. But is this true only for the fragmentary works? And in fact how safely can one distinguish between his incomplete and his finished works? In
the marble relief at the Bargello, the upper arm of the
child, along with the Madonna's left hand, is almost flat,
and the background figure is equally evanescent. Only
the two principal faces radiate in full and smooth relief.
This lack of a standard level of execution adds immensely
to the life of the work. It also denies the difference between the temporary and the final.

19 June

The pilgrimage to Florence reveals what by now must be
called the twilight of the great originals. On a dark day,
Masaccio's *Trinity* in Santa Maria Novella, so thoroughly
known from reproductions, remains nothing but a black
patch on the wall. His murals in Santa Maria del Carmine
are obstructed by scaffolds. The Raphaels are removed
from the Uffizi for restoration. Plastic shields protect
other beloved works from the hands of the visitors but
also prevent their eyes from seeing anything but their
own reflections. The dirt of centuries hides the colors,
and the gloom of the churches plunges them into darkness. Michelangelo's *David,* high upon his pedestal but
pelted by the flashes of the cameras like a new Sebastian,
barely manages to keep above the surging crowds. The
local guides scream in what a Roman friend of mine calls
"the new Tuscan dialect," broken English pronounced
with a heavy Italian accent. Visits to the Venus of the
Medici are limited to three minutes. The harassed pilgrim
stumbles home to his unhurried sessions with the lucid
reproductions in the art books.

In the Pazzi Chapel and also in San Lorenzo, Brunelleschi girds the interior at shoulder height with a dark belt made of the silky gray *pietra serena,* a local stone. By overruling the separation of the lateral chapels from the central hall, this gray ribbon binds the whole space in a lively melody of ins and outs, a closed ring of expansions and contractions.

20 June

The only Greek temple on Sicily that still looks complete and that still is nested in the undisturbed beauty of its natural setting is the small miracle of Segesta. Yes, it is complete, although it has neither a roof nor a walled core. The Doric colonnade and the outlines of the gables describe a visual totality, just as in a drawing the geometry of a cube is fully caught by the lines of its edges. The temple stands halfway up a slope of cultivated land. There are vineyards and plots of brown earth woven in rolling bands of gentle alternation and reaching high up to where, paradoxically, they end in the sharply torn skyline of the mountains. Within this swell of hills stands the temple, firmly right-angled but wrapped in the shrubbery of the *ginestra* with its thousands of yellow, perfumed candles. Seen from below, it is a golden apparition, deposited like a jewel box of the gods on a green carpet.

The unreality of the transparent little monument is much enhanced by the contradiction between the completeness of its visual shape and the lack of all actual enclosure. Approaching it, one hears that the columns twitter with the voices of swallows, and one sees little nosegays of wildflowers sprout from the cracks of the architrave and along the ridges under the open sky. The columns have the cylindrical rigor of human mathematics, but their golden surfaces have been eaten into, to re-

veal a mineral bark that hands the marble back to the
natural world from which it was quarried.

Palermo—the tired and defaced remains of ancient greatness reminded me of an observation by Boris Vian: "And
he noticed a large square surrounded by buildings that
dated from the Middle Ages but had aged since." In the
midst of the ugly apartment blocks and the jeering traffic
of its clogged streets, it is as ludicrous as it is sad to think
back to the Norman kings and to the realm of Frederic II,
who for a historical moment made of the Mediterranean
island the center of the Western world, the synthesis of
the Arabic and the Christian cultures it was so eminently
suited to be. Demoted from the status of a navel to that
of an appendix, a neglected liability of Italy, Sicily made
me speculate playfully that if Dante lived there today, he
would design his *Comedy* in a wholly different form. Inferno would be everywhere, although dotted here and
there with the jewels of lost Paradise, while Purgatory
would be all in the future as the promise of possible sal-
vation.

27 June

Boris Vian's *L'Autonne à Péking* is the closest to a Mack
Sennett slapstick comedy I have ever seen in a novel, with
the difference that the film comedy shows a unitary world
in which the unreality of the happenings follows logically
from the unreality of the human figures that execute
them. If one of those puppets with their rolling eyes
and walrus mustaches is hit over the head, nothing but a
purely mechanical effect can result. Puppets do not bleed.
Vian's characters, however, are known to us mostly
through their speech, which is sufficiently human so that
all those decapitations, amputations, and rapes look surrealistic. Those men and women are people as we know

315

them, but they are inhabited by mechanisms that can only be broken, not mourned. They behave out of character when now and then they complain or repent.

9 July

A friend of mine, an architect, points out that the weaknesses of a design show up at the corners, that is, at the places where basic elements meet. The completed work must function as a whole, but it is inevitably made up of components that are invented, studied, and shaped one by one. Even in great architecture one notices examples in which, say, a church's nave and its crossing are not prepared to meet each other—the corner columns or posts do not fit their neighbors. The skill of overcoming such patchwork and of uniting all elements in one overriding structure is a challenge to designers and composers in all the arts and, for that matter, to organizers everywhere else.

10 July

Conducting is the natural response of unrestrained listeners. They act out the music with their own limbs and bodies and, in fact, seem to generate it by molding the air. Perhaps, although I do not really believe this, conducting was born when some privileged enthusiast jumped on the podium to pull the music bodily out of the players.

Our philosophers are plagued by the temptation of wanting to appear expert in all the arts and sciences, from which they extract their theses. This has led to a phony specificity now in fashion among professors of aesthetics. The philosopher cites the third movement of a late Beethoven quartet or the Master of the Barberini panels for an observation trivial enough to be sufficiently illustrated by a folk tune or a calendar landscape.

The large profile of Giacometti's brother Diego is narrow like the blade of an axe when looked at from in front, and yet it is the very opposite of a relief. The broad shoulders indicate that the narrow front of the face is the main view. The profile is all that remains of the head's volume, afflicted by the cruelty of the empty air.

11 July

The guilt feeling so common among survivors made my late friend's daughter write, "Perhaps I can try now to understand my parents a little better." I replied by telling her I was not sure that parents are to be understood. They are, I said, a part of your living conditions, which you want to know and appreciate. It is as though you grew up in a valley surrounded by mountains. You learn to predict the behavior of those mountains and how to adapt to it. You love or fear or trust them, but do you need to understand them? It is different with your children, for whom you are responsible and whom you may be able to guide.

27 July

What in the arts is called an "original" is never more than an approximation. Paintings retain only a semblance of their pristine state. The written score of music preserves little more than the basic properties of pitch and rhythm, and performances offer nothing but versions of the intended composition. And what are the referents of words in literature more than rough hints at the images in the writer's mind? Thus in the arts, as everywhere else, communication is only partial, because even the most perfect form is never more than an attempted embodiment.

Will our literary analysts ever stop confusing the world of a work with the reality it represents? Suppose a great writer were a tribesman, ignorant enough not to know

317

the connection between pregnancy and conception. And suppose he wrote a play or novel whose network of causal arrows did not include the fact of the father's paternity. Would the wife's child be nevertheless the son or daughter of the father? Most certainly not. The biological tie, if introduced into the story by a busy reader, would add a wholly new vector that would overthrow the characters and their relations. It would destroy the work.

The characters of Stendhal's novels remind me, strangely, of those white asbestos mantles that made light in the old gas lamps. Purified by fire, the delicate little cylinders illuminated the room with their transparent glow. Similarly cleared of all the contaminants that clutter our novels today, Stendhal's men and women glow in the purity of their passion, their innocence and intelligence, their ambition, pride, and brutality.

1 August

I have maintained that abstract thinking finds its imagery in the realm of spatial relations. A similar idea was recently expressed by another psychologist, with the significant twist that in his opinion the spatiality of thinking is nothing more than an evolutionary leftover from the days in which the brain's activity was limited to orientation in the environment. Some people will go a long way to avoid realizing the persistent usefulness of the analogy between the interrelations of concepts and the configurations of space.

15 August

My grandson and I were drawing pictures of our beach cottage on its hill surrounded by trees. Since we were sitting three hundred feet away and the day was dark, he had trouble discerning all details. I said to him, "What

you don't see, you don't have to draw!" but realized soon
how difficult it would be for him to follow my advice. It
has taken Western painters many centuries to acquire the
liberty of leaving out something they know is there. It is
a brazenness not easily adopted by anybody entering the
practice of art afresh.

17 August

How disillusioned I felt when I learned that the meteor
showers of our summer nights are made up of particles
often no larger than grains of salt! Our regular stars,
looking no different than the luminous dots on the ceiling
of the planetarium have been revealed long ago to be distant giants, although I do not see them as gigantic. It is
difficult to describe a visual experience in which the perceived size and distance of objects remain unchanged yet
are qualitatively affected by what one knows about them;
but this is what happened in my mind's minor cosmic crisis when the falling "stars" were revealed to be motes like
the dust lit up in my room as the sun shines through the
window.

I have always resisted collecting musical recordings, much
as I appreciate undisturbed listening. The degradation of
music from events rooted in their place and time to objects that can be stored, pulled out, and handled at will
strikes me as demeaning. Demeaning and also ghostly, in
that the prompt availability of a particular group of musicians playing a particular work is so absurdly improbable
as to be either fairy-tale magic or illusion. I am greatly
bothered by recordings used at weddings or funerals, occasions at which presence should never be a mere fake.

2 September

Not without good reason do chamber players perform
from the score whereas soloists memorize their pro-

grams. The completeness of a concerto or song lends itself to being grasped and retained as a whole even though
supported by accompaniment, but an instrument's part in
a trio or quartet has meaning only in the context of the
total work. It tends not to be "a good part" in the gestalt
sense of the term because it has no completeness of its
own. Chamber players do know many a piece by heart,
but the shapeless fragment on the page resists independent appropriation.

25 September

Sometimes as I handle my little electric coffee maker, I
am distracted and forget to put in the water, or I leave out
the filter, or fail to put the cup in its place, which makes
the coffee pour over the table or, in the worst case, could
make the machine's metal cylinder explode. The damage
is rarely great, but I shudder to think how similar must
be the small manipulations required of the technicians
who control the nuclear generators—small kitchen stuff
in a quiet workroom, and the leisurely carelessness suggested by such a setting. It is different in surgery, where
the presence of the human body makes it harder to forget
one's responsibility. But those remote dials and buttons—
a little slip, and a whole section of the world blows up.

3 October

I feel about my violin as a man does about a woman
whose beauty he feels he does not deserve. The elegance
of the instrument's curves and proportions, its delicate
weight, and the precision of its shape—how do I dare to
hug such perfection with my chin? We went to the concert of an elderly famous virtuoso. He waddled onto the
stage, half penguin, half turtle, but as he lifted his violin,
its voice began to vibrate and to sing, and the skillful ornaments rose like soap bubbles. It is this sort of sound

that the Baroque curves of my wooden lady has in mind
as she suffers in captivity.

14 October

It has been observed that the great artists do not fit the
styles to which the history of art conforms otherwise.
Michelangelo is neither Renaissance nor Baroque, and do
we place Bach with the cheerful constructors of Baroque
music or the Romantic moods leading to Beethoven? But
the giants are not simply beyond classification. They do
have their place in the history of art as bridges between
what preceded and what followed them. Is their freedom
from membership a necessary condition for the powerful
personal vision that is so deeply familiar to our own and
so awesomely alien?

17 October

A German scholar told us that Goethe based his view of
the origin of volcanic minerals not so much on scientific
evidence as on the symbolic implication of the facts. To
believe that basalt was thrown up to the surface by erup-
tions from the fiery core of the earth would place our
world on a turbulent foundation, and Goethe disliked
revolutions. It occurred to me that throughout his many
explorations of nature, Goethe practiced science in the
manner of a poet. He treated the facts of nature as metaphors of the human condition. Just as he refused to see
our earthly existence placed on any but a granitic foundation, he attacked Newton for his theory of color with an
irrational outrage because the immaculateness of the color
white had to be protected from the accusation that it was
composed of darker shades and was therefore impure.
This was not simply a debate on two scientific theories
but a quixotic knight's campaign in defense of virginity.
In the same vein, one might surmise that Goethe's search
for the intermaxillary bone, the missing skeletal link be-

tween man and animal, was inspired by his admiration
for the beauty of organic evolution, and the same could
be said about his vision of the primordial plant, the *Ur-
pflanze,* from which all other plants were to have derived.

5 November

When Mary tells me about the geology of our region, my
image of our home ground changes. No longer are our
buildings and streets based on an anonymous but solid
foundation. Our dwellings become a mere surface cover,
like the hair or fur overlaying the skin of a body. The true
center of life is now inside, revealed by the scientific dig-
gers and pervaded by gigantic struggles of rising and falling, squeezing and crushing, on the top of which we precariously ride, lifted and lowered by petrified waves.

24 November

No cosmological theory will look good as long as it
speaks of a single universe surrounded by a void. How
can one conceive of a lawful world in which an event
comes about only once and at one place? Since the same
laws are likely to exist everywhere, the same events must
come about everywhere also. That is, in the beginning,
things will happen either everywhere or nowhere.

25 November

A physical therapy clinic looks much like a mental asy-
lum in the movies. In the large ward an occasional person
lies or stands or sits, absorbed in moving a limb mechanically, raising an arm, stretching a leg—an action motivated by no visible purpose, a mere obsession. Nobody
notices his neighbor, but from behind curtains one hears
soft conversation or even a giggle, so close to the ear, yet
invisible, like the hushed life in an ancient Japanese
prince's palace.

3 December

The harmonious unity of body and mind is an illusion for
the young and the healthy. When the body is handicapped
by disease or accident, it reveals itself as a stranger. How
rarely is the suffering deserved, how rarely does it follow
logically and predictably from the behavior of the mind.
It hits us out of the blue, like something meant for someone else. And how ignorant we are of what is needed to
defend us! Experts must be called in to help. We discover
that we have been closely cohabitating with obtuse matter. Yeats says of his soul

> What shall I do with this absurdity—
> O heart, O troubled heart—this caricature,
> Decrepit age that has been tied to me
> As to a dog's tail?

> ("The Tower")

🌿 1984

12 February

When they passed each other under the trees of the fogged-in park, the old gentleman said to Mary, "Kind of a mistical morning, isn't it?"

14 February

On the rug in the middle of the large basement room there stands all by itself a garden chair, arousing a surrealist shiver. Ready to receive the sitter with open arms, the chair seems pathetically blind to the emptiness around it. Since it is deprived of its function, it displays the expression of its gesture all the more clearly, like an abandoned woman unaware of her loss.

25 February

A fable for adjustment psychologists. There once was a professor who also played the violin but so badly out of tune that he sometimes was half a tone off. No accompanist could put up with him. Then one day he found that one of his students would modulate on the piano to the

key to which he happened to have shifted—a well-
adjusted player!

Susanne Langer begins her chapter on music in *Philosophy
in a New Key* with the assertion that a Greek vase is a
work of art whereas a handmade bean pot is only an artifact, albeit it may have "a good shape." And Nikolaus
Pevsner starts his book on European architecture with the
sentence: "A bicycle shed is a building; Lincoln Cathedral
is a piece of architecture." This is ostensibly so because
only the latter is designed for "aesthetic appeal." My own
conviction has always been that unless you recognize aesthetic expression in all good form, simple or complex,
natural or man-made, intended or unintended to be art,
you will never touch the root of art, which grows from
the soil of universal perceptual expression. To look for
the distinction between art and nonart is like seeking the
cutoff point between plainness and beauty.

At times, themes for notebook entries stand in line
waiting to be used, and then again there are weeks and
months without any such demand. I notice that when periods are meager, it is not because I lack ideas. The nour-
ishing cues seem to be always around. What matters is
the difference between times when I have, as it were, my
tentacles out, and the ducts are open between observation
and readiness to respond, and other times when I watch
and learn and think without the response urging me to
write. I suspect the same is true for "inspiration" quite in
general. Experience lies patiently in wait until the poet
puts up the sign Open For Business.

As we stood admiring the amaryllis, a young woman, recently married, confessed that she felt the large size of the
flower to be obscene. I retorted rashly that size did not
matter, since, for example, the vaginal shape of an orchid
remains the same, whether it is tiny or huge. And yet our
friend was right, because it is only when the flower enters

the size range of human shapes that it addresses us in a disturbingly private manner, remote from the neutral contemplation we can afford when the object is too small or too large. Something like this is true also for sculpture and painting.

29 February

Our playing place was surrounded by a fence. Our parents had to pay for a key if we wanted permission to spend our days in the wildly overgrown park, which differed so abruptly from the big city surrounding it. The children who "belonged" were like a secret fraternity, distinct from the rest of the neighborhood. Leaving the daylight of the clean city streets, we entered the messy shadow under the old trees and made our way through the shrubbery on narrow "Indian" trails. Hidden in the thicket and accessible only to the more select children was the Temple of the Ants. The Temple of the Ants was a gazebo, of which nothing remained but the fluted columns on a cracked concrete floor. The wood of the columns, spotted with the leftovers of a red stain, was punctured and mined by wormholes. In and around the columns traveled the ants, exuding an invigorating alcoholic odor and crawling over us as we huddled on the floor. Our favorite game was "The Stonecutter's Family," our image of proletarian living, which let us indulge in the rough speech and the bad manners forbidden in our middle-class homes. For refreshment we assembled at the cottage of the caretaker, whose wife sold goat's milk, warm from the animal; so I can claim that, like Zeus on Mount Ida, I was suckled by a goat.

4 March

When the cat, sitting on your lap, looks deeply into your eyes and you in turn look deeply into his, there is so direct a contact from being to being that the distinction be-

tween human and animal vanishes. Rather than see a
specimen of a different breed, one sees a curiously
masqued face, as at a costume ball the bizarre outfit of a
partner does not hide the appeal of her searching glance.

15 April

In terms of pure optics, two images are of the same size
as long as they subtend the same angle. But a small face
seen at short distance on a home screen may nevertheless
create a basically different impression than a large face
seen at a large distance in a movie theater. It may create
an intimacy not obtainable in remote projection.

22 May

In the foreground of the news photograph a delightedly
smiling president shakes hands with a visiting general.
Two young men, although standing immediately behind
him, are entirely removed from what is happening in the
foreground. Intensely concentrated, they scan the scene
around the president, on the watch for enemies. So totally alien are they to what is going on that they tend not
to be seen, just like the men in black who in full view on
the stage of the Japanese *bunraku* theater guide the puppets. And just as the puppets create the compelling illusion that they act by their own inherent volition, the
president seems to perform completely at liberty, even
though his every move is prescribed and controlled by
watchful puppeteers behind him.

5 June

I complained about the dancers' leotards smoothing the
articulation of their bodies out of recognition. Are we
much better served by the living skin, which in the same
objectionable manner glosses over the interaction of the
muscles, so illuminatingly displayed in the flayed *écorchés*

328

of the anatomists and artists? What is the best relation between the integrating sweep of the overall form and the individual statements of the components?

24 June

The Latin *virtue* acquires its ethical meaning quite gradually. Even today it preserves its sense of power and strength in expressions like "by virtue of." I am told that something similar is the case with the Greek *agathon,* which means "good" only secondarily and stands, first of all, for "successful" or "important." Here then we have verbal resoundings of the late arrival of ethics in the human community. Primarily there is the rule of power, by which everybody obtains what he is strong enough to take from the weak, the way plants and animals struggle for survival. Righteousness and goodness develop later, by way of the enlightened self-interest of group and individual.

25 June

There is a fundamental difference between creatures that take messages from the eyes of their opponents and those that do not. A cat or dog trying to find out what you are up to searches your eyes and thereby proves he knows that the world is run by intentions, which can be discerned before they turn into behavior. This amounts to recognizing the existence of the mind and its role in the world of bodies. Birds or squirrels, on the other hand, can react only by observing consummated action—a limitation that distinguishes them in principle from our society of humans and higher mammals.

The hit-and-run technique of these notebooks gives me the enjoyable freedom of recording without hesitation thoughts and facts that may be true for the moment but would not stand up to broader, more thorough scrutiny.

Here they pass muster, rather than being smothered at birth.

18 July

When Mary took a picture of the Leaning Tower of Pisa, she tilted her camera a little to make sure she got it all in. The picture turned out to be disappointingly perpendicular. The leaning had compensated the leaning.

30 July

"And a mouse is miracle enough to stagger sextillions of infidels" (Walt Whitman, *Song of Myself*).

3 August

The efficacy of the "soap operas" on the radio derived, as I showed in my analysis at the time, from the twofold image of woman presented in the stories: the powerful, wise guide of the distressed, and the perturbed victim of her own troubles—that is, the idealized woman of the wish-dream, and the merciless portrait of the listener. Would it be shocking to point to, as the great prototype of this formula, the double image of woman in medieval religious imagery: the Virgin Mary, ruling helper and wise counselor, and the red-haired Magdalen, shaken by her passions—the woman one would like to be, and the one in whom one can recognize oneself?

7 August

When the Canadians endeavored to support the arts of the Inuit (Eskimo), a controversy ensued between the ethnographers and the people in the arts. The latter accused the former of treating the sculptures and graphics of the natives like harpoons and snowshoes, mere implements of a practical culture. Instead, they maintained, those works should be thought of simply as art and be put in the company of art elsewhere. I fear that this would expose the Inuit to unfair competition and blind us to an essential virtue of their work. The value and dignity of Inuit art are in no way diminished by being considered those of folk art. Although some of their artists have developed a strikingly personal style, they would be done an injustice by being compared with a Barlach or Klee. The two generations of artisans in a culture that bases its view of life essentially on survival—love and fight, birth and death—move us by their fresh grasp of those simple essentials. It is in the nature of folk art, however, that it fulfills itself in the shaping of those simple themes, whereas the conceptions of Western artists are fashioned by a rich tradition of imagery, ideas, and individual variation.

Inuit art is still fully integrated in the ecology of collective life and would be misread if considered in isolation. Such isolation would confirm us in our habit of looking at works of art as though they were cut flowers, unrelated to the soil in which they grew.

8 August

The cube and the cylinder are the archetypal standards of sculpture. The cube reduces roundness to the four basic surface views from which visual conception takes off. Through a gradual synthesis of those basic views the conception returns to a later version of the roundness that the carvers of totem poles and early icons derived from the cylinders of the tree trunks.

10 August

Curiously shocking are the representations of a sculptor at work in drawings or reliefs of the early Renaissance. Because the artist and the infant angel he is carving both look like creatures of the same kind, the one no less alive

331

than the other, we see one being go at another with a
pointed or sharp-edged weapon, handled not with the
passion of an aggressor, however, but with the care of a
surgeon thoughtfully bent over his work. And indeed,
carving is unique among the methods of creation in that
it shapes beautifully animated beings by cutting, piercing,
and drilling—a fearsome union of two elemental impulses we would rather keep safely separate.

11 August

Cellini's assertion that a sculpture must show eight views
illustrates a phase of the transition from cube to cylinder
I referred to earlier. Obviously, those eight views come
about when the four upright edges of the basic cube are
chamfered on the way to roundness.

My life has been that of an amateur, an amateur husband
and father, an amateur scientist, teacher, and citizen—a
person impelled by his predilections without much of a
need to bow to a sense of duty.

12 August

The views of a colleague of mine angered his father so
badly that the old gentleman was once driven to exclaim,
"If I had a son, I wouldn't want him to have a teacher like
you!"—an utterance that plunged the son into a pro-
longed meditation.

Every time I begin to play, I rub my bow faithfully with
rosin, and every time I use my carving tools, I hone them
with a drop of oil on a whetstone; but I have no idea
whether the rosin really smoothes the sound or the
whetstone really sharpens the chisels. Similarly, from the
morning to the evening, from brushing my teeth with
salt and bicarbonate of soda to drinking real coffee to stay
awake and decaffeinated coffee to sleep, I perform one rit-

ual after another without the slightest proof that any of those agents does its duty. Since controlled experiments exist only in the laboratories of the scientists, nothing better than faith is available for my conduct.

28 August

As an airplane warning, a red light blinks on top of the tall building, pulsating on and off all night—a skyscraper with a heart.

Electronic candles produce flickering lights when the faithful, after depositing their donation, touch one of the red plastic containers with a thin metal wand. I feel that it is all right for a red indicator lamp to light up when the elevator is approaching, but the imitation of the flicker is an appalling fraud when the life of the little flame it replaces is supposed to embody a bit of immortality. Once again, the gift of Prometheus yields to the Age of Edison, and the symbolism of a burning fire is replaced with an imitation.

14 September

The best color reproductions of works of art have a quality the originals cannot match. They present the work as such, freed from the context that modifies it wherever it is seen. The original, altered by the viewing distance, the accidental lighting, the partial transparency of the cover or container, and the surrounding space, is never more than an impaired reminder of the work. To be sure, the hospitality of the physical setting has the advantage of embracing the artifact as a fellow creature: it lets it share our space and dwell within the reach of our touch; whereas there is a supernatural chill about the absolute presence of the reproduction. Perfection does have its price.

20 September

An anatomist reports that Michelangelo's rendering of
the surface muscles in the human body is astonishingly
faithful. Actually, what is more astonishing and what distinguishes the great artist from a mere skillful copyist is
that in Michelangelo's drawings all those subtle bumps of
the torso and limbs fit the overall expressive form and
thereby create a readable visual statement rather than a
mere accumulation of correctly reproduced detail. To do
full justice to the model without being seduced by it is an
ability granted only to the few.

30 September

"A new dog on the block," we said when a lady with a
white poodle walked past our window. Of course, the
lady, too, was likely to be new. Do dogs differ more from
one another than do ladies?

14 October

The art-historical game of accounting for works of art by
deriving them from earlier ones has been amply applied
to Picasso's *Guernica*. Recently again a German book described its resemblance to paintings by Goya, Delacroix,
Rousseau, and Dali; and an American writer relates it to
Rubens's *Horrors of War*. The resemblances do exist and
may even be due to direct influences; nevertheless, they
may not prove what the clever detectives want them to
prove. I suspect that the pictorial tradition of the West
contains a limited number of themes and formal devices,
which produce a general family resemblance rather than
account for the specifics of a particular work. One might
want to know more about those commonly shared idi-
oms of the Western visual language.

I read that the founder of the American Museum of Natural History, Albert S. Bickmore, had his official portrait

composed of three photographic shots, one straight from in front, one straight from the back, and one in profile. He insisted on this whimsical procedure because that was the way anthropologists documented the heads of their thousands of Eskimo, Indians, and Ainu. Reduce the live expression of a human face to the measurements of the skull and you have a better illustration of how science differs from art than can be found in many philosophical essays on the subject.

Our hopeless ambition to find the physiological equivalents of the items of consciousness. True, we are getting closer to discovering the connections between elements, by which we account for our world as a network of relations. Such a weave of nerve cells, however, captures no more of the true nature of the conscious event than does a computer of the event it is computing. The mechanism of the computer does not account for the difference between the timetables of airlines and the medical symptoms of diseases; it only delivers the links between the items. Similarly, neurology may tell us by what connection we learn that a kind of mushroom is poisonous, but it is still miles away from accounting for the particulars of a mushroom or a poison. Only when we come to distinguish the two brain events under the microscope shall we approach success.

17 October

At the height of a Bach fugue, the play of the overlapping voices submerges in a mere texture of pulsating sounds. Is this the upper limit of hearing, which cannot keep pace with the supreme complexity of invented form and thereby effects the tragic defeat of the great artist betrayed by his medium? Or does artistic form ultimately transcend all particular action and attain the final uniformity of being?

335

25 October

An experimenter has found that a square-shaped room looks smaller than a rectangular one of the same area. This seems to me to rehabilitate the children who are accused of immaturity when, in Piaget's experiments, they assert that a tall and narrow beaker contains more liquid than a squat one. The children, like adults under comparable conditions, respond to a genuine perceptual phenomenon, which happens to be in conflict with the physical facts.

27 October

As long as the sandhill cranes crowd the waters of the marshes, they look approachable in their busy Japanese manner. But when they float over our heads as black heraldic shapes against the sky, flattened and with stretched legs and necks and entirely immobile in their conceptual symmetry, their presence is transfigured into an awesome emblem. They are revealed as spirits temporarily adopting a bird's guise, like the ancient gods walking among the humans.

31 October

I was reminded of the sophomoric question of whether a tree crashing in the forest makes a noise when nobody is there to hear it. I was alone in the house; Mary had to leave for Florida, and the cat was boarded with the vet. As I was making noises in the kitchen, it occurred to me that nobody was there to hear them, because hearing is receiving messages and my own noises were not messages to my ears, since I knew all about them. Thus my noisy rummaging was uncannily nonexistent, unheard of.

13 November

In drawing from the figure, competence shows, as it does
in architecture, where the parts of the whole meet and are
made to get along with each other. When the reclining
figure twists at the hips, it is not too difficult to draw the
chest and the head facing you and also the buttocks and
legs toward you, but it is desperately hard to make the
ones turn believably into the others.

19 November

After visiting us in Ann Arbor, a German friend, the
sculptor Albrecht, wrote in a letter: "Your wood carvings
were a particular surprise to me. I had no precise or definite expectation of what they would look like but did assume that they would be done in the clear and surveyable
manner of the writer I know. Instead I found them all but
'obscure,' in spite of the light color of the wood, and not
at all deduced, planned, composed. I think of them as the
roots for your broad and enlightening works in the field
of the arts and psychology." I had to smile, because I am
fairly sure that the romantic darkness so generously attributed to my little figures is due to nothing but an amateur's inability to make the wood match his *concetto*.

20 November

Verbal language uses chains of things to describe perceived events, which offer no similar segmentation. Subject and predicate, as two separate and coordinated verbal
objects, have no obvious analogy in the relation between
a person and what he is doing. Somebody's activity is not
a separate thing but one of his properties. Similarly, a
proposition such as *before* or *next to* is not a thing separate
from another thing to which it applies, but a temporal or
spatial property of that thing. Hence the difficulty of

young children in parsing spoken sentences into words, let alone syllables or phonemes. A recent Russian study found that when a preschool child was asked how many words there were in the sentence "Galya and Vova went walking," the child asserted that there were two words, namely, "Galya went walking" and "Vova went walking." If this does not teach us that imagery is the primal fact of language, what will?

26 November

In drawing class the teacher asked the students to assume with their own bodies for a few moments the position in which the model was posing. This made us replace the immobility of the viewed body with the play of muscular tensions perceivable inside ourselves and helped us discover a similar dynamics at work in the shapes before us.

18 December

The term *mixtura,* used in the days of Augustine to describe the union of spirit and body, is close enough to what we mean by *gestalt;* and the *unio inconfusa,* as a description of what happens when parts organize properly in a whole, is still useful. *Mixture,* in the more common sense of the term—occurring, for example, when two liquids are mixed—is rightly rejected as an "ugly confusion," not because it pollutes the spirit by involving it with the body but because the whipping of ingredients into a uniform mush degrades structure. A mush is not a gestalt; at best, it represents the limiting case in which the components have been milled into indivisibility. A gestalt derives its nobility from being a structure of defined elements. The prime instance is not that of parts vanishing in the whole and thereby losing their identity but rather the state of affairs in which each part displays its double nature, its being in and by itself and that within the whole. The theological problem of how the spirit can

338

enter the body without losing its dignity is therefore a general gestalt problem. There is no contradiction between an entity being one thing in itself and another in context.

21 December

What matters about the Eucharist is not whether it is thought of as an actual transformation of bread and wine into the body of Christ (which reduces it to an inferior superstition), or as a mere symbol of Christ's presence (which bleaches it into a mere metaphor), but that the gift is received not only with the mind but also by the body, the way full love is a union of body and mind.

26 December

The curious difference between recognition and recall lets us detect the smallest change in a familiar object but leaves us incapable of evoking an image of that same object in memory. What, then, enables us to make a drawing of, say, a horse and judge its correctness with some precision? We accomplish the feat by transforming recall into recognition, that is, by judging the drawing as to whether we recognize in it its subject.

27 December

I cannot help finding meaning in the coincidence of my reading about the psychological effect of the doctrine of Incarnation and directly afterward finding a book on how people respond to home computers. Being told that the human body had become the vessel of the divine spirit made the faithful attribute a new beauty and dignity to their own bodies. And today, having been given machines that act and talk reasonably, they wonder whether their own minds are machines. But it does make a difference, doesn't it, whether such an epochal revelation suggests a heightening or a lowering of the human status.

✿ 1985

When the Department of Visual and Environmental
Studies was founded at Harvard in 1974, we dreamed
of an integrated course of studies that would introduce
undergraduates to the visual aspects of our world as a
whole. Painting, graphics, and sculpture were to be
taught as reflections of social and individual life, as ways
of understanding the world. This meant bridging the
gaps between the fine and the applied arts and viewing
them in the context of architecture and landscaping. It
meant exploring the visual aspects of knowledge and
thought and the similarities and differences of art and science. It also meant recognizing functional objects as carriers of meaningful expression and understanding, and
paintings and sculptures as objects designed for enlightenment and deepened awareness. The history of art and
architecture was to be taught as the social, political, and
cultural history of the world manifested in its visual crea-
tions. This educational approach was intended to be more
than the usual art department and the opposite of voca-
tional training in the arts. It called for teachers with a
wide-angle conception of their task and for students
understanding the need for a broad synoptic foundation

as the basis for their particular future profession. It was a dream, but one worth recording.

12 January

There is art for art's sake and art for English departments. In the latter category are works with provocative subject matter, preferably Surrealist, without much pictorial imagination but with lots of lack of obvious meaning. Karl Kraus called it "Auf einer Glatze Locken drehen."*

19 March

After spending the morning on cleaning the house, she bicycled to the art school to model. At five dollars an hour, frozen into the beauty of a goddess, she joined the timelessness of the Greek marbles while watching the clock surreptitiously.

21 March

To celebrate the three-hundredth anniversary of Bach's birth, a local church hosted a twenty-four-hour-long nonstop performance of his organ works, thereby desecrating the church, the composer, and the spirit of music in one sweeping demonstration of the deplorable fact that in our country quantity is still considered the safest measure of quality.

5 April

The airplane trip to the South took less than three hours, but the cultural difference was marked. When I asked the hostess of the breakfast room whether they had a non-smoking section, she said reassuringly, "No, we don't.

* "Using curlers on a bald pate."

342

You can smoke anywhere you please!" And when I explained, she repeated, a shade more coolly, "No, we don't. Here you can smoke anyplace." Semantically the meaning of "you" had shifted from me to the more acceptable rest of humanity.

10 April

A first acquaintance with Jane Austen and her *Pride and Prejudice* introduced me to a society in which people are concerned entirely with each other's character and behavior. They have no true occupation other than that of dealing with one another, no further task in life. Those private struggles of the leisure class continue in the later novels of the century but apply by then more often to men and women concerned with their missions and ambitions and coping with their chores. Think of Balzac, Flaubert, Tolstoy, or Zola. Austen's book also reminded me again of how difficult it has become for us to see the novelists of those years as "realists." Her characters are walking concepts, highly stylized abstractions, which nevertheless come to life. She is much closer to the authors of *Les Liaisons dangereuses* and *La Princesse de Clèves,* much closer to Stendhal than to Dickens.

25 April

In Indian sculpture the sensuous women's heads and limbs and the sections of their torsos tilt and bend to indicate their ardent pursuit of action and passion. Only the balls of their breasts, like all spheres, are exempt from oblique distraction. With the immobile stare of a hypnotist their nipples fixate the viewer, summoning and captivating him but also keeping him sternly at his distance.

By 1877 the coming and going in the city streets of Impressionist painting is uncomfortable enough for a painter like Gustave Caillebotte to make him stabilize his Parisian

343

scene with the stark axis of a green lantern in the very
middle of his large painting *Place de l'Europe on a Rainy
Day*. Also the wedge-shaped apartment block in the background faces us head-on, like the bow of an ocean
steamer, stopping the traffic with its uncompromising
symmetry. While the ladies and gentlemen with their
umbrellas still busy themselves on the glittering wetness
of the pavement, the approaching rigor of Seurat and
Cézanne is forecast in those safety measures of solidified
form.

9 May

When Clifford Geertz describes the new methods of the
social sciences as dealing with society on the model of
games or theater plays or literary texts, he seems to envis-
age nothing more serious than a change of procedure. Future generations, if such there will be, are likely to take
notice of these analogies as symptoms of a dying culture
that had come to see the reality of existence as a mere figment of the imagination, no more valid or tangible than
dreams and speculations.

13 May

A young teacher said to me, "Since I am just beginning,
how will I know when it is time for me to stop teaching?" After a moment of thought I replied, "When you
hear yourself talking, it will be time for you to retire."

Ann told me that once, in a provincial museum in France,
she heard two of the guards talk to each other. "How
come," asked one of them, "so many of our paintings are
pitch-dark?" The other replied, "That's because in those
olden days they had very little light."

16 June

A Canadian artist sent me a slide of a painting of his representing a bud about to open. The religious quality of

this epiphany, although not claimed by the artist, is all the
more evident when it appears enlarged on the screen. The
revelation of the large in the small has always seemed to
me one of the most striking religious manifestations—religious in the sense of proving to the eyes that an intelligent perfection of structure exists well beyond the range
of human utility. To realize that an intelligence worthy of
the brain of man pervades nature in the small and in the
large, and well beyond the range of human control, is to
recognize our own limitation in a world that is admirable
not because we made it but because it made us. One need
not share the primitive superstition that this admirable
world was created by a superhuman being. In fact, its
having come about through forces that are no mere magnification of our own, as those of a divine Creator would
be, but are before and beyond anything mindlike makes
for the very essence of the shudder I am willing to call
religious.

An art therapist described in one of her papers a young
client so passive in her dealing with the things around her
that when she wanted to color the backside of a piece of
paper with her crayons, she strained to reach around the
paper rather than turn the paper itself. A similar constraint of the mind would be laughed at as an unrealistic
stupidity in a film by Buster Keaton. We would also ap-
plaud the gag as ingeniously invented to symbolize the
helplessness of our coping with tasks that would offer no
problem to a superhuman mind. But the therapist's report on the pathetic inability of the client, caused not by
a lack of intelligence but by the blinding tyranny of her
fears, reminds us once again of how closely allied are
tears and laughter.

20 June

It is true that many of the connections pointed out by
Heidegger derive from similarities of words existing only

in German—such as *thing* implied in *necessitating* (*Ding* in *bedingen*), or *gift* in *pouring* (*Geschenk* in *einschenken*). This limitation, however, does not necessarily prove that the connections are not generally valid. Every language offers revelations not obtainable from others.

30 June

The split between the self and the outer world goes right through our bodies. The dancer's vision must be translated into the language of the body, which recommends certain motions and vetoes others. A young cat plays with his tail as though it were a toy; and in our own handling of our bodily resources, even singing and speaking entail the enlisting of physical instruments that do not always oblige.

10 July

The initials "OK" were the signature of Oskar Kokoschka. Every time I use the two letters to mark my approval of one of my editor's changes on the galleys of my next book, I sneakily credit myself with the small creative act of impersonating one of my favorite painters.

11 July

I get the impression that in some recordings of classical music, the sound engineer adds crescendos and decrescendos of his own by fiddling with his knobs. This pernicious interference with the phrasings of the performers reminds me of a similarly despicable practice in the printing of etchings. Old-timers in printing workshops, with the connivance of the artists, used to do some finger painting of their own on the plates by adding shadows and highlights with a sweep of the thumb, thereby supplying deficient images with volume and drama. The better artists of course insisted on clean prints whose chiaroscuro was created entirely by their maker's own graphic powers.

16 July

A stroke of genius by Alessandro Manzoni, when in his *I Promessi Sposi* he calls his archvillain the *Innominato,* that is, the Unnamed One. He has him enter the scene when the evil plots against the innocent young couple reach their climax. The villain's name is known and whispered with awe by everybody in the story but is withheld from the reader like a taboo, thereby veiling the man in an almost superhuman mystery. Appropriately, it is he who is suddenly struck with repentance and converted to brotherly love by the mere sobs of the saintly heroine—an improbable event that turns the novel into a legend. And as the nameless evil shadow concretizes into a distraught sinner, the legend lapses temporarily into sentimental fiction.

Most evenings, Mary is the first to enter the bedroom and switch on the lamp on the night table. When last night I happened to do so in her stead, she walked in after me and switched as usual, thereby turning light into darkness. Her habit has been programmed in motor memory, which, unaware of light and dark, knows only acts of handling.

7 August

The belief that what is not acquired by learning must be inborn as a native endowment dies hard among psychologists. A recent example: when it was found that young children needed no previous training to recognize outline drawings of simple objects, psychologists concluded that such understanding must be due to a special inherited ability. Once it is known, however, that perception consists in the grasping of structure, outline drawings should be understood as facilitating recognition rather than as presenting the child with a special task. Discovering form in the complex, noisy images of physical reality is obviously the much harder task, requiring more, not less, of a psychological explanation.

14 August

All through their little lives and in the generations before them, the goldfinches have made a laborious living by waiting for the thistles to ripen their seeds, searching for them over a wide territory, and then extracting them. Now that we have installed a plastic cylinder filled with thistle seeds, the finches flock around the new source of food like the seasoned devotees of a department store sale. It took them no more than a week to make the historical leap from a hunting culture to modern commercialism, which supplies resources in bulk, ready for the asking and removed from their natural suppliers.

26 August

As the birdfeeder hangs suspended from a branch of the tree, the scaffold of wooden arms around the rising trunk creates a spatial grid for the social organization of the birds. They fly in, approach boldly or keep at a distance, in awe of some aggressive male, view the chances from some elevated lookout or sneak in from below. The social order is externalized in a symbolic pattern of spatial relations but also crisscrossed constantly by the irrational yellow flashes of individual impulses.

1 October

The sightseer's automobile turns the magnificent hills of Idaho into a visual fugue. The curving knolls of cultivated fields become a sliding sequence of overlapping waves. The chocolate brown of the plowed slopes, the

golden stubbles, the timid green of the winter wheat—
a symphony of colors that would enrapture Scriabin.

It is certainly the same pianist whose playing pervades the
corridors of the hotel every morning when I walk to
breakfast. I know the touch of his fingers, his phrasing,
his repertoire. Yet although he is omnipresent and invisible—like a local divinity—in lobby, hallway, and restaurant, he is surely absent from his recordings and probably
far away, otherwise employed, or perhaps no longer
among the living. A ghostly emanation of his departed
mind rules the roomy spaces, full of strangers who do
not notice.

Shortly after the small airplane took off from Seattle,
there emerged from the cotton-wool field of clouds the
top of Mount Rainier. Since the snow on the mountain
was the same white as the clouds, the sight was that of a
wintery and empty planet, its snowscape dominated by
the splendid peak.

The giant white pine in the Idaho forest goes back to the
days of Christopher Columbus. The five hundred years
of its life have been filled with catastrophes, wars, revolutions; but untouched by any of them, the great tree has
risen perfectly straight, like a temple column, not in history but in sheer abstract time.

What I have called the law of differentiation in the development of visual form may also hold for the history of
Greek tragedy if it is true that the chorus, at first the only
content of the entire performance, was later reduced to
the more differentiated role of "the ideal spectator or the
people against the princely region of the scene," as
Nietzsche has it in *The Birth of Tragedy*. The chorus became a collective individual, an intermediate phase in the
articulation of the dramatic medium. Just as in visual
form the shape of the primary circle is the universal, un-

differentiated matrix, so the chorus as pure verbal address
is the primary shape of dramatic performance, executed
by the still anonymous, unassigned actors.

10 October

Analytical Cubism ought to be seen as a late and last
manifestation of the Impressionist dismemberment of
shape. It transforms the atomic elements to which Impressionists had reduced the visual world into extended
geometric units. The loose fabric of touches of color becomes a framework of blindly interpenetrating shapes.

12 October

Van Gogh's imagination was limited to the translation of
views taken directly from nature or from compositions of
other artists, which he turned into his own beautiful
idiom of shape and color. His most famous painting,
Starry Night, has always bothered me with its stilted arti-
ficiality. One cannot paint in the dark, and so the painting
must have been done from memory. Van Gogh's talent
did not include the inventiveness of Gauguin's, who created landscapes and actors found nowhere but in his own
imagination. Van Gogh can cease to surprise me, but
Gauguin keeps captivating me as only the great ones can.

7 November

In the midst of all the shabby chatter of Maupassant's *Bel
Ami,* the account suddenly rises to the lamentation of the
old poet, Norbert de Varenne, his complaint about death
lurking behind all aspirations and pleasures. This moving
speech can be used as a fine contrast to the Madwoman of
Chaillot's pep talk in praise of the joys of life when she
addresses the young man who had attempted to drown
himself.

350

Are there works of art that, although successfully completed, stop short of final compositional balance? In Matisse's *Dance* of 1909, the three figures on the right do not
seem to be at their final places. By calling for changes in
spatial relation, they force the viewer into the time dimension, the motion of the dancers' roundelay.

1 December

Not only the blind but we, too, have memories of nonvi-
sual activities. Lying awake at night, I often occupy myself by remembering melodies which I mentally accompany by noting the sequence of the places the tones hold
on the strings of the violin. Since when I actually play, I
do not see what my fingers are doing, because my eyes
are on the music, my memory images of the playing are
equally tactile. In my nightly consciousness, a disembodied something leaps from place to place on an equally invisible fingerboard.

2 December

The stories told by my teacher, Max Wertheimer, in his
writings are fables rather than scientifically documented
episodes. When he tells what happened when he visited a
school class or when two unequal partners played a game,
the story may derive from a kernel of actual happening
but is conceived principally as an embodiment of theoretical positions assigned to invented actors. Thus when we
read how a self-centered secretary described the setup of
her office team, it is clear from the systematic nature of
her description that, like the cricket and the ant in Lafon-
taine, no such person ever spoke, but that she is an animated abstraction, the pure model of the mental image
resulting from a particular social attitude. There is nothing fraudulent about this procedure. It is good pedagogy,

although something of a problem arises when an actual historical figure, such as Galileo or Einstein, is chosen for the plot.

3 December

The decisive experience that turned me forever against learning to drive an automobile came when I was in my teens: a cousin asked me to sit down on the driver's seat of his car and step on the accelerator—"As soon as you do that, the car will move—it's as simple as that!" I did step on the gas pedal, and the frightening experience of the big metal box taking off and running away with me stopped me from ever meddling again with motorized vehicles. A bicycle was all right because it was I who generated its motion, but I was not willing to be kidnapped. As children's toys have changed increasingly from tools of action to contraptions that run under their own power, I wonder whether this change reflects the passivity of a consumer society that prefers being served to doing its own serving. All my life I have been reluctant to delegate power to other people.

9 December

In his fight for animal rights, the philosopher Tom Regan distinguishes between direct and indirect duties. Respect for the rights of animals, he says, is not only an indirect duty, based on our concern for the feelings of compassionate persons, but a direct one, owed to the animals themselves. Fair enough. Regan limits his claim to mammals; he is not sure about the lower animals. But what about objects? Should we respect them only to protect their owners from loss and distress? Should I be free to smash my violin, to tear up my Manet etching, to step on a flower? Is the respect for the integrity of objects different in principle from that for sentient creatures? Vandals are so frighteningly inhuman not just because of the damage they do to people but because they are without the love for existing things.

30 December

Figure 8a is a part of Figure 8b—a striking example of how thoroughly an object's character may be changed when it is fitted to another context. By itself, it is symmetrical around a tilted axis and entirely flat. In its new setting it conforms to a vertical/horizontal framework, and its crossings have been undone because their components are moved to different planes in depth. This also wipes out the central square.

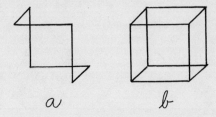

Figure 8

❧ 1986

7 January

"The wise man's eyes are in his head; but the fool walketh
in darkness" (Eccles. 2:14).

One can give the measurements of a person and thereby
leave out all that matters. Boccaccio describes Dante:
"Medium height, long face, aquiline nose, large jaws,
lower lip more prominent . . ."

10 January

In the early drawings made by children, elements are
combined by mere addition. A head, a neck, or an arm is
independently complete, uninfluenced by what happens
next to it. Similarly, at early levels of "primitive" thinking, processes such as dying or coming to life are not
understood as modifications of the body but as mere additions or withdrawals. Diseases invade and possess the
body like incubi. The soul is an independent entity applied to the body or taken away from it. Functional modification is a concept of a higher order. In the arts also,
the modulation of shapes comes late.

2 February

I happened to read a French translation of the Czech
writer Kundera's novel *The Unbearable Lightness of Being,*
and it occurred to me that in English it might be a quite
different book: a fairly thin story of young people during
the Russian Occupation. In French, the same book reads,
more appropriately, as a kind of choreographed game of
chess, whose figures are wood-carved types and whose
actions are strategic moves.

13 February

It is of interest to the students of gestalt theory to note
how the term *Prägnanz* is used in general German practice. I translate from the art historian Kurt Badt's book
on Delacroix: "Prägnanz is a particular degree of visibil-
ity, needed for the represented subject to make itself rec-
ognizable as never happens in reality, so true that its appearance serves the viewer to intensify his own vital
power of cognition."

11 March

At the newsstand of the hotel there was a rack with attractive magazines on display and on top a sign in large
handwritten letters saying No Reading Please!

25 March

Mary tells that when as a camp counselor for a group of
Detroit children she walked with them through the
woods to give the city dwellers a first taste of nature,
one of them asked her, "Miss Mary, is this also America?"

28 April

When Flaubert says of the maid Félicité that "for such souls the supernatural is quite simple," he points to a fundamental fact of the nature of religion. Before the unnatural split between what is taken to be true and what is believed by mere faith, the known world reaches without a break from the reality of the everyday to the miraculous and all-powerful.

In another story, "Herodias," Flaubert presents a beautiful example of the metaphor made flesh. He says of the head of John the Baptist that "since it was very heavy, they had to take turns carrying it."

29 April

Freedom and liberty—the verbal meaning of the words is the same, but a great difference is created by sound and rhythm. "Freedom" is an unhampered outcry, sharpened by the squeakiness of the long *ee*. "Liberty" is a dactylic skip performed by three short vowels and made even more playful by the first and third being almost the same, so that the step taken forward returns to its base.

It had never occurred to me that the figure representing Matthew in Caravaggio's painting could be anybody but the boy bent over the money at the end of the table. The simple visual logic of the confrontation between the two figures in profile, the standing Christ and the sitting boy, at the two ends of the canvas, the target of the pointing hands, the symbolism of the light mobilizing everybody but the chosen one, who is wrapped in his detached darkness although distinguished by his brightly checkered sleeves, the greatest distance between the caller and the person least likely to be called—all this seemed so evident that only a recent scholarly article alerted me to the unexpected fact that so far art historians had taken the bearded man to be the chosen apostle. Why not trust the common sense of the eye?

26 June

There is a habitual hesitation in British as well as in Italian conversational speech, but the two mannerisms are so unlike as to express a fundamental difference between the mental attitudes of the two peoples. British conversation falters and stumbles in tentative spurts, timid, unsure, and embarrassed, as though the road of verbal intercourse were so rough with insecurity that one could not dare to proceed directly or as though addressing the other person outright were somehow vulgarly unsubtle. Italian speech, on the contrary, forges ahead in a carefree stream but likes to indulge in generalities that lack tested concreteness. Therefore the sentence, after barely hinting at its argument, is made to evaporate into a drawn-out nondescript noise, pretending that any further substantiation of the thought would be so obvious as to insult the intelligence of the listener.

27 June

In the United States the street traffic moves in abstract, geometrically simple lines, straight or curved but smooth and steady, as fits the thinking of machines. Everything runs on invisible rails. On the crowded roads of Europe cars behave like people. They wind their way through a stream of neighbors, with their eyes constantly open to the quick turns and stops of their fellow vehicles. They rub shoulders, crawl through irrational crannies, stop short, push ahead a little, and give way again. They have minds and senses and talk to one another with blinking lights and angry horns. Split-second situations that would precede catastrophic clashes in America are the normal constellations of Old World traffic.

Zola's *Thérèse Raquin* reminds me again that in the great novels of the nineteenth century, the realism of faithful description is compensated by an almost trivially obvious symbolism, which raises the down-to-earth scene to the flimsy height of a cheap myth. The icy corpse of the drowned husband lying forever in the bed between the adulterous murderers; the scar of the struggling victim's bite that begins to burn painfully on Laurent's neck when he puts on his wedding shirt; the paralyzed mother, unable to move or speak but alert like revengeful Destiny to the inevitable self-destruction of the criminal couple; and even the movielike darkness of the alleyway where the drama takes place—it all could not be less realistic, steeped though it is in dripping reality.

29 June

The cat Toby scratches at the closed door in an attempt to remove the obstacle. But he also comes to know that scratching serves as an auditory request. When we hear him scratch, we open the door. Thus in the evolution of intelligent living only a brief span of learning separates action from signaling. By doing the one we discover that we are doing the other.

A rickety elevator took us up to the scaffold, at arm's length from Michelangelo's paintings on the ceiling of the Sistine Chapel. So near are the gigantic figures that they evade the viewer's sight, and one marvels once again how the painter could have executed shapes that are so distorted when viewed from up close. His picture of the Great Flood, however, also contains figures that are only a few inches high and therefore impossible to see from the floor of the chapel. They remind us that not all art is made to be seen; to give it physical presence, be it ever so hidden, seems to have sufficed. But then again, as we explore from our unnaturally close location the vigilant eyes of Michelangelo's giant faces, we find that we cannot meet their glance. Those divinely shaped eyes look right through us, all the way to the distant worshipers below.

Controversy has been raging about the ongoing restoration of the paintings. That morning, we listened to an influential Roman painter's vehement denunciation. The darkness of Michelangelo's vision, shrouded in mystery, he said, was being shamelessly denuded. To me it seemed that he mistook the dirt of the centuries for art's sacred intangibility. In my view the portions of the ceiling by now cleaned were a true revelation. I saw Michelangelo's paintings for the first time in their historical company. Gone was the shadow world of tawny figures by which a sculptor seemed to have invaded the domain of pictorial surfaces without much relation to what other painters had done before him or would do later. Now a new watercolor freshness, liberated blues and greens, evokes a kinship not just to the frescoes of a Piero della Francesca but to the metallic coolness of a Tintoretto as well. Michelangelo emerges as a painter among painters at his place in his time. Also, by contrast with the cleaned portions of the ceiling, the paintings as we have known them look to me by now too remote to fill the cavernous cube of the chapel's interior space. With the power of their restored colors the paintings begin to occupy that empty hollow. One tries to imagine what the impact of the *Last Judgment* will be when, with its original brilliance, it will advance across the room from the back wall toward the visitors as they enter the chapel at the other end. Once again the vision of that formidable ultimate day will be truly upon us.

Our modern languages seem to have lost some of the ease with which medieval Latin characterized the abstractness of concepts. We would hesitate to call the essence of being alive "animality" or the essence of being a stone "lapidarity"; Thomas Aquinas does so without trouble. Even the German translator must resort to the awkward

Steinhaftigkeit, while *Lebendigkeit* suits his language but is not quite an abstract concept.

In books on architecture, among them one of my own, the Church of Santa Maria della Pace in Rome is described as a small jewel combining the neatness of the Quattrocento with a Baroque porch that protrudes in counterpoint to the active shapes of an articulate square. In reality, however, one now easily misses the sight as one wanders through the narrow streets near the Piazza Navona. The walls that shape the little square are blocked by a disorderly spread of cars, and as one winds one's way through the rubbish of cramped living, one turns around to discover the soiled columns of the porch, deprived of the space it was designed to invade and occupied by a tramp who lies asleep in front of the church entrance. When the crystalline inventions of architects are made into stone and thus changed from *forma* into *materia,* they are like concepts whose tidiness is sullied by the rude disorder of usage.

5 July

For every figure I make a small Plasticine model. Its shape and expression have a finality of their own. But then, when I look at the piece of tree trunk or branch from which the figure is to be carved, I am struck by the cylindrical obstinacy of the wood. Its closed shape looks uncooperative. And in fact, what comes from the labor of the chisel turns out not to be very faithful to my little model. Rather it is a monster, born from my effort to force the figure upon the reluctant segment of the tree. What I should try instead, of course, is to view my wood obediently and cut into it as told by its nature, guided at most by my remote image of unspecified dynamic hints that are willing to take the shapes they find.

6 July

What I admire as truly ingenious in the Caravaggio of the Palazzo Barberini is not the horrible realism of Holofernes' bloody head or even the psychologically brilliant blend of loathing and determined savagery in the face of Judith. It is rather the powerful clasp with which the bony hand of the old crone, Judith's companion, squeezes a piece of cloth. This involuntary and unfunctional gesture gives an insuperably direct expression to the tension aroused by the murder. What meaning would there be to the ugly slaughter without that tension, that awareness of the gruesomeness of the heroic deed and the liberty it promises?

Have I made a note of the three stones that lie always on my desk while I write during the summer? Found on our beach, they are a phallus of grey granite, symbolizing creativity; an egg with white and blue streaks, also of granite, for fertility; and a tetrahedron of black basalt, for rationality. They keep my papers from flying off the desk when they are tempted by the wind.

16 July

Years ago, the day after his first child was born, I ran into Robert Fitzgerald, the great translator of classical poetry. "What is it like?" I asked him. "It is extraordinary," he replied. "Something ought to be done about it."

17 July

A tilt of the head goes a long way in enlivening the human figure. By a slight deviation from the vertical, the comic-strip cartoonist indicates that a character is humbly sensitive and considerate, as distinguished from the stiff-necked villain. And the saintly Mother Teresa tilts her head in her devoted listening to God and her willing adherence to her mission.

Gustaf Britsch offers the concept of *Ueberbestimmung* to describe the misinterpretation by which, for example, the simple early circle in a child's drawing is interpreted as a head, or a "tree" is taken as, say, an oak. This corresponds to what I have called misplaced specificity, namely, the false conviction that a pictorial representation implies the same completeness as its model. "What is Rembrandt's *Aristotle* thinking about?"

21 July

Sometimes at darker moments now, I feel as though I continue playing the accustomed role of my life because I happen still to be around. It is as though the husks of things are replacing the things themselves, as though the top keeps spinning until the impulse for its rotation will cease and the top drop and stop for no particular reason.

For several years every summer the song sparrow has come to sit on the same peak of the juniper bush, proclaiming his territory at the top of his voice. Is the same bird surviving those several winters? Or is he obeying a tradition in his family? Or if he follows an instinct, how sharply pinpointed is that impulse? Does it prescribe our juniper bush, or does it drive the bird, more in general, to choose an outpost surveying the scene, a sort of Cape Sunion for birds, as we, too, choose promontories and hills for our temples and palaces?

23 July

In one of De Chirico's melancholy vistas (*Autumn Meditation*) a walking cane, left behind, is leaning against the classical but desolatedly bare arcades. As the only residue of human presence, it attracts my attention because it reminds me of my own favorite cane, the one with the silver handle, bought for me as a birthday present in San Gimignano and supposed to have belonged to the bishop of Volterra. I keep losing this beloved object on my travels; I lost it twice this summer on a one-month journey to Europe, but so far it has been returned each time. So there it stands, leaning against the Italian wall near a decapitated marble statue of a woman. That is what is left of me.

6 August

Goethe, in *Wilhelm Meisters Lehrjahre,* says in praise of a country mansion: "All furniture and tableware was in harmony with the whole; and though I generally have found that the architects seemed to have been trained at the school of the pastry cooks, in this case the pastry cook and the dinner-table designer had been trained by the architect."

14 August

The delight of the first evening turned into a nightmare in four days. We were touched by the smiling devotion awakened in the young parents, the total surrender of their usual articulate earnestness letting them communicate with the little creature that understood only motion and sound. And we were captivated by the child's eager attention to new faces, his tireless curiosity, which made a miraculous puzzle of a shoe or a wheel, his struggle to break the fetters of gravity, to raise his head and to crawl. But after we had been coerced for four days by the power of the little deity, deprived of our freedom to reason and to speak, we came to feel that we were being subjected to an evil spell that sacrificed our humanity to the irresistible dominion of a small demon. It was a vision of mutilation, threatening an aging mind that is haunted anyway by the fear of losing its own vital powers.

The tranquillity of domestic animals keeps us from remembering how breathless a vigilance is required for the
ordinary pursuit of life in the wild. Watch a goldfinch
hastily pecking his seeds while his head darts in all directions to make sure that interferences from anywhere can
be responded to with lightning speed. How much fortifi-
cation of the environment it took to protect us from a
way of life in which constant mortal danger is a pervasive
condition!

As far back as I can think, I have been visited from time
to time by what I have called "my hotel dreams." I find
myself lost in an alien environment where I cannot reach
my destination and cannot leave. My room is crowded
with strangers; I cannot find the bathroom; I am due to
take a train in five minutes, but the stairs to the station
end against a wall or in darkness. The setting of these
dreams varies endlessly, but the basic theme remains the
same through the years. It is as though the Gnostic vision
of the stranger on earth is revealed unconsciously, even
though during daylight hours I feel comfortably at home.
Is it that I have never quite overcome the decade of the
diaspora, now so far remote in the past?

Goethe's novel *Wilhelm Meister* is interspersed with long
musings about human behavior and the state of the
world. Instead of describing them as thoughts, Goethe
presents them as monologues, Shakespearean or in the
manner of opera arias, by introducing them with "He (or
she) 'exclaimed.'" This raises the pronouncements to an
even higher level of abstraction than does the theater: the
presence of a stage shifts the entire performance to an ele-

vated level of abstraction, whereas in the novel the monologues stand out against an otherwise worldly course of
events.

28 August

Like the murderer returning to the site of his deed, the
cat Toby returns to scratch at the place on the living-
room carpet where he threw up his food days ago. What
has already been forgotten by the world survives in the
more sensitive conscience of the sinner.

29 August

Ungratefully I compare the doubtful profit I have received from the infinite resources of what I have heard,
read, and seen with the few tangible benefits gained by
learning about small matters—little tricks that have since
facilitated every day of my life. Some forty years ago at a
faculty party the president's mother-in-law, a sturdy British lady, kneeled on the floor in the midst of the cocktail
crowd to teach me patiently how to tie my shoelaces with
a double knot that could not come undone by itself but
would yield quickly to a single deliberate pull. It changed
my life and has made me remember the lady every morning with an explicit thought of thanks.

In the center of Brueghel's painting with the magpie, the
gallows stand like an entrance gate before the landscape.
The legs of the wooden structure are placed parallel to the
frontal plane; but by the time they reach the crossbar at
the top, they have turned 90°, now pointing into the
depth of the landscape. This vigorous twist of orientation
turns the scaffold into a diagrammatic indicator of the
two principal directions of the pictorial space.

29 September

Hegel's discussion of poetry can mislead readers when
they mistake his distinction between poetry and prose to

refer, as we commonly do, to two forms of linguistic use, the bound and the unbound form. Instead, Hegel clearly intends by *poetry* the artistic use of language, be it in a poem or, say, a novel, while he means by *prose* the expository use, as in a factual report or scientific treatise. This teaches us that even a poem can be purely expository, for instance, if it is written for a mnemonic purpose, but that there can be poetical qualities to just about any form of writing, done in whatever form to whatever intent.

19 October

The hotel where the psychologists held their convention had replaced the traditional room keys with a card from which a computer reads the room number. As I walked along the corridor, I could see half a dozen people trying in vain to make the card open their room doors. When I tried mine and had the same trouble, I came to understand what was the problem. As a psychologist, I took it for granted that the computer, as a kind of mind, would need a little time to read the number on the card. Instead, the mechanism works only if the card is pushed in and pulled out again at lightning speed. The computer, being a supermind or rather no mind at all, is beyond our comprehension.

In the evening the busy drive along the Chicago lakeshore becomes a kind of X-ray image of its traffic. As one looks down on it from the tenth floor, nothing remains but a flow of thousands of light dots, turning the ribbon of the coastline into a true artery of pure abstract motion.

28 October

Ants, fruit flies, and other small creatures probably do not need the incentives of pleasure and pain to do what is needed for procreation and survival. Presumably, instincts acquire those premiums of reward and punishment

367

at the level of evolution at which animals have developed
the will to do or not to do things. From that level on upward, why would anyone want to survive or multiply if
doing what comes naturally were not rewarded with
pleasure and the avoidance of pain?

5 November

In a book on Chartres, the author distinguishes between
the primary structure, the walls and rafters and arches,
which carry the building's body, and the secondary elabo-
ration of the surface, the shafts and ribs and cornices. In
part, this distinction is purely technical and historical, in
the sense of what is statically basic, what was built first,
etc. But there is also a corresponding visual distinction
between the basic skeleton of the composition and the
fleshing out, and the two distinctions do not necessarily
coincide. Consider the example of Mies van der Rohe's
office building in Chicago, where externally applied ribs
are used by the architect to make the underlying structural scaffold visible from the outside.

7 November

"The painter's brush consumes his dream," says Yeats in
"Adam's Curse."

25 November

When at an advanced age one cuts down on eating, one
discovers that the sensation of slight hunger is actually
more agreeable than the satiation produced by much
food. Hunger is desire, a striving for an outer goal,
which amounts to feeling alive, whereas with satiation
desire has ceased and the interest in what the world has to
offer has been extinguished. Like all fulfillments, this is a
final state, a sensation an old person has reasons to avoid.

· 1986 ·

6 December

Nietzsche says of Anaximander that he was the first
Greek to ask, "Wie kann etwas vergehen, was ein Recht
hat zu sein?"*

11 December

Our neighbor in the back, about a hundred feet away
from our bedroom window, has taken to irradiating the
outside of his house at night with an eerie green light,
which makes it look like a huge television screen. Removed from material reality and transformed into an image, the house now looms as an apparition in the dark,
floating in the nowhere. If persons were to appear before
this backdrop, one would expect them to perform the
hideous antics of comedians or commit a picturesque
crime.

The Italian *Vogue* magazine printed an interview we recorded in Milan. It ends with my saying that my life has
been one of contemplation rather than of action; and
since I watch the artists, who are contemplators, I am
twice-removed from active life "perchè guardo quelli
che guardano."† I am, I told the interviewer, the little owl
perched on the shoulder of Athene.

* "How can something pass away that has a right to exist?"
† "Because I observe the observers."

Designer: Barbara Jellow
Compositor: Graphic Composition
Printer: Maple-Vail Book Mfg. Group
Binder: Maple-Vail Book Mfg. Group
Text: 11/14 Bembo
Display: Bembo